The Deeds of Daring Diggers on the Somme

1916-18

Florence Breed

About the Author

Florence Breed lives in Donald, Victoria. An active local historian, she hails from Cornish stock and is the author of *A Devonshire lad : from Mullacott to Jeffcott*, *Woodbine wives from World War I*, *Forgotten heroes of the South African war 1899–1902*, *From Gallipoli with Love* and *Old Cornish Tales*.

Published in Australia by Sid Harta Publishers Pty Ltd,
ABN: 34 632 585 203
17 Coleman Parade, GLEN WAVERLEY VIC 3150 Australia
Telephone: +61 3 9560 9920, Facsimile: +61 3 9545 1742
E-mail: author@sidharta.com.au

First published in Australia 2021
This edition published 2021
Copyright © Florence Breed 2021
Cover design, typesetting: WorkingType (www.workingtype.com.au)

The right of Florence Breed to be identified as the Author of the Work has been asserted in accordance with the Copyright, Designs and Patents Act 1988.

The Author of this book accepts all responsibility for the contents and absolves any other person or persons involved in its production from any responsibility or liability where the contents are concerned.

All rights reserved. No part of this publication may be reproduced, stored in a retrieval system, or transmitted, in any form or by any means without the prior written permission of the publisher, nor be otherwise circulated in any form of binding or cover other than that in which it is published and without a similar condition being imposed on the subsequent purchaser.

Breed, Florence
Daring Deeds of Diggers on the Somme
ISBN: 978-1-925707-74-8
pp448

CONTENTS

Introduction and Facts of The Great War	v
How It Began	vii
The Angel of Mons — 1914	xvii
Lord Kitchener	xxi
in Praise of Our Soldiers	xxiv
at Last — to France	xxxii
Good-Bye Australia!	xxxiii
Eager to Leave Egypt	xxxiv
Keen to Reach France	xxxiv
Index and Soldiers' Names	xxxvii
Training in Egypt	1
Land of The Pharoahs	2
Cairo — Bedrechein Village	5
Sergeant Arthur Clifford "That Unforgettable Train Journey"	7
Sapper Harold Willey That Wonderful Train Journey	13
Private Frank Lee	18
Army-Nurses are The Heroines of This War.	22
The Battle of Jutland	25
Carnage at Sea	29
A Charlton Lad, Private A. M. Draper (7th. Battalion) Describes What Can Happen in The Trenches.	31
Private Mick Mcinerney (of Witchepoole) Kempston Hospital.	33
Arthur Clifford Writes:	36
Private Tom Cavanagh, (of Watchem) Writes to a Friend Miss Anne Pickering.	43
Battle of Fromelles, 1916	46
Just An Old Felt Hat	48
Sgt-Major H. Daniels Tells How He Won The V.c.	62
A Phenyl Bath 1916	68
Oh, Pozieres, Resting Place of Heroes.	71

Our Brave Infantry	72
The Horrors of War	77
Mongrel Curs!	80
The Western Front 1916	82
Fovant Training Camp — On Salisbury Plain, England	91
Attack On Pozieres Ridge	94
Private R. T. Arundell (of Charlton) — 1916.	105
Pozieres	107
Wounded at Pozieres	111
~ Like The Rock of Gibraltar ~	116
Saved By A Wallet	117
Before A Battle	120
Wounded at Pozieres, On 4th. August, 1916.	127
A Black Day For The Germans	128
Sergeant Arthur Clifford, M.m.	130
Sgt. Arthur Clifford	131
Mouquet Farm	131
A Charge at Mouquet Farm	136
Blown in Halves	150
Mud On the Flers Battle-Fields — November. 1916	153
Living With the Pigs	163
"Please Pass Conscription."	167
Australia's Light Horse Brigade	169
The Historic Charge of The Light Horse at Beersheba	175
Proof of A Soldier's Death	183
"Somewhere in France".	185
An English Opinion of Our Soldiers	186
in The Mud at Flers — 5th. November, 1916.	191
Moo-Cow Farm	197
A Trip Across The World	201
- Stonehenge -	208
A Soldier's Death	209
"Don'T Worry" / "Be Happy"	210
A Real Bed	211
Thank God For The Y.m.c.a.	215

Hard Nuts	216
Mud — Mud — Mud	220
A Winter's Raid in February, 1917.	221
A Fighting-Soldier at 50.	222
"Somewhere in France".	226
"He Died As A True Soldier Ought to Die."	229
His Last Letter Home	232
Killed By Their Own Guns!	235
"Troopship Ballarat Sunk By Submarine."	238
Arrival at A British Camp	244
Bullecourt — April/May, 1917.	245
Wounded at Bullecourt	253
Wounded at Bullecourt — On 3rd. May, 1917.	257
Stalemate in The War	261
Messines — June, 1917.	263
The 3rd. Australian Division in Attack	264
The Second Battle of Bullecourt	271
Battle of Messines 7th. June, 1917.	272
Battle of Messines	274
Bullecourt and Messines	278
The Battle of Menin Road	285
Over The Top	287
War in The Air	288
Some Near Misses	292
On Board A Troopship	299
Private Edward, Palmer Pearse	305
Stretcher-Bearers	308
Running Across A Battlefield	312
A Runner On The Battlefields	313
A Runner's Lament	316
The Kind of Letter That Parents Dread to Receive in Wartime	318
Experience of A Soldier On The Somme Battlefields.	320
The Conscription Referendums in 1917 — Majority Votes For 'No' Was 184,832.	322

The Big German Offensive	325
Extracts From War Letters (1917-18)	327
A Runner's Lament	337
An Honor For Australla France.	340
A Lull Before The Storm	342
"Somme" Mud	346
Over One Hundred Tanks Took Part On That First Day	352
Letter of Condolence	356
Eating Cats and Dogs	360
Spanish Influenza Pandemic	362
Telegram That Ended The War	366
Peace.	367
The Finale of World War 1	369
Our Gallant Dead	371
"Their Names Shall Last For Evermore"	373
Who Really Won The War?	373
Surrender of German Fleet	379
Conclusion	383
An Australian On Peace Day	387
Spanish Influenza Pandemic	389
The Story of Two Lientenants	391
Bridal Statistics	394
Shot at Dawn	396
A Maiden's Prayer	397
The World's Oldest Man	401
Waiting For A Stretcher	402
Influenza, The Post-War Killer	404

INTRODUCTION AND FACTS OF THE GREAT WAR

If this book does nothing but give people a better awareness of the gratitude we owe to Australians involved in the great European conflict, it will have done something worthwhile; for there is nothing more hurtful than ingratitude!

I trust that this collection of. writings from our local "Diggers" will help people realise the terrible price paid by all soldiers in the First World War, just for the ambitions of a few greedy men.

In my collection of soldiers' personal recollections, entitled "From Gallipoli With Love", is that first great drama in Australia's brief history, when ANZACS shed their blood upon foreign cliffs.

This collection follows, to tell about "Diggers" who fought in Belgium and France for the causes of Freedom and Justice. They faced machine-guns (a new device for mass killing) and the horrors of chemical warfare (a new scientific, diabolical way to exterminate). They had to smoke cigarettes to calm their nerves and to cover the terrible stench of the killing fields.

They could not protect their frozen bodies from the cruel weather, whieh caused seas of MUD that imprisoned them and even drowned them: and when they heard about the negative results of Australia's two Conscription Referenda, their cup of sorrow must have been full.

We know that the Australians were used as "shock troops" (which was a form of compliment from the British Headquarters). "There are certain divisions," said Haig's Chief-of-Staff, "who when given a job to do, will do it. The Australians fall into that category."

Let us not forget the wonderful Australian Light-Horsemen to whom the same praise must be given they faced sand, heat, dust, thirst, Turks and Arabs, in a war-zone that was no less dangerous, bringing so great credit to the name of Australia.

Their famous bayonet charge over two miles of open ground at Beersheba, without faltering (although machine-gun bullets mowed down many of their comrades), must surely rank among the world's great deeds of courage.

The following words of the participants themselves are the best introduction to their book: the honour is all theirs; and we are simply the blessed beneficiaries of their selfless deeds.

HOW IT BEGAN

The First World War began in August, 1914, and if we want to blame one person for lighting the fuse that started this massacre we could name a fanatical 19-year old terrorist called Gavrilo Princip. He was a Bosnian Serb who pumped bullets into the Archduke Ferdinand and his wife, Sophie, as their car passed him on the streets of Sarajevo. It was June 28th. and both his victims died within minutes.

Most historians agree it was those two bullets from a terrorist's gun that triggered the war — resulting in four years of slaughter and suffering as Europe blew itself to pieces.

A MUDDY BATTLEFIELD ON THE SOMME

Remember Gallipoli 1915

A GALLIPOLI SOUVENIR

LT. GEN. SIR. W. R. BIRDWOOD
"The soul of Anzac."

BRAVO ANZACS!

RINGS THE WIDE WORLD WITH THE FAME
AND GLORY OF AUSTRALIA'S NAME,
VALIANT SONS OF BRITAIN TRUE
OUR GREAT EMPIRE PRAISES YOU!

AND TO HISTORY SHALL GO DOWN
NEW ZEALAND'S LOYAL AND BRAVE RENOWN,
ZEAL IN EVERY NOBLE HEART
ANSW'RING PLAYS A HERO'S PART
CLOSER BINDS OUR EMPIRE'S TRACKS
SONS OF BRITAIN – BRAVE ANZACS.

— Willmer

Britain declared war on Germany on the 4th of August, 1914

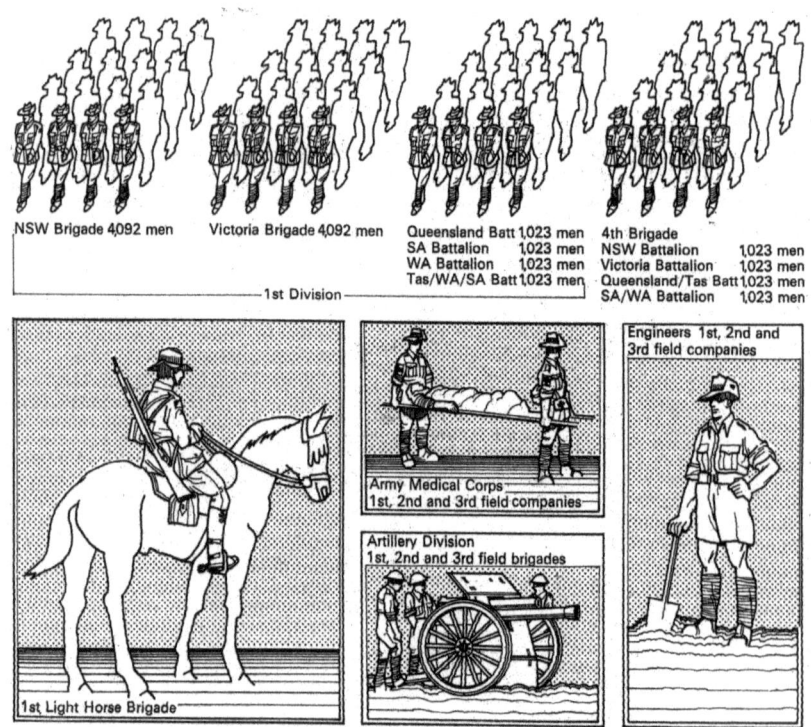

IN 1914 AUSTRALIA HAD 20,000 VOLUNTEERS to form the A.I.F. (Australian Infantry Force)

The Somme mud.

ANZAC — A word invented by an English clerk who was tired of having to write the words 'AustraJian and New Zealand Army Corps' on all the mail that passed through his hands. This word not only reminds us of the great loss of men in war, but also of their courage and endurance in the face of adversity; it means a love of one's country and a faithful duty to it; above all, this word represents mateship and good humour in times of great hardship, as well as a sense of self-worth against dreadful odds.

Tyne Cott War Memorial Cemetery — Belgium (photo D.E.Breed)

King George V, in World War I, set an example to the people with his optimism, courage, patience, humanity and self-sacrifice. He visited industrial places to encourage ammunition production and to praise those hard-workers.

(1865–1936)

1875–1934

Civilians flee as German armies invade Belgium — 1914

Wounded British soldiers in the Retreat from Mons — 1914

THE ANGEL OF MONS – 1914

It was in August, 1914, when powerful German hordes invaded neutral Belgium, bringing death and destruction to a peaceful population. "Destroy everything and spare none!" was the order given by megalomaniac, Kaiser Wilhelm II, to his large army — and so we read of the cold-blooded murder of harmless old men, women and children in several Belgian towns.

By the middle of August, Britain's Expeditionary Force had landed in France with the words of King George V still ringing in their ears: "You are leaving home to fight for the safety and honour of my Empire. Belgium, whose country we are pledged to defend, has been attacked, and France is about to be invaded by the same powerful foe." No wonder the French people greeted our soldiers with enthusiasm, even learning the words of that popular British war song, "It's a long, long way to Tipperary".

By the 20th, August that great Prussian war-machine had already crushed Antwerp, Lille and Charleroi and reached the capital city of Brussels. It was here that the Belgians (and the rest of the world) saw the "goose-step" for the first time in history when a mighty, conquering army marched through their streets.

Although our British forces had quickly travelled north to join up with their French and Belgian allies, unfortunately the Germans had a great advantage in numbers and by the 24th August our soldiers fell back after suffering tremendous losses. The Germans were advancing south towards Paris with a strength of about 300,000 men; whilst the British were holding a line of about 25 miles with less than 1., 00,000 men. One can imagine the eagerness with which the Germans advanced towards the next town, of Mons to wipe out the hated British.

In the words of the would-be conqueror of Europe, Kaiser Wilhelm II, to his army, "Devote your attention to the treacherous English and walk over General French's contemptible little army".

However, at this point our hard-pressed British forces were ordered to retire to avoid further losses — and it was during this retreat from Mons that an amazing incident was observed by many soldiers (and their officers) who spoke of the descent from on high of an angelic army which came to their aid.

Naturally, not every eye-witness describes this Heavenly intervention in the same way — some thought they saw St. George on a white horse leading the angelic host, whilst others spoke of a blinding light desoending between the two opposing forces which scattered the advancing German cavalry and stopped their oncoming infantry.

Interestingly; another version was given by German prisoners-of war who described more than just a single event, saying that several times they saw in front of the English forces·, phantom bowmen led by a towering figure on a shining white horse.

Another story by British soldiers describes three angelic-beings hovering in the air over the German lines and thus providing protection and an inspiration to them.

Of course, in hindsight we have to wonder why none of these eyewitnesses came forward at the end of the war to have their names and experiences recorded in official documents. However, it is a sad fact that few of the-soldiers who fought at

Mons survived the war because they were killed later in Flanders, or on the Somme.

My father and many others who fought in that terrible war, believed in the Angels of Mons — maybe because the British firmly believed in the justice of their cause and were not surprised that angels gave support to them against such a brutal and wicked enemy.

There is no doubt that the British Third Division was in great danger of being annihilated and needed to retreat from Mons to avoid being cut to pieces. They were in great peril because the German cavalry was rapidly advancing and very much outnumbered our forces.

Was it just the ordinary soldier who saw this miracl? What about the officers who were there? Well, there was one (unnamed) general who did state when questioned that he had been at Mons during the retreat. He described how when the German cavalry was advancing upon our very much outnumbered forces, suddenly he saw a bright cloud descending.

It placed itself between the German and the British forces. In the cloud he saw bright objects moving about, but could not say if they were angels. (Maybe the general was short-sighted.) He did say, however, that the moment the cloud appeared the Germans stopped and their horses began rearing and plunging out of control.

Another officer, Brigadier-General John Charteris, was also with the British Expeditionary Force in France and an observer as the men retreated from Mons. In a letter home, dated September 5th 1914, he wrote: -

"There is a story of the Angels of Mons going strong through the

2nd. Corps, of how the angel of the Lord on the traditional white horse and clad all in white with a flaming sword, faced the advancing Germans at Mons and prevented their further progress.- I realize that men's nerves may play weird pranks on their imagination at such times, but all the same this angel of Mons interests me — and I want to know more about it."

These days we realize that shell-shock can affect the state of mind of soldiers in battle, but why did so many of soldiers who were eye witnesses (both British and German) talk about seeing angels and ghostly bowmen? Could they all have suffered from delusions?

Today we live in an age where science and technology rule our lives, so maybe that strange luminous cloud that descended between the two armies was a natural phenomenon caused by the swampy ground along the Mons canal which was a coal-mining area with many water filled ditches and drains. Could these physical features have caused some kind of luminous cloud and bright lights?

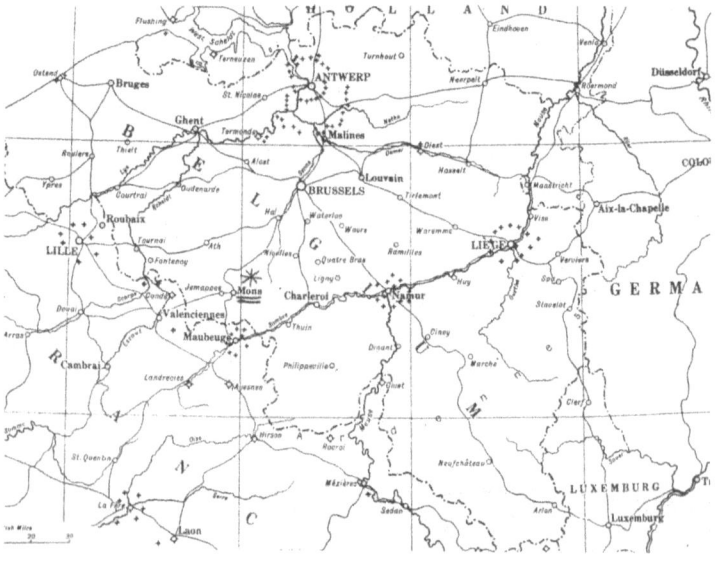

LORD KITCHENER

The famous British recruiting poster, used during the 1914–18 War.

During the First World War, 66 Victoria Crosses were awarded to Australians.

IN PRAISE OF OUR SOLDIERS

It was the soldier, not the poet,
Gave us freedom of expression.
'Twas the soldier, not the preacher,
Gave us freedom of religion.
'Twas the soldier, not Trade Unions,
Gave us better work conditions.

And 'twas the soldier made this country free,
Not party politicians.
Freedom from Want, Freedom from Fear,
And Freedom of Speech which we hold dear.
'Lest We Forget' are words we say
When marching every Anzac Day.
So keep alight that undying flame
To honour those who deserve great fame.
F. Breed.

*Wedding Day at Midsomer Norton
27th June, 1917 (married whilst on leave)*

Residence of the Right Hon. Joseph Chamberlain M.P.

Griffith writes "I was staying at this Australian Auxiliary Hospital in Harborne, Birmingham."

An Australian soldier

Dear Mum
        When you get this I'll have gone out.
I want you not to fret.
Remember that a life spent in a good cause is not wasted.
Be glad your son thought enough of his people and the country he loved to give his life for them.
I hope you and Dad have peace for the rest of your days.
Tell the boys that if ever Australia needs them not to get cold feet. Tell them it's better to die game in a good cause than to be numbered amongst the slackers.
Don't forget Australia is the best place on earth. You know the longest life is but a drop in the ocean of eternity. Find solace in the thought that we'll meet in heaven
Kiss Dad goodbye for me and remember how often you've said 'Thy Will be done'. Goodbye Mum
                              Yours to the last
                                  Jackie

Australia's First Conscription

xxxiii

AT LAST – TO FRANCE

In the Spring of 1916. the 1 Anzac Corps gladly left behind the burning sands of Egypt and set sail for France. From the Port of Alexandria they sailed across the Mediterranean Sea, enduring the agonies of sea-sickness once again. But worse still. was the ever-present peril of German submarines which our soldiers nicknamed. "King Billy's Tin Fishes" — (this was their disrespectful title for Germany's megalomaniac King William. known as Kaiser Wilhelm). Our soldiers wore life belts all the time. even using them as pillows when they slept.

***

On March 23rd. the Troopship. MINNEAPOLIS, was torpedoed but. luckily, she was empty, having already landed Australians on French soil.

***

Australian soldiers were famous for their boisterous, high spirited and independent behaviour — which is why they made such bold and daring soldiers. Therefore, fearing that they would indulge in riotous behaviour. the British Authorities refused permission for them to look around Marseilles, or Paris. In fact. our Australian troops were rushed straight from the docks and entrained up north to the Flanders battle fields. The tragedy is that so many of them were killed before they had an opportunity to visit these places.

***

This long train-journey through France was a unique experience, for it enabled them to view some wonderful scenery as well as meet the kindly inhabitants. The French gave them a great reception. in spite of the language barrier.

GOOD-BYE AUSTRALIA!

EAGER TO LEAVE EGYPT

" SAND IN YOUR BOOTS AND ON YOUR FOOD."

KEEN TO REACH FRANCE

Photos- Geddie Pearse Collection

The Pyramids of Egypt

Daring Deeds of Diggers on the Somme

Cairo

INDEX AND SOLDIERS' NAMES

Aldag. 240-2
Alexander, C. 1 1 8-120
Allardyce, J. 66-7
Arundell, R. 1 16
Baddock, F. 243-5
Ballarat Ship. 228-23 1
Blencowe, F. 84-5
Buchanan, P. 215-7
Budge, H. 278-81
Bullecourt. 234
Bunworth, J. 254
Campbell, A. 224
Campbell, W. 122-3
Cannard, M. 318-9
Cannard, S. 191-2
Cavanagh, T. 64-5
Cavell, Edith. 46
Charlton soldier. 142-4
Clifford, A. 35-9, 57-63, 82, 95- 101, 106- J 12, 136-141, 235-239
Coningsby, E. 269-270
Condolence. 290- 1
Crone, H. 257-9
Crouch, A. 1?7
Daniels, H. 79
Dart, 0. 77
Davison, W.
Dickie, R 105
Draper, A. 54
Duggan, B.124-5
Eating cats/dogs 316-7
English opinion 184

Felt hat. 68-73
French philosophy. 205
Fraser, J. 183
Fromelles. 78
Galeka ship. 186
Gilchrist, C. 285
Griffin, R. 121
Grogan, C.
Gullett, H. 233
Haase, R. 1 89
Harrison, L. 193, 272-4
Hogan, M. 87-8, 126-7
Hogan·, R. 162
Jacka, A. 32 1
Jackson, A. 47-8
Jacobson, J. 182
Jutland Battle.
Kewpie Doll. 1 87
King George V. 150- 1
Lee, F. 44-5
Loel, B. 154-6
Leok, J. 160
Lewis, H. 194-6
Light-Horse. 168- 177
Lofts, C. 290- 1
Map of Somme. 131
Mcinerney, M. 55-6 91-2 Messines. 248
Monash, J. 310
Mouquet Fann. 142-4
Mulquiny, N. 213
Newstead, C. 185
Newton, E. 220-1

O'Brien, D.	133	Simpson, L.	134-5
O'Donnell, J.	249-53	Smith, A.	132
Olive, G.		Somme Mud.	188
O'Meara, M.	161	Storer, H.	214
Pearse, E.	282-4	Summerfield, A.	33-4
Perry, H.	222	Taylor, C.	255-6
Phillips, W.	198-203	Training in Egypt.	30-2
Platt, H.	332-6	Treahy, J.	218-9
Phelps, F.	206	Trollope, E.	226
Pozieres.	86	Tyers, F.	210
Ross, D.	117	. War in the Air.	263
Rowe, P.	204	Wilkinson, F.	260-1
Runners.	286-9	Willey, H.	41-3, 157-8, 163-5
Salisbury Plain.	232-3		
Sherrin.	146	Willey, V.	166-7, 190-1, 268, 293-4
Short, P.	302-4		
		Williams.	128
YMCA.	209	Young, F.	305-8 Young, H. 266-7
End of War	323-342		

Silent, they lie in their last long line while the lark sings overhead.

TRAINING IN EGYPT

Upon the evacuation of Gallipoli, our Australian and New Zealand Corps (ANZAC) was sent to Egypt. Here, our soldiers could rest after their ordeal and then train and reorganise to meet the " real enemy" (as they called the Germans) . They found themselves camped out in the desert at a place called Tel el Kebir — which the soldiers complained was a long way from the entertainments ("tempting fleshpots") of Cairo. Their camp was near the famous battlefield where, in 1882, a large British Force under Lord Wolseley defeated an Egyptian revolt led by Arabi Pasha.

The desert at Tel el Kebir and Moascar had a hard surface — not thick, soft sand — so it was a better surface upon which to do route-marching and infantry practice.

* * * *

During January, 1916, reinforcements from Australia began arriving in Egypt to join the veterans of Gallipoli. The following writings give us a good idea of what it was like in Egypt during this time of preparation.

THE THREE PYRAMIDS OF GIZEH

LAND OF THE PHAROAHS

Private A. G. Summerfield (8 th. Battalion) writes home about his arrival in the "Land of the Pharaohs".

Tea in a Glass,

Mena Camp, Egypt, 1916

Dear Son and Annie.

Mena Camp. EGYPT.
1916.
Just a few lines to let you know I am alright. I was very bad for a few days with Ptomaine poisoning. which I got through eating sardines. I was never so bad in all my life. I did not think I was ever going to stop retching; and with the pain in my stomach I did not know what was wrong. I was suddenly took bad at 12 o'clock one night.

Well. I had a good trip across on the boat. We were a bit down hearted at first when we were told we were coming here (instead of France). but I am glad in one way that I am here. as Egypt is a very interesting place.

We are camped right behind the Great Pyramids and the Sphinx. The pyramids are fascinating for it is marvellous how they were built. They are made of great stones — not exactly stones but rather great lumps of rock — and they are as big at the top as at the bottom.

They are 4.000 years old. I have been in one. The entrance is cut out of solid rock; and the room where the King and his family are buried. is also cut out of rock. The walls and roof are built up with granite — all polished and beautiful — and it is a mystery to me how it was done.

We had a guide with us who showed us where the mummies were stolen from. You are allowed to climb one of these pyramids. but I have not been up yet.

I got your letter dated 3rd. November, at Port Said. and was sorry to hear about Uncle Joe Bailey; yet it is a blessing he has gone.

We are camped 10 miles outside Cairo and we got here at 10 o clock in the morning the day we arrived? It is pretty cold here of a night. but hot in the day.

A TYPICAL EGYPTIAN SCENE

I have been into Cairo once. It is a big place and has some bonza buildings. but it has some real break-ups that ought to be destroyed. I had tea in town and what do you think they gave me my tea in? They brought it in a glass — like a wine glass, only much bigger.

There are some bonza bridges over the Nile River; one bridge must be at least a mile long. and it is all made of iron.

The money here is called "Piastres" — and a million of them is only worth a farthing!

We get mostly camel here as meat to eat. Donkeys and camels do most of the hard work. and they use horses for the Taxi-Cabs. These horses are beauties (Arabian).

I went for a swim today in the baths of "Mena House". This place is really a big palace, but it has been turned into a hospital for our troops. It was alright. too.

Remember me to poor old Mick if he is still alive. Hoping you are all well as it leaves me — and with love to all. I remain, your loving brother, ARTHUR."

PRIVATE A. G. SUMMERFIELD (LATER} IN THE TRENCHES IN FRANCE

CAIRO – BEDRECHEIN VILLAGE

FROM ARTHUR CLIFFORD'S DIARY

"Last night several boats moved off up the Canal, and five others came in and anch ored in the roads. About 8 o'clock, the pilot came aboard and we ?oved in to the wharf.

It was very amusing, for as our boat was creeping along the waterside, Port-Police were trying to hunt the niggers off the wharf. They had a difficult job, so had to use their canes pretty freely on the poor beggars.

When we got close in, some of the chaps started throwing their spare clothing overb oard just to see the locals jump into the water. Very often, two or three of the poor beggars would get to the article of cl othing at the same time, and then there would be a fierce argument and a fight in the water. A lot of the kids were diving for the coins we threw in.

Quite a lot of chaps disembarked and got away in the train. Our Company, with several others, got off the b oat and into the train by

10 o'clock. The native porters helped us off the boat with our equipment and stacked it away for us and even wiped the dust

off our boots. Of course, they wanted a tip — and didn't forget to salute us when they got it.

On our way through Suez, ab out 1,000 kids ran alongside the boat wanting Bakshish (money). T'was about here we saw the first donkeys. Two soldiers were riding them and one got a nasty spill.

The native drivers run behind with sticks and bang into the donkeys for all they are worth.

SERGEANT ARTHUR CLIFFORD "THAT UNFORGETTABLE TRAIN JOURNEY"

20th. March, 1916. This morning we steamed into Marseilles, after dodging submarines on our voyage across the Mediterranean Sea from Egypt. night we anchored outside the harbour.

It is a very pretty place, but very hilly. The buildings reach down to the water's edge. There are a lot of ships in port; and from the amount of smoke over the town, there must be a large number of factories. Just alongside our berth is the LAKE . MANITOBA which an-ived yesterday from Suez, crowded with Tommies.

Monday, March 27th. I must tell you about the trip from Marseilles to Flanders. This was a railway journey we shall never forget. First, we travelled in a westerly direction along the coast and then up the hills. We could look down on the houses and streets and gardens. It was a pleasure to see the smiling faces and neat appearance of the people. They gave us a splendid reception all along the line; running from their houses, and waving, and throwing kisses to our fellows hanging out of the train windows.

What struck us most from the start, was the pretty, tiled cottages and the cleanliness of everything. The people and children were all so neatly-dressed, and everything was a strong contrast dirty, stinking Egypt. It was a sight to see houses perched on the slopes of steep hills; and every little corner is made to grow plants and no ground is wasted.

On the first part of the journey we passed through a good many tunnels, some of them a few miles long. At midnight, the train stopped and we got issued with a dixie of tea each. There was mm in it, but it was very acceptable all the same in the cold night air. We passed through Lyons, and crossed the Rhone — which is a fine stream of water with seven> fine bridges across it. We saw little of the town as we passed through it too quickly, and anyway it was hidden by the hills.

We were continually passing through villages which are very close together. Most of these places have vineyards; and when the vines are loaded with leaves and grapes it must be a wonderful sight. There seem to be no big trees about, though some of them are quite tall and most are covered with ivy. The woods look so lovely with trees growing close together and the ivy covering both the trees and ground.

The trees themselves have no foliage just now as the winter is barely over; but in some parts the leaves are beginning to sprout. On the edge of one of the woods we saw a pheasant — the first I had ever seen — and it was so close to the line we had a clear view of it. He was a bonzer bird, beautifully-coloured and larger than a big rooster.

About the middle of the afternoon snow started to fall in very large flakes, but as soon as they touched the ground they melted. It was the first snow I had ever seen.

Tuesday, March 28th. We got as far as Dijon tonight. We stopped there for some time and the people threw oranges, cakes, apples and such things, while we shied back our cigarettes and hard biscuits. We got hot tea again at midnight and we were glad of it as we were cold and uncomfortable. All the same we managed to get a bit of sleep — a couple curled up on the floor between the seats and the rest put their feet onto the opposite seats. It was a tight squeeze and we were stiff and sore, but that's nothing — we'll get worse yet !

Two days in the train carried us into a snow-blizzard, which seemed so strange after the hot and dusty sands of Egypt. When we got out of the train next morning, the boys happily snowballed each other with the same accuracy they had thrown hand grenades at the Turks.

All morning the train ran alongside the Seine River. It looks deep, with barges working up and down it. There is lovely scenery along this river. The banks on either side are thickly-wooded, and here and there a Chateau, or old castle, the sort one expects to find in this country and one can imagine the same sort in England.

Our first disappointment in France was when we expected to go through Paris, but instead the train turned off 12 miles away and carried us past that fair city. We could see the Eiffel Tower in the distance and would have liked a closer view; so we vowed to see the capital of France another time, or die in the attempt (and many did die).

Wednesday, 29th. March. Our rail journey through France was marred today when one of the men fell whilst attempting board the moving train. He must have slipped on the snow and ice and missed his footing. He fell beneath the moving wheels and was buried in the town where the accident occurred.

From here on the country is not nearly so hilly. There are few hedges and no fences. Wheat and oats are the main crops, and the farmers are busy with their ploughs. The ploughs are pulled by white bullocks and they are big, powerful animals. Further on we saw mules and donkeys pulling the wagons. Their horses are splendid animals, nearly all grey.

Near Amiens we ran into several snowstorms, and the ground, and trees, and buildings were all white. All along the line about these parts we saw French soldiers — Cavalry and Infantry — and they look jolly fine fellows. Most of them are in their service uniform of light blue coat and trousers with a grey steel helmet. The sentries had red trousers, blue coat and cap. At one stop we met a Frenchman with the Military Cross of France (Croix de Guen-e)on his jacket.

We expected to reach our destination tonight after three days on the railway, but we did not reach it until 3-30 a.m. on Thursday mor:,ning. There was a very heavy frost so it was jolly cold on the train. However, we soon had our blankets rolled and our equipment gathered up, and were outside as soon as it was daylight.

Thursday, 30th. March. We had breakfast, biscuits and bully-beef and jam. We are fed up with these things. The biscuits are as hard as bricks and it takes a long time to chew them and they hurt your gums. Soon after 5 a.m. we left the siding and started for our new home. We had to march many miles to our first billets as we lost the way and went several miles along the wrong track.

At last, we found our way on to the right road and passed through a good many villages, and soldiers were billeted in most of them. Our village is Rebecq, and we were jolly glad to get there. We arrived at 11- 30 a.m. and were flat out! We c anied heavy packs and 120 rounds of ammunition, and after a week on board the boat, and the long, long train journey, our feet were too soft for the 12 miles of hard roads.

Friday, 31st. March. However, we are in very comfortable quarters. MyseH and 23 others are camped in a barn, with plenty of straw to lie on, water handy, green fields _to look at, and good roads to walk on. We have white people to look at, even if we can't talk to them. All of us are pleased to get away from filthy Egypt. We hear the continuous rumble and booming of the big guns, and no doubt it will not be long before we get closer to them and have a little to say in the fighting which is going on.

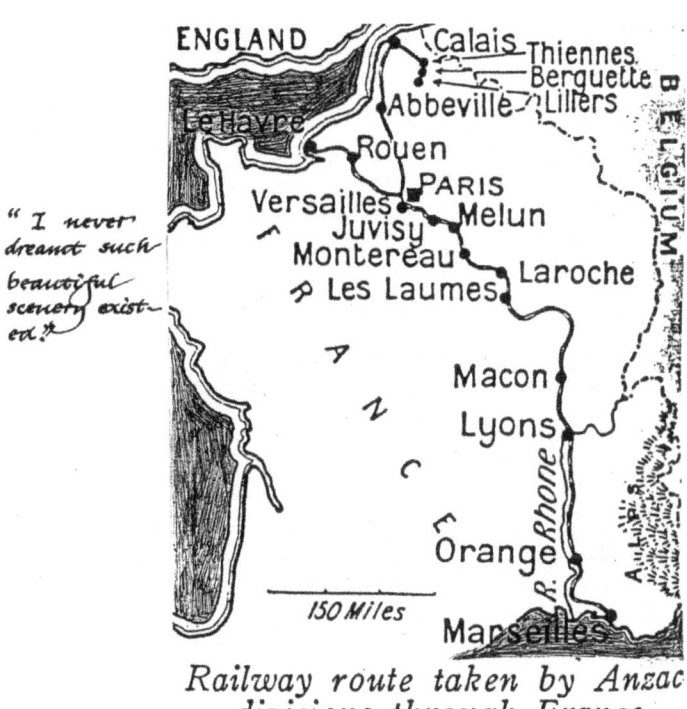

Railway route taken by Anzac divisions through France

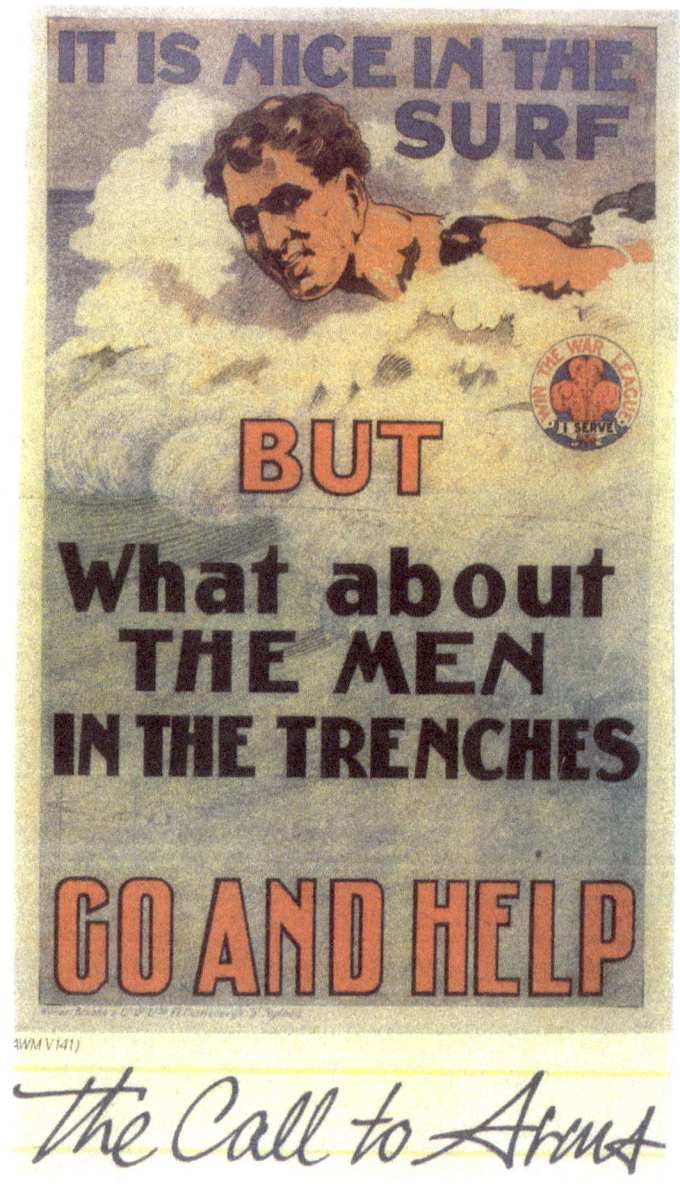

SAPPER HAROLD WILLEY
THAT WONDERFUL TRAIN JOURNEY THROUGH FRANCE

Dear Mother,

We embarked on the troopship Scotian, a fine big boat of 14,000 tons and belonging to the Allan Line. Why all the haste, I do not know, as we did not leave the wharf until 7a.m. on the Monday morning.

At that homur we weighed. anchor and steamed out of the harbour, all glad to leave that rotten place Egypt. Our quarters on board were under the foc'sle and in cabins 6 feet by 6 feet, and four men in each. We were all issued with life belts, and had to wear them all day, and sleep on them at night.

Our meals were something awful and not fit for pigs to eat. I was on guard one day, and my duty was to keep a watch for submarine periscopes, but we did not see any.

I must give the British Navy great praise for looking after us, as every few hours a Destroyer or Patrol boat would pop up from nowhere, and come alongside to see who we were; and after being satisfied, would steam out of sight in quick time.

The first few days of our sea-trip to France, the sea was calm; but on the last day (Saturday) it got a bit rough and some of the boys were seasick. We sighted the French Coast about 3 p.m. on Saturday, and steamed into (Marseilles) Harbour about 9 p.m. What a lovely sight it was with all the different-coloured lights along the bay.

At 10 p.m,. we dropped anchor, and when we awoke on Sunday morning all of us were anxious to view this beautiful city. It is surrounded by great mountain ranges, and the white houses have red? Wed roofs which contrast with their dark background. Quite a change from the .dreary yellow sands we had been used to for so long.

At 3 p.m. on Sunday, we disembarked and marched about 3 miles to a rest-camp. The French people gave us a great welcomei cheering us all along the streets. We arrived at this camp and had tea — then orders came that no one was to leave camp.

Well, this was no good to brother Victor or me, so we took French leave. I will never forget how we managed to escape. We climbed over brick walls, through. private garden.so along gutters11 through glasshouses and greenery and finished up by running through a railway tunnel about 000 yards long.

We hopped on the first train that came along, not knowing where it was going; but Luck favoured us as it took us right into the heart of the city. I cannot tell you much about this city as we did not arrive there till 8 o'clock — and the last car left for the camp at 9 p.m.

What we saw of it was beautiful, and quite different from the dirty streets of Egyptian cities. At 9 p.m. we caught the last car for the camp, and then had some more fun trying to get back inside.

Monday — and Reveille is at 3 a.m. After breakfast, we march to the station and entrain in cattle trucks to start our three days' journey. At 8 a.m. our train whistles and we are off.

We travel around the outskirts of (Marseilles) to the foot of the great ranges and receive tremendous cheering from the

French people as we pass along. We also get a lovely view of the harbour.

Our next wonder is, how are we going to get over these high mountain ranges? But our question is soon ans?ered when we enter one of the great tunnels. Now we begin to wonder if we shall ever see daylight again, as it seems as though we have been in darkness for hours. I was in.formed that the tunnel is close on 4 miles long.

Out of the tunnel and we find ourselves among the hills, and looking down on valleys, all lush and green. The railways about this part must have cost thousands to construct, as in many places there are steep cuttings through solid rock.·.

We pass through beautiful countryside for hours, and are not the least tired of looking at the scenery. I thought we had some beauty spots in Victoria, but we cannot compare them with the beauty of these parts? One can understand now why the French are fighting so hard for their country, as it is all worth it.

Our first stop of any importance is Aries: from there we pass up through Vallence to Lyons. Through this part we follow the River Rh one tot many miles, through country under intense cultivation. One thing very noticeable was the number of old men, women and children working in the fields.

Lyons is a fairly large city, and it w as here that we first saw young women acting as tram-conductors.

Night now comes on and we are all sorry. We do not stop on account of this, but continue our journey in the dark. I forgot to mention that we have our meals in the trucks, bully and biscuits and wash it down with water (Good oh!)

Some little fun now starts, as there are 30 of us in a truck, and the problem is how are we all going to get a sleeping berth? After some little arguments we settle do? — some with their knee& up under their chins, others with their feet resting on another's head, and others not resting at all. All we wanted was some oil and we would then have been the "dinkum" sardine. All growling, but not downhearted.

Our next stop is Macon; and from here we pass through Chaton and on to Dijon. Dijon is a very busy railway town. Here we saw young women acting as station-porters, also loading the engines with coal, and they were as black as the Ace of Spades from the coal dust, but as happy as lords.

Leaving Dijon we pass on through the grape country, through Sens, and to within a few miles of Paris. How disappointed we all were when we learned the train would pa- round the outskirts of Paris. We passed through Versailles and could just see the outline of the Eiffel Tower against the sky.

On the third day, and we are still in the cattle truck and living on bully and biscuits, but now getting a drink of tea. Our first stop on that day was at Amiens where we began to meet the English soldiers who are billeted in every village.

Leaving Amiens we pass on throup Boulogne to the outskirts of Calais. Here we branch off towards (Hazebrouck) and what a busy line it is, with train after train of war material of all kinds.

Our next stop is (Thiennes) and from here we pass on through (Wlttes) to (Roquetoire). It is now 10 p.m. and we disentrain, have a cup of tea, and march about three miles to a farm house. H ere we are billeted in large hay barns, and are· real comfortable.

We are only a few miles from the Firing-line, and can hear the roar of the guns and see the shells continuously bursting. I believe we are to go into the Firing-line at the end of this week, so by the time this reaches you we will have served our first 16 days in the trenches on French soil, and then we have a rest for 16 days.

I am sending you a little souvenir of France (a handkerchief sachet) which I purchased in a little village just outside Ypres, also some view-cards of a town close to our camp. Do not worry about us, dear parents, as we are in splendid health and hope to see you in 1917?

PRIVATE FRANK LEE

He was killed in action on the Western Front.
"Somewhere in France" 1916.

HERE WE ARE AT LAST
Dear Mother,
Just a few lines to let you kn ow that things are going all right with me. You will see that I am now in France and right amongst it. We waited in Egypt long enough, but here we are at last.

France is a fine place. We landed at Marseilles and then spent about 58 hours in the train. We passed through some of the most beautiful country one would ever wish to see. The Rhone valley, with the river runnlng beside us, was just a picture.

Of course, it was Spring-time when we came through, the best time of the year to see the country. The barley was just brown, the oats and, wheat just in ear. and the grape vines bright-green. There were no big patches of crop like one sees in Australia. No more than a few acres of each.

Then there would be grape vines, or vegetables — with no fences, all hedges. Always there were plenty of trees, mostly tall poplars. It was Just like a great· park we were travelling through.

We have fine scenery here, too, of a night, like a great fireworks display — only it is a lIttle more rowdy. There are rockets going up all night and they light up the trenches like electricity, while bright searcbllghts travel across The sky looking for aeroplanes.

Then the dull thud of. the guns some distance off, and the loud bang of those close at hand that make the very ground shake. Then comes the shmp rat-tat-tat of the machine guns. Altogether, things are pretty lively here of a night.

Some of the houses that the shells have hit make a terrible picture. Most of them have tiled roofs and are built of brick — very few wooden houses are seen — and a few shells soon make them a heap of ruins.

We never get twilight in Australia like it is he re. It do es n ot grow dark until just after 10 o'clock, so it is a v ery short night.

The first shell fire we saw was when we were about 15 miles from the firing line — it was one evening and they were firing at an aeroplane. We could see shells bursting all round an aeroplane, which was only a small spe ck in the distance. But they must be very hard to hit. I have not seen one hit yet.

The other night we were in reserves, in a big barn, and a battery of ours behind us was banging away, sending the shells over. The row woke me up, but I had dozed off again when suddenly a few German shells came over and almost got our barn; in fact, a few pieces of one did hit it, so we had to get out lively.

All the reports we get show that our side is advancing, so things are going well. We get fed well here — better than we did in the desert in Egypt. I got your last letter just before leaving Egypt.

We had a good trip over, though there were plenty of rumours of submarines. We stopped at Malta for a couple of days, but were not close to the pier so no-one could get ashore. It was on a Sunday and we were allowed to go over the side for a swim during the afternoon. It being fairly hot, there was a big crowd of us in the water of Malta harbour.

Marseilles is a big city. We were about an hour-and-a-half coming into its harbour, passing small lighthouses and buoys about a mile from the shore: and yet we were passing the city the whole of the time. But we were not allowed to see any of it for when we got off the ship they marched us from the wharf straight on to the train which left about 10-30 in the evening.

We passed Paris about 12 miles off, and all I could see of that famous city was the Eiffel Tower sticking right up over everything else. It must be very high as we could see it quite plainly

Well, Mr. Wortley, there is nothing more to write about at prese nt so must close. Remember me to Mrs. Wortley, and all."

PTE. F. LEE

PTE. F. LEE

Nurse Edith Cavell was shot by the Germans for helping English, French and Canadian prisoners to escape from Belgium. She faced her executioners bravely, saying, "Patriotism is not enough. I must have no hatred or bitterness in my heart towards anyone."

Miss Edith CAVELL
COWARDLY MURDERED
October 12th 1915

ARMY-NURSES ARE THE HEROINES OF THIS WAR.

SISTER A. C. JACKSON (of St Arnaud) describes her work in France.

First Australian General Hospital, FRANCE.
7th. May, 1916.

For ten weeks no Australian mail has come through since we reached France on April 5th. I am now on night-duty. At first I was on all alone with just the help of four orderlies. We had only a few Australian patients; but since then we have had several convoys arrive.

We now have several hundred patients all Tommies and King's Own Scottish Borderers. We always get them in the sm all hours of the morning; and they have generally been on the Red Cross train for seventeen or eighteen hours.

They come from Armentieres and near Ypres. They are evacuated from the clearing-hospitals up near the firing-line. These men are kept in the Field Hospitals for forty-eight hours, but as there are no nurses there (only orderlies) the result is they are very dirty.

The staff up there work day and night, and have only time to do the dressings. So we have the task of digging off the trench-mud and dirt, and the train dust. To add to that, the fifty who have just come in were absolutely unmentionable with vermin.

The poor old Tommies are all worn out! They went to sleep before I could get them half-sponged. At 2 a.m. I called up more nurses to help me. Some of the men were poisoned by gas; others were burnt by bombs bursting near them.

It is real active service here, and the splendour of the Heliopolis Palace Hotel in Egypt is a thing of the past. Here we sleep in huts which are only tiny cubicles, 12 ft. by 6 ft. Two sisters occupy each hut; and for beds we use the camp-stretchers which we brought with us from home.

We just have four bare walls, and supply everything ourselves. We bathe in a hand-basin, which is very trying. At present, as I am on night-duty, I sleep in a tent holding seven of us. There is nothing in it but the beds. We dress in the huts.

It is very cold here today, and last night we nearly froze. No fires are allowed after April 1st. (by British Army Regulations) no matter how inclement the weather. I think it will snow today. Snow is quite a common thing here.

Chilblains are the order of the day because we cannot keep our hands and feet warm. Yesterday we had to sleep in an empty tent in the medical lines because our night-tent was having a wooden floor put in it. Then, about 1.30 a.m. we were awakened by the noise of twenty orderlies putting up tents right against us.

Red Cross train and ambulances

I was about to go to bed at midnight after writing this letter, but we have just received word that a convoy of wounded is coming in at 4 a.m., so everyone is. bustling around preparing hot water-bags and blankets. It is now snowing and the cold is intense.

Of course, we are feeling the cold more after Egypt's heat? The cook is up all night to supply hot w ater and drinks. My patients are too ill to leave, so I have my supper in the small bell tent attached to the big tents I am in charge of. Twenty-four beds are squeezed into each tent, and they are all bad surgical eases.

Sometimes we buy little things for supper as one gets so tired of cheese, bully beef and biscuits. You see, we don t h ave our mess catered for. We do it ourselves. We e ach pay a franc a day for extras, and with this we buy jam, butter, bread and vegetables. We do not have fruit or any.luxuries.

Everywhere here the most rigid economy is practised — such a change after the lavishness of the East. Pineapples are 4 francs each, potatoes are 2 fran cs each, sugar is 9d. a lb. and butter is 3/8 a lb. — so you s ee how dear things are.

Now I am about to put on my sou'wester and mackintosh and rubber boots, and take my old hurricane-lantern by the hand, and sally forth to do a round.

I h ave a poor English boy with half his shoulder blown off by
a h igh explosive shell, and an amputated arm; and the re are various cases of gas poisoning, too gruesome to m ention.

THE BATTLE OF JUTLAND

It was after nearly two years of war that the plans of hvo great sea commanders led to " The Day" — or " Der Tag" as the Germans named it. Bristish Admiral Jeilicoe and German Admiral Scheer would at last face each other in battle and two great navies would confront each other in a fight to the death off the coast of Jutland.

On board HMS Malaya was my father, aged 24, in a detachment of the Royal Marine Light Infantry (Plymouth Division). He was a corporal in the gunnery section of that great battleship which sailed out of Rosyth Naval Dockyard with four other dreadnoughts — Queen Mary, Warspite, Valiant and Barham — heading for the grey waters of the North Sea.

These five ships made up the 5th. Battle Squadron and,vere due to rendezvous with the rest of Admiral Jeilicoe's fleet off the coast of Denmark. Somehow plans,vent rather haywire when this squadron ran into thick fog — and my father would never forget "What happened next.

As the fog lifted, HlVIS Malaya and her companions suddenly found themselves face to face with Admiral's Scheer's battle cruisers. Barham and Valiant took on two of them, while. Warspite and Malaya took on the nearest three.

They scored hits with their 6-inch guns, but unfortunately my father's ship was trailing behind the others and came under fire from at least four of the enemy ships. She Was hit seven times and the awful scenes on father's ship would remain with him for the rest of his life.

However the Malaya did not sink, but steanred ahead with the rest of the 5th. Battie Squadron to their appointed meeting-place with the British Grand Fleet. make no mistake, the winner "would rule the waves" and help to bring an end to the Great War (1914-18).

When at last they finally confronted the German High Seas Fleet, the World saw two of the largest navies in history slugging it out in a fight that lasted 24 hours.

It was a terrible battle, bringing sudden death to thousands of sailors arnd lvlarines. Sometimes a thick fog hid the two mighty antagonists from each other's view, yet throughout that day (31st. of May) the battle raged relentlessly,vhile these huge dreadnoughts hurled one-ton shells at each other.

The Malaya was at first very lucky because German shells,vere just falling around her, covering the ship with spray, but without a direct hit. " Neverless than three ships firing at us — sometimes more, was how father remembered it.

Then the Malaya successfully hit one of the German destroyers that came within 6,000 yards — and sank it with several more of her shelis.

However, her good luck could not last for ever and eventualiy the Malaya received a serious hit on two of her gun turrets manned by the Royal Marines. When shells explode on deck they rip through the armour plating like a knife through cheese, smashing and igniting the ammunition; and as that dreaded cry "Fire!" goes through a ship one can just imagine the results.

Men are trapped inside the watertight doors and burn like moths in a flame; and when a shell bursts on a gun it sets fire to the cordite on the trolieys nearby, causing severe casualties. Blackened bodies are scattered everyvvhere.

HMS Malaya had 168 killed and 63 wounded after the Battie of Jutiand, but in spite of severe damage she managed to limp over 300 miles back to Rosyth Dockyard.

At the end of the day, the German High Seas Fleet slunk home like a pack of beaten curs to the nearby port of Wilhelmshafen. Yet before the British ships crossed the North Sea back their British bases, Admiral Jellicoe on the 'Iron Duke' signalled that all ships must stop and get ready for a tradional burial at sea for the corpses. My father said he never forgot those awful sights and often described them to my mother.

Many of the dead remained where they had fallen, dismembered and charred, at their posts. It required a strong stomach to collect and identify the corpses and prepare them for burial.

Each mutilated form was placed in a hammock with a shell tied onto the seaman's boots for weight to ensure the body would remain at the bottom of the ocean; and the Last Post was sounded by the Royal Marine buglers as each shipmate was plunged into the waters.

On the hardest-hit British ships, such as my father's ship HMS Malaya, the burial services could not be concluded quickly as the sheer number of corpses to be disposed of was intimidating and a long drawn out affair. Father witnessed many of his shipmates plunged into the dark waters as one by one the corpses slid overboard.

Years later he told my mother that the most awful part of those sea burials was the sight of corpses (who did not sink immediately) floating in an horizontal position; and then, as the weights attached to the seaman's boots took effect, the corpses changed themselves into an upright position, with about half of the canvas showing above the water as if the poor dead sailor wanted to salute his mates and take a final look at his ship.

All that day funeral services were carried out for the men killed in action. Bodies were placed in turn beneath the Union Jack to be slid off into the sea as their shipmates sang that great hymn, "Abide With Me".

It seems the same respect was not accorded to the enemy's sailors because father remembers his ship steaming through hundreds of floating corpses, most of them wearing German uniforms.

A recently-published book about the Battle of Jutland written from the German perspective, argues that Britain lost the Battle of Jutland — in my opinion that is as bad as denying the Holocaust ever happened.

The truth is that after the battle it was the British Grand Fleet left in control of the seas while the Germans fled for their lives back to Vilhelmshafen where their sailors mutineed, refusing to come out again and fight. Or as one witty journalist wrote at the time, "If the German Fleet has assaulted its jailor, why is it still in jail'?"

Without doubt Britain lost more ships and more men than the Germans, but it is courage, not superiority of numbers, that wins a battle. Britain lost seven ships along with 6,907 men a The Germans, on the other hand, lost three ships with 2,551 killed.

But the fact remains that after returning to Wiiheimshafen there was mutiny amongst the German sailors — their morale had been snattered — and for the rest of the war they and their ships never ventured out again upon the high seas to confront the Royal Navy.

It was indeed the greatest naval battle in history and those who were there — such as my father — even if their lives appeared to return to normal, would never be able to erase those shocking scenes from their memories. In his dying moments my father would keep repeating, *"Pass up lyddite, pass up shrapnel!* 11

CARNAGE AT SEA

HMS. "Malaya " in Portsmouth Harbour

H.M.S. MALAYA IN PORTSMOUTH HARBOUR

A CHARLTON LAD, PRIVATE A. M. DRAPER (7TH. BATTALION) DESCRIBES WHAT CAN HAPPEN IN THE TRENCHES.

IN THE LINE AT ARMENTIERES June, 1916.

We have just finished fifteen days in the Front-line of trenches. I came out of it fairly well, but I got one nasty crack on the nose from a splinter of a shell. I thought I had lost my nose for a while, judging by the quantity of blood there was all over my face, but after I got it dressed and a bit of sticking plaster on it, I went back to the trenches.

I lost two of my best mates, P. C. Smith and Mitchell. Poor Smith got blown. up with a shell. Our cook had just come back from a holiday in England, and brought up the food to us. He said he would like a shot, so someone lent him a rifle and he stood up at the parapet. He just had one shot, and the next minute he fell back, shot through the head.

My Company has not lost many men this time? Poole and Lionel Pennyfeather are all right. I see Tom Williams and Tommy Ryan are back home after being wounded. Good Luck to them, because this is worse than the Gallipoli fighting.

Here, you have the biggest guns in the history of the world, firing upon you day and night, and they make holes you could put half of Charlton in. And the gas — it is terrible. And the liquid fire. And the weeping gas they send over to try and blind you. But we are prepared with helmets and goggles for both. The boys look weird characters with steel helmets on, but they stop many a hard crack on the head.

PRIVATE MICK MCINERNEY (OF WITCHEPOOLE) KEMPSTON HOSPITAL.

A RAID AT ARMENTIERES 1916.

I got a very severe shell wound In the shoulder. It caught me Just near the back of the neck and cut a good furrow Into the left arm. There Is a bone broken In more than one place, but I am going to have an operation and expect to be all right shortly.

I cannot describe to you the way we are treated in hospital for It Is Just like being at home. All the English people are so nice. They bring us cigarettes, fruit, flowers and everything to make us comfortable and happy; and I can assure you they are successful.

Here Is a brief account of how I came to get my wound. They called for volunteers to raid the German trenches. So I, with many others, volunteered; and I was vety pleased when chosen. We had a little special training and then we were fattened-up for the occasion. The aim ls to wear out the enemy.

On the 29th. June (1916) about 10 o'clock, we crawled the first 300 yards on our stomachs and then laid flat while our artillery played on the enemy's trenches. The gun-fire was terrific, shells were going to and fro over our heads In thousands.

When our guns ceased firing, we rushed their trenches. We had less than 100 yards to run, but Fritz lit that ground up with bombs, shrapnel and bullets; and every man In our party who did not fall (wounded or killed) got Into the Fritz trench. There were no nervous men In our little raiding-party on that night.

We took a good many prisoners because the Germans we met didn't put up much of a fight, that ls after we got into their trench. In fact, a few that could speak English indicated they were very glad to surrender and get out of the war.

Just as a few of the last of us were getting out of Frttz's trench, one of our mates got badly knocked about, so we lifted him out and began dragging hlin back. But the ground was so rough With shell-holes and sltppery-mud that we could scarcely keep on our feet, so we trted pulling him along. We had only gone five more yards when I got my souvenir.

Needless to say, I was no more use to the party, or to the wounded man, so now my only ambition was to get back to our '-own trench: but 400 yards looked a very long way to travel across No Man's Land under very heavy fire. However, delay meant danger, and I didn't want to wake up In Berlin.

I crawled from one shell-hole to another and you can imagine how I felt. _ Just before I reached our trench I got a crack from a bit of shrapnel on the neck, but It hit me with Its flat side and so It only burned and bruised a little. I do not know yet how the others in my raiding party fared.

I was very pleased to arrive at Eastbourne (on the South Coast of England) and with the wonderful treatment we are getting, I expect to leave here fit — and to be in France at the finish of this war (which I do not think Will last more than another seven or eight months).

The British organisation for handling the wounded is simply marvellous. I will be here for a long time yet; and apart from a ltttle pain, we are all as happy as kings here. : lt wasn't too bad In France. In fact, when we were out of the trenches we used to have a good time.

The British and French are pushing ahead In great style.

"RED AND WHITE DIAMONDS"
(24th. BATTALION)

Standing, L. to R.
Private Webb (Machine-Gunner)
L/Cpl. Swetman (Machine-Gunner)
Private Smith (Trench-Mortar)
Sitting (L. to R.)
Gunner Beckham
Corporal Arthur Clifford

ARTHUR CLIFFORD WRITES :

RESTAIRES

Just after we started, we saw an aeroplane being fired upon by the Germans. It was up a great height and the shells seemed to be bursting all round it;. b ut it just sailed on and seemed to take no notice. There must have been over 100 shells fired at it. We have seen several German Taube machines, but they keep up a great height; almost out of sight above the clouds.

Our different Companies marched along the road, leaving at 8-minute intervals, until within sound of shell-fire; and then we split up again and platoons went on at 2-minute intervals, until finally the men advanced in single file. The Royal Scots were all out of their billets anxious to march off; and so we took their places.

Our huts are within easy reach of enemy shell-fire, and if the Germans wanted to they could knock the Hell out of us; but I suppose they know if they started. that game our Artillery would return it to them with interest.

The day after we arrived they sent a good many shells whistling over our heads into Fleurbaix, where they set alight to a house in which our Artillerymen were billeted. There are a lot of our own Artillerymen planted all round us here and some of their guns are quite close?

Our Firing-line was a high wall of sandbags built above the ground; for this part of Flanders is very marshy, and trenches dug into the ground b ecome hopelessly waterlogged.

Once I was out examinlng some breast-works and barbed wire entanglements, when a big gun went off near me. I ducked down behind the parapet like a shot b ecause I thought old Nick had got me.

Our sister battalion (the 23rd.) is in the Fro nt-trenches now. One evening a m achine-gun got one of their office rs and he was buried the d ay b efore yesterday. I was on guard at a comer of the road that day and the cemetery is opposite, so I saw the buri al.

About a mile down the road is a village which we can observe from our corner-post, and we saw about six shells burst on the road where s ome pioneers were at work. One poor chap was killed instantly and several others wounded.

Poison-gas used by the Boche on this Front is a horror for us. Its victims are filling the Ypres cemeteries. But our artillery discovered that exploding shells can break up the gas clouds.

[*Aussie humour prevailed, even over poison-gas, and our soldiers used to joke* : "The Germans are smoking cheap tobacco again; here comes their smoke cloud)

Yesterday we marched into a town, about 4 miles from here, and we had a lovely hot bath and got a change of underclothing each. It was alright to get rid of the "chats" as some of us had a whole regiment of them.

We always have to crawl out early in the morning at 4 ·o'clock and "stand-to" in the trenches for an hour, but we always go back to bed afterwards. At dusk we have a "s tand-to" as well. There's usually a bit of cannonading and musketry at both these times. We go into the trenches tonight for ab out five days, I think. We have all our "duds" packed up, and we cleaned out the huts for the next lot.

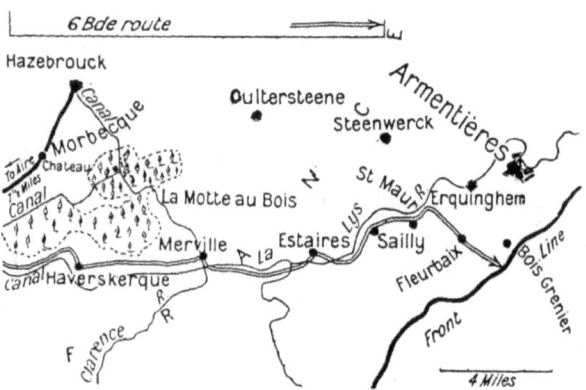

Yesterday, a mate called Jeffrey was only about a dozen yards from our post when a lump of dirt hit him on the arm and frightened the wits out of him. Some of the chaps in the dugout called to him and asked if he was hurt, and he replied, "I don't know — yet". When he said that, it did sound funny.

The rats here are big enough to defend the trenches on their own. When we sleep in the sandbag-shelters, hungry rats run all over our faces and even nibble our noses and fingers. They are far more annoying than the Huns.

On Wednesday, Fritz sent over half-a-dozen shells, but they did no damage. On either side of us they "socked" it in each day, but I don't think anyone was hurt. We got no more shells this week, but it rained nearly every day and night. Thursday night and Friday was the only decent weather we had.

We were due to come out of the trenches on Good Friday and thought we would have a good time since the day was so fine.

But we were doomed to disappointment, for it started raining at sun down and continued all night.

Well, about 9 o'clock the 23rd. Battalion took over our posts and off we went through the muck. It was as dark as pitch, except when flares went up. We made good headway, although the duckboards are only about 15 inches wide and there are several feet of water beneath them; so if you step off them it's ten to one you sink in stinking muck up to your waist.

In the long, winding communication-trenches, at some places the water was over the boards. In the dark we slipped and sprawled in all directions and every now and then some poor, tired beggar would miss the duck-boards and down he would go — up to his neck in slimy water. I, myself, was very lucky and only got my boots full of mud, three times.

However, at last it came to an end — and we were very glad for our eyes were aching with trying to watch where we were going. The muddy roads were covered with slush and water, too. The chap in front of me was just boasting about how lucky he was to come through the trench without getting a spill, when over he went into a hole of water up to his waist.

We got into billets in Fleurbaix about 1 a.m. and slept soundly in the partly-demolished houses. We are a bit crowded, but we are dry and have a fire-pot in the middle of the floor so we can dry our clothes. On Saturday we got up about 9 o'clock and had our breakfast which was bread, butter and jam.

After dinner we went down the town to buy some things. We got some jolly fine postcards, nice little handkerchiefs, and some tucker. This town of Fleurbaix is in an awful state. About 19 out of 20 houses are cornplete wrecks, many are burnt down, and very few are fit for habitation. The Germans must have stuck a jolly lot of shells into it.

We had a good day on Easter Monday, but a sad accident occurred later. An officer in the 22nd. Battalion was instructing his men in the use of hand-grenades when a bomb exploded in his hand. The poor chap and one of his men was killed instantly.

PRIVATE TOM CAVANAGH, (OF WATCHEM) WRITES TO A FRIEND MISS ANNE PICKERING.

At the beginning of 1917, this poor soldier had his leg blown off – and died at a dressing-station, 24 hours later.

A REASON FOR MARRIAGE, FRANCE. 1916.

"The mail has just, come in and both of us fared pretty well. I think your brother (Bert) got a dozen letters and I got ten; so you can be sure we had a good read; and, what is more. I believe we know as much as anyone does about what has been happening around Watchem. Bert also received the two cakes you sent him, and they were lovely.

We have been having a fair time in France so far, although it is pretty wet I honestly believe it rains here 364 out of 365 days of the year. What a vast difference between this country and Egypt. At the later place we were over our boots in SAND; and here it is just the reverse because you sink up to your waist in MUD and SLUSH, and very likely you have to call to your mates for assistance to pull you out.

Although it is Summer here now, it does not seem to make much difference for it is still <u>raining</u>. I will never forget last Friday night as long as I live because it was our first experience in the trenches in France.

We started off from our billets shortly after dark, and for the first mile or two it was not too bad; but when we came to the Front-line it was just the reverse.

The trenches here remind me very much of the water channels that run through the country about Watchem; and when they are full you can imagine what it would be like walking on a 15-inch wide plank, balanced just above the surface of the water.

We enjoyed the trip thoroughly, I don't think! There was not one of us that did not get a good soaking. You would walk along safely for a few yards, and then SPLASH! Sometimes you would fall in feet first, and at other times, head first. We got there alright, but I believe it would have paid a fellow to swim, as we swam nearly half the way as it was.

If old Kaiser Bill could have heard the language that night, he would have turned the game up at once. It would have done him good to hear some of the Australian swear words — and I don't mind telling you we are champions at the game.

I see where some of the Watchem volunteers got a good send-off. Good luck to them! The pity of it is that there are not <u>more</u> of them, for there are thousands needed here as replacements for

the wounded and dead. I also see there have been a good many marriages of late around the district. I think that a lot of these men are frightened of Conscription coming into force, and they know married men are exempt from war-duty.

Today is the 15th. of June (but they wouldn't let us put the date at the top). I suppose your brother told you that we are now both attached to the Artillery? We have a little gun of our own and every time we send Fritz over some "Iron Rations" he gets real vexed and aims all sorts of things back at us — anything from "Coal-Boxes" to "German-Sausages".

"Coal-Boxes" are big, high-explosive shells; and the "Sausages" Fritz sends over are not like the ones you buy at Waddell's Food Store. Oh dear, no! They are BOMBS threaded on a straight piece of iron; and after one bomb explodes the rest bounce away to another place, where another bomb goes off — and on it bounces till all the "Sausages" are finished.

Fritz sends over another sort of bomb known locally as the "Rum-Jar" as it is about the size of a gallon demi-john. He has been sending over a lot of them lately because we have been stirring him up.

We had a great laugh the other day when Fritz was sending over shrapnel and we all made for cover. One of my mates was a bit slow and he had the misfortune to stop a piece. It never broke the skin at all, but it raised a lump, the size of a marble. He stands up to take his meals now and he gets very cross if we ask him the reason why!

I will sign off by saying I promise to write as often as I can — if Fritz Spares me — so do not be anxious about us. I assure you that the only V.C. most soldiers want to see, is the Victorian Coast.

Private J. Allardyce writes from 'Somewhere in France' to his sister, Mrs. J. Moore, of Donald.

BATTLE OF FROMELLES, 1916

Our boys of the 15th. Brigade had a go at the Germans on the morning of Wednesday, 19th. July. Our heavy artillery opened fire on the Germans and blew their trenches to pieces, as well as a lot of their big guns. We kept pouring it on till 6.30 in the evening when our boys fixed bayonets and jumped out of their trenches.

My 60th. Battalion led the charge across a distance of 500 yards, through long grass, ditches and barbed wire (which was very plentiful having been hidden by the Germans in the long grass).

Well, our lads had only gone 200 yards when the Huns trained their machine-guns onto them. Huns just sat on top of their parapets and worked their machine-guns which were positioned no more than 50 yards apart. Those bullets poured down from the Sugar Loaf where the Germans had built concrete fortifications containing machine-guns that could fire down upon our men as they crossed the plain of the Laies.

The German bullets played havoc amongst our men, and very few of them even gained the first line of German trenches. Major McCrae was killed almost immediately and all our officers were quickly picked off by the enemy. Almost every officer and N.C.O. of my 60th. Battalion lay dead or wounded on the plain of the Laies River.

But a few of our men who were not hit, got there and took some prisoners, bound them up, and then quickly advanced to the second line of enemy trenches. However, the

Germans counter-attacked and our men, not having sufficient reinforcements, had to turn back and beat a hasty retreat.

The noise of the big guns was deafening, I can tell you. Out of 2,000 men in our 15th. Brigade, there are only 200 left to tell the tale. Some were cut to pieces, whilst others were killed or seriously wounded. I will never, never forget it. My 60th. Battalion was wiped out in its first encounter with Fritz.

The cowardly Huns even fired upon our wounded as they walked slowly about to ease the pain they were suffering. I helped to carry in the wounded and we gave them hot tea before they were passed on to the hospitals. The majority of them are now in England.

When our roll-call took place the morning after this attack, only 61 men from my 60th. Battalion answered to their names, although the Battalion was nearly 1,000 strong before the attack. I saw some German prisoners brought in and they were well-clothed, fine, big men who looked well-fed. We captured 350 prisoners, including a Major and a Captain.

At present, I am busy carrying rations up to the Front-line and it is night-work, of course. We start about 11 p.m. and go on till about 3 a.m. and then we turn in to rest. But I cannot sleep much during the daytimes for the noise of the big guns.

Fromelles was the greatest battle that has been fought and the Australians have made a great name for themselves. There is a lot to do yet to get rid of the Huns who are just like ants, attacking in their thousands. I am done up with the sights I have seen, especially when I saw the pitiful state my mates were in.

The heroes of our 15th. Brigade did not fail, for no infantry in the world could have crossed No-Man's Land under those conditions. Wave after wave of exposed men were mown down — 7,000 troops were recklessly thrown away in one night. It was a suicidal attack.

JUST AN OLD FELT HAT

This story is a view of the Battle of Fromelles from close quarters — for only after the danger had passed were soldiers able to tell the truth about this tragedy in their letters home. The battle took place in Northern France on the 19th. July, 1916, and in that stiff fight our soldiers displayed amazing courage and outstanding gallantry, yet in the end it proved to be Australia's bloodiest military loss.

Amongst an enormous collection of war memorabilia in Canberra's Shrine of Remembrance one can find tragic souvenirs of this very battle; and perhaps one that paints the most poignant picture of Fromelles is just an old felt hat lying in an alcove upon a dusty floor.

This felt hat was actually worn by an Australian soldier when he and his comrades made a courageous dash across No-Man's Land towards the line of German machine-guns and consequently he was cut to pieces by a withering hail of bullets.

Apparently, the first two waves of men from Australia's 15th. Brigade went over the top wearing <u>steel helmets</u>, but the following two waves of men advanced with <u>felt hats</u> on their heads.

I noticed a small hole in the crown of a faded, mud-stained hat on the floor — perhaps caused by the very bullet that ended a soldier's life as he charged across the plain of the River Laies.

"Honestly, what good is a felt hat and a bayonet against a line of blazing machine-guns?" I muttered, gazing sadly at such a tragic souvenir.

Thousands of British, French and Australian soldiers were slaughtered on July 19th. in their brave attempt to cross the River Laies and capture enemy trenches, but no soldiers in the world could have survived such a continuous rain of machine-gun bullets falling down on them from the German fortifications (known as the Sugar-loaf).

It was more than two years after the Armistice in 1918 when several military felt hats were found in the mud of the river and carefully brought back to the Australian War Memorial for preservation. The same search-party also found plenty of skulls, bones and torn Australian uniforms scattered about everywhere beside the Laies — and nearby lay the bones and bits of uniforms belonging to British soldiers.

The attack at Fromelles against well-entrenched German lines cost the 5th. Division almost 7,000 troops in one night and was therefore the biggest slaughter Australian forces had ever suffered.

A witness of what happened at ground level is Private John Allardyce who wrote a letter to his sister describing his part in the Battle of Fromelles. He tells her how his 60th. Battalion was wiped out in its first encounter with Fritz.

"We boys of the 15th. Brigade had a go at the Germans on the morning of Wednesday, 19th. July. Our heavy artillery was given the job of pouring a full bombardment upon the enemy's front trenches to blow them to pieces. At 6-30 in the evening we fixed bayonets and jumped out of the trenches.

My 60th. Battalion led this charge across a distance of 500 yards, through long grass, muddy ditches and barbed-wire entanglements, but we had only gone 200 yards when the Huns trained their machine-guns onto us. Bullets poured down from the Sugar-Loaf where the Germans had built concrete fortifications.

Major McCrae was killed almost immediately and soon nearly every officer and NCO of the 60th. Battalion lay dead or wounded on No-Man's and. Out of 2,000 men in our 15th. Brigade there are only 200 left to tell the tale. Some were cut in half by their own artillery. The cowardly Huns even fired upon our wounded as they walked slowly about to ease the pain they were suffering.

When our roll-call took place the morning afterwards, only about 70 men answered to their names, although my 60th. Battalion was nearly 1,000 strong before the attack."

Private John Allardyce also wrote that he helped to carry in the wounded from No-Man's Land — and gave them hot tea, laced with rum, before they were passed on to the hospitals.

It seems that he could not resist the cries of the wounded because several times he went back into No-Man's Land, risking his own life, to drag bodies out of the mud near the German entanglements and carry them back on his shoulders to safety. "Don't forget me, Cobber!" was the cry of many wounded soldiers to the brave rescue parties searching amongst the dead.

Another man who tells his view of the same tragedy was Lt. Colonel Ernest Albert Harris. He had already served with distinction in Gallipoli during 1915 where he had been an inspiration to his men; for when the troopship "Southland" was torpedoed in the Aegean Sea he made sure all his men were in the life-boats before leaving the sinking ship himself.

In a letter to his wife, Lt. Colonel Harris describes how (on the 19th. July) he led his 59th. Battalion in one of the first waves of attack upon the German fortifications, only to be pinned down by machine-gun bullets. His men could get no further than half-way across No-Man's Land and he could clearly see from his position the wounded men of the 60th. Battalion crawling back. He sent a message to General Elliott (who was behind the lines) saying that the men could go no further without being slaughtered, yet Elliott ordered him to continue the attack. Consequently, the unnecessary slaughter continued and Colonel Harris himself was wounded by an exploding shell as he rose to lead his men forward to certain death.

(Some years after the war General Elliott committed suicide; so perhaps it was his decision at Fromelles made in ignorance of the real situation that troubled his conscience.)

Another soldier in that terrible place at the same time as Lt.-Col. Ernest Harris (59th. Btn.) and Private John Allardyce (60th. Btn.) was Major Frederick Percy Williams (58th. Btn.) who described July 19th. as *"a day of horrific casualties"* and *"a day of desolation"* saying that he was engaged the whole night *"administering hot drinks of beef-tea to the wounded".*

Major Williams served as a chaplain throughout the war and later he wrote about Fromelles in his diary: — *"Our casualties were very heavy. In the morning the division returned to its original front line, having taken about 400 German prisoners...... Our 15th. Brigade was immediately relieved. They had been without food for 24 hours, so we cut up some bread and cheese in hunks and the rum we mixed in the tea. They did relish it...... We left a big number of dead out in No-Man's Land. The total casualties killed, wounded and missing amount to 7,800 in the 5th. Austalian Division.*

"Artillery duels were still going strong as we commenced the task of bringing in our dead...... I found Chaplain Maxted at the end of

one trench, all hunched up, but quite dead. I attempted to straighten his body, but was seen by the Bosch who turned their machine-guns on me, so I had to retreat." Major Frederick Percy Williams was awarded the Military Cross and after the war returned to his vocation as a priest in the Anglican Church. He died from a heart attack in 1939 while playing bowls in Ballarat.

The Battle of Fromelles was indeed a foolhardy and senseless attack on the German lines and the loss of life was so great that many of our allied soldiers were hastily buried in mass graves dug by the Germans outside the village of Fromelles.

Those of us who have lived through the terror and darkness of a war know as the years pass how that terrible darkness becomes just a dim memory; yet do we ever completely forget its horrors?

One of several felt hats found in the mud of the River Laies.

Unknown soldier wearing a felt hat

A German signpost directing its soldiers to the village of Fromelles

The huge scale of Australian losses at Fromelles and, a short while later, at Pozieres almost defies the imagination. The first Australians had arrived at the Port of Marseilles in March, 1916, and we know from letters written by those soldiers how they marvelled at the beauty of the French countryside as their trains rolled north to the combat zones of Belgium.

A little later they were sent down to help the British and French on the battlefields of the Somme; and the previous letter from Private John Allardyce vividly describes that terrible suicidal attack upon the German line near the village of Fromelles and how his 60th. Battalion lost 16 officers and 741 men of other ranks.

The felt hat (pictured overleaf) was one of several picked up years afterwards in front of the Sugar-loaf; and an Australian visiting the area said, *"We found the place full of our dead. In the sector west of the Laies River and east of the Sugar-loaf salient, the skulls and bones and torn uniforms of our men were lying about everywhere."* C. E. W. Bean's official history of the war states that only the first two lines of some companies had been provided with steel helmets, whilst those in the third and fourth lines were wearing their felt hats.

Allardyce also tells you in his letter how he went out and helped to carry in the wounded. *"Don't forget me, Cobber!"* was the cry of many helpless soldiers lying out in No-Man's land. The 15th. Brigade may have failed, but no infantry in the world could have survived the intense fire of machine-gun bullets raining down from the German fortifications (known as the Sugar-loaf) along the opposite bank of the river.

Another Donald man who fought at the battle of Fromelles was Colonel A. E. Harris. He led his men of the 59th. Battalion in one of the first waves of attack upon the German line, only to be pinned down by a withering hail of bullets. He sent back a messenger to Elliott saying that his men could go no further without being slaughtered, yet Elliott ordered him to continue the attack. Consequently, the unnecessary deaths continued and Colonel Harris himself was wounded by an exploding shell. (Some years after the war Elliott committed suicide.)

> PRIVATE GEORGE OLIVE, in this letter to his mother, writes about his experiences while fighting in France during 1916. He was recovering from his wounds in a hospital at Tunbridge Wells, Kent, England.

Well, all goes well with me. I am getting along nicely, the wounds on my cranium are healed, leaving only the eye to mend. Ere another month has passed, it may be possible for me to return to Belgium to seek my revenge. As to our doings during the past month I have told you practically nothing, but I am not to be blamed for this; the censor is to blame. On February 4 our regiment left Salisbury Plains amid great excitement, naturally. All were then well pleased, as our stay there was not too pleasant. In those days, however, we little knew what lay ahead, or we might not have been quite so pleased. A few hours journey by train brought us to the port, Avonmouth, near Bristol, where we were herded on an old cattle boat, arriving at Saint Nazaire on the 14th inst. after experiencing some dirty weather at sea. The old tub rolled and tossed everywhere, and what with the crowd of troops and horses, it was unbearable. The seas smashed over the boat, washing away some of the stalls, and killing several animals.

We had a terrible job looking after the brutes, at one time there were as many as six down side by side. We did not fare much better either — no sleeping accommodation, and only bully beef and biscuits to eat. Most of the chaps did not need that as they were so sea-sick. Here again my luck in being a good sailor stood me in good stead. None were sorry when we were safe on land again. Saint Nazaire is down the Bay of Biscay so, of course, we expected bad weather. Disembarked on the morning following, and by 5 p.m. we were on a cattle train bound for the scene of action. Here again we were herded like sheep. On the journey across France we enjoyed it, however, as we crossed from the Bay of Biscay to the Franco-Belgian border, thus seeing much of France, skirting Paris, though we passed such large cities as Rouen and Nantes. The peasants were very kind, giving us wine, fruit &c.

After 48 hours journey we arrived at Hazelrouck — you will frequently see this town mentioned during the war—and forthwith commenced a march to a village called Caestra. Here we stayed until the 23rd, then moved onward to Erquinghen, some 18 or 20 miles away. No marching for me, though, as I was in charge of a team. It was on this journey that I rode a horse till he almost dropped. He was left at a farm where we halted but died next day. Like a good soldier he practically died in harness — the boat trip settled him. Here, not far from Armentieres, we first experienced the trials of the trenches. On the night of the 26th we moved, and after paddling through mud and water for miles, took over trenches from some British troops. Never will I forget that experience, wet almost up to the knees and unholy cold; plenty of work to do, sentry duty, barb wire and listening patrols, two hours, two off. The latter were the worst, the only cover being dug-outs with muddy floors. My feet troubled me most of all — becoming numb, it Was impossible to get them warm enough to allow one to sleep. Glad were we when morning came. These were very quiet trenches, scarcely any bullets flying about. Now and again we would send them a few to remind the Germans that there was a war on. They replied with rifle grenades but our artillery gave them to understand by well directed shells that it would be wise to desist. This was only a trial for us, as we came out of those trenches after 24 hours. None were sorry, either. Next day we were recipients of a few shells which fell too near our billets to be healthy. On March 2 we moved to new billets at Bac St. Maur, and the following day our brigade began work in earnest, taking over some tenches. My work, driving a team with rations and munitions, began here. Once, with a transport officer, I had to run the gauntlet of a flying daylight trip with parts of the machine gun. The roads had been shelled that morning, and you can guess it was risky, because the German trench was plainly visible, and the C.O. would not allow me to take the limber back before dark — more able to make a run then if shelled. All passed satisfactorily, however. For the next few days we had a fine time. We machine-gun drivers, with our teams, were billeted away from the rest. We were like the Lost Legion — never bothered at all. It came to an end all too soon. On March 10th our first section casualty occurred; not serious. Further down the great battle of Neuve Chapelle was being fought — our only part being to keep up a rapid fire to stop the Germans attempting to make attacks. Again we moved, nearer the fighting line at Levanti, staying two weeks, and then went to

Estaires for a rest. We enjoyed our stay there. Only once whilst there was our rest disturbed, when German aeroplanes dropped a few bombs around us.

On April 7 we went to Cassell, and on the 15th began the march which ended so disastrously to our division — in casualties only, not in honour by any means — that from Cassell to Ypres. The first day's march brought us to Keewoorite, after passing through Poperinghe. Up with the lark in the morning we reached Ypres, Belgium towards evening, and moved into trenches taken over from the French. A rotten night for driving — dark as pitch, raining heavily. Eventually we arrived back at our billets about four in the morning — practically at it 24 hours without a breather. Ypres we found to be a doomed city, a beautiful old place, once the capital of Flanders, and where the Kaiser promised himself he would be crowned King of Belgium. To my mind he should be crowned King of Hell. After three days in Ypres, large shells began to fly all round but they did not bother us. More objects of interest were they than anything else. Every 15 minutes we expected them, and were seldom disappointed. We could hear them coming some distance off, pass overhead with a whistle, then crash; no harm to us. But the city and civilians did not always fare so well. For many of us this was the beginning of the end. We were shelled day and night, yet we managed to visit all parts of the city, the once famous Cloth Hall and the cathedral, now a mass of ruins. Ypres has a bad name among the troops, as the trenches ran around V shape, being in range of German artillery on three sides.

All went well until the fatal 22nd. During that afternoon we were surprised to see Zouaves, rifles and guns, returning to the city. We learned that the Germans had broken the French line by gas, and the Highland Brigade was exposed on the flank. The order for our men to stand to was given. Shells were falling everywhere. Unfortunately I had to drive with the guns and munitions, but we thought nothing seriously wrong. We laughed and joked the same. All the time the bombardment never ceased. The star shells lit the sky until it was as light as day, aeroplanes dropped coloured lights on our guns, giving the range to the enemy. It was dark when we were ordered to positions. We went to the Yser canal, and attempted to cross a bridge scarcely wide enough for a limber. Stuck with the team, I expected a tip into the water, but by breaking the bridge, managed to back out. The troops went on, and I returned, later on coming to a growing crop. The wagon having previously been emptied by the section, I awaited further orders. Hell was let loose! Our boys had encountered the advanced line of the Huns! Bullets and shells everywhere, many shells not exploding, and wounded pouring back. I was there all night, not that I wanted to be.

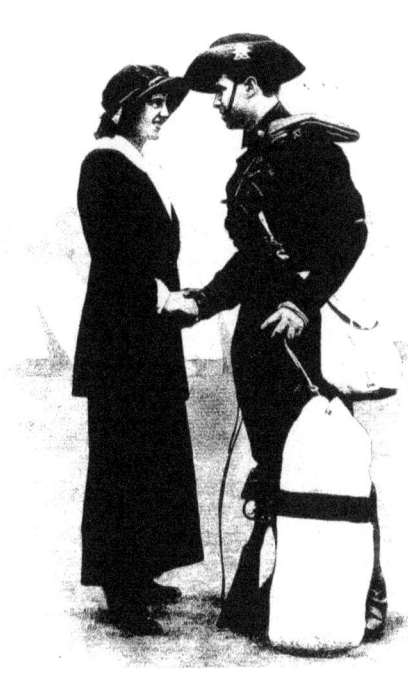

A MOTHER'S FAREWELL

GOODBYE MY SON

Sapper Oscar Dart (of St. Arnaud) who is serving in the Field Engineers, writes to his uncle, Mr. G. Edwards, of Bealiba.

"Somewhere in France". 1916

MUDDY TRENCHES

"I have got to the dinkum game at last. I don't think any of us were sorry to leave Egypt's sand, natives and camels. We had a five days' trip on the sea. then a four days' train ride through France to a small village where we billeted for a fortnight.

Then we were reviewed by Lord Kitchener, and marched past General Joffre of the French Army. When we were marching to the front we did about 25 miles in two days — carrying full packs which weigh 50 or 60 lbs.

It was very wet and muddy in the trenches at first, but the weather is getting finer now.

It is supposed to be very quiet on our front, but it gets a bit lively at times. I have got past the stage of ducking my head when a bullet whistles past it but I can't say that I care too much for the sound of the shells."

"FAIR SAILS THE WIND FOR FRANCE"

Re-interred soldiers at Fromelles

SGT-MAJOR H. DANIELS TELLS HOW HE WON THE V.C.

Now I had been out of the trenches into No Man's Land so knew what it was like — a continuous stream of fire in which no troops could hope to live and jump the wire. So shouting as loudly as I could to be heard above the din, I called out to Lt. Pennyfeather, "But, Sir, we can't do it — no one can do it. We must have the wire cut."

"Very well," he called back. "Send the wire-cutters out at once. We have orders to take the wood."

I knew well the terrible risk of cutting wire in the face of a withering fire, so how could I pick out two or three men and command them to go out to their certain death? It wasn't right for me to give such orders. But something had to be done as we had been commanded to take the wood at all costs — and until the wire was cut that order could not be carried out.

To try it would be to be murdered. Still, somebody must go out and cut that wire. Suddenly, it occurred to me that I must go. I passed the word along for my chum, Tom Noble. "Tom," I said, "we must go out and cut the wire."

He nodded. "I reckon we'll deserve a medal if we do," he said. "We'll get a German bullet apiece more likely," I replied. We each got a pair of wire-cutters and then shook hands.

"If you die, I'm going to die, too," said my chum to me. I made some sort of reply to him and then said, "Ready? Come on then."

Together we jumped up onto the parapet of the trenches and

directly we showed ourselves the German bullets came quicker and thicker than ever. But bending down and running as hard as we could we reached the wire in safety.

The first thing we did was to drop down on our backs. We set to work at once. Up shot our hands and 'snap, snap,' went the wires under the pressure of our cutters. I don't know how many German rifles and machine-guns blazed away at our quick-moving hands, but it must have been hundreds. The rattle of the guns and the ping of the bullets were incessant. We were out there for 7 or 8 minutes. Well, we cut all the low wire we could reach while lying on our backs and then we had to get up to reach the 'breast wire'.

We stood up and I knelt down on my right knee — and we seemed to have the most wonderful charmed lives as bullets went everywhere but into us. We had almost finished when — plug — they caught me in the left thigh. Over I rolled onto the ground and almost as I fell I saw Tom go down as well.

"I'm hit in the chest, old man!" he called to me, but his voice was faint. I believe he was unconscious almost at once, yet 3 or 4 times he tried to rise up and finish his cutting job. I yelled out to him to lie down and keep quiet, but he didn't hear me. He never said another word to me after he called out that he was hit.

Tom was the bravest and best man in the world. Not being able to help him, I rolled over and fell into a shell-hole. Then I got 2 hard biscuits from my pack and with them and a field dressing made a tourniquet and so stopped the bleeding from my wound. Some time later I was picked up and carried in.

"We must go out and cut the wire."

Sergeant Claude Castleton, AIF, brings in wounded men across ground swept by intense machine-gun fire. He was killed and received a posthumous award of the V.C. for his gallantry.

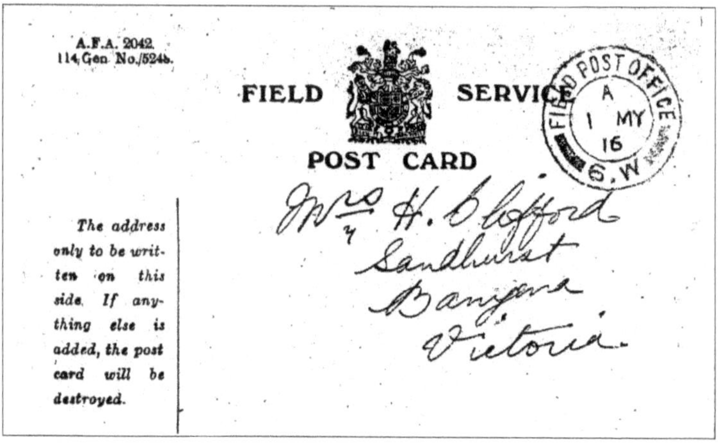

A.F.A. 2042.
114 Gen. No./524b.

FIELD SERVICE
POST CARD

FIELD POST OFFICE A 1 MY 16 6.W

The address only to be written on this side. If anything else is added, the post card will be destroyed.

Mrs H. Clifford
Sandhurst
Banyena
Victoria.

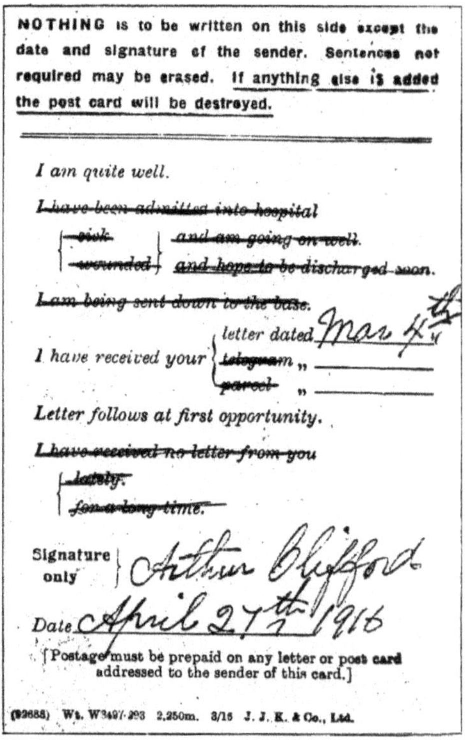

NOTHING is to be written on this side except the date and signature of the sender. Sentences not required may be erased. If anything else is added the post card will be destroyed.

I am quite well.

~~*I have been admitted into hospital*~~

~~*sick*~~ ~~*and am going on well.*~~
~~*wounded*~~ ~~*and hope to be discharged soon.*~~

~~*I am being sent down to the base.*~~

I have received your *letter dated* Mar 4th
~~*telegram*~~ „
~~*parcel*~~ „

Letter follows at first opportunity.

~~*I have received no letter from you*~~
~~*lately.*~~
~~*for a long time.*~~

Signature only Arthur Clifford

Date April 27th 1916

[Postage must be prepaid on any letter or post card addressed to the sender of this card.]

(93688) Wt. W3497-293 2,250m. 3/16 J. J. K. & Co., Ltd.

A brief reassurance from a soldier in the field to his auxious folks at home

Private Fred Blencowe (of Birchip) writes home from "Somewhere in France".

A PHENYL BATH   1916

Dear Mother, As a pal is going to England, I am seizing the opportunity of writing to you some news that I can tell — for any other kind would be censored.

Leaving Egypt in teeming rain, we embarked for France. On board we had to have a life-buoy in our hand at all times, owing to a sister ship having been torpedoed on her return voyage from France — fortunately, she was not carrying troops at the time. (*This was the* MINNEAPOLIS.)

After a week's voyage we landed at Marseilles and then entrained. It was an interesting trip. By the way, when ordered to move, we Infantrymen are never told where we are going, or how long it will take.

From Albert we marched about six miles to (*Dernancourt*) in very heavy rain, and we did get wet. For a week we camped in sheds and barns — these are the soldiers' HOTELS — and we had plenty of straw to sleep on.

After marching all day we arrived at our billet; and when we were nicely-settled, an officer came in and informed us that we would have to get out as he wanted the barn for his sick horse. We told him in no uncertain terms what he could do with his sick horse, and we never saw him again. I think the horse must have died, for he did not ask us to move a second time.

From here we started marching again, and were on the road

for a couple of days until we arrived, footsore, at the Somme. But billets were found for us every night. Then we went into the trenches. It is quite a home here compared to what it was in Gallipoli.

We have six days in the trenches, and then out for the next six days. It is very interesting to watch the aeroplanes being shelled.

I am amazed how the French people bravely stick to their homes; and I am surprised how they live within only two miles of the Firing-line, and always in constant danger from the shell-fire.

The other day a village was shelled, and in addition to some of our soldiers being wounded, three little French children were killed.

We go on a march tomorrow again, but I cannot say where. The food issue is much better here, although some days the food is a bit short. In that case we go to bed and sleep for a meal, or we find a coin and toss up to see who gets it This only happens while we are in the trenches.

I am feeling very fresh this afternoon, having just returned from having a hot phenyl bath and a change of clothing. Phenyl is necessary as we are not vermin-proof.

One day there was a dozen of us in a sap when a six-inch shell struck the end. We had a fall of earth, a flare, and enough smoke to make a fellow keep his mouth shut. There was a scatter of legs, but another mate and myself were buried. The other chap was buried completely, but I managed to keep my head out.

Cross bars and shovels were soon put to work and we are both alive to tell the tale. It caused one poor fellow's death. He got such a shock that he became paralysed down one side and died on the way to England.

It is spring-time here and glorious weather. I read in a Berlin newspaper that by fighting the Australians the Germans are fighting with the scum of the earth. What jolly beastly wretches to call us SCUM!

All the villages around here have been heavily-shelled, so that only a few scattered bricks show where once there was a home. I saw a house set on fire from shells, and the women and children were carrying away what few little possessions they had managed to save. It was a pitiable sight indeed, and illustrates the real sacrifice of war.

We are now camped on the banks of a river, and some distance back from the Firing-line. We are doing drill every day, and we are sick of it. So far, the trenches here are the best places to be. At this moment, the Germans are popping some 9-inch shells about four hundred yards away — and I am pleased they are no closer.

OH, POZIERES, RESTING PLACE OF HEROES.

In July, 1916, the Australians were sent south and put into the Great Battle of the Somme to help the British in their "BIG PUSH" to break the German-line. Our tenacious Diggers pushed forward the British line, but suffered terrible casualties, mainly around the shattered village of POZIERES.

Just after midnight, on July 23, the 1st. Division attacked and took POZIERES; but beneath the heavy enemy bombardments, "every inch of soil around POZIERES was washed with Australian blood".

An eyewitness described the survivors of the 1st. Division as "looking like men who had been in Hell. Each man looked drawn and haggard, and so dazed they appeared to be walking in a dream, and their eyes looked glassy and starey".

At POZIERES HEIGHTS the 2nd. Division endured hours of relentless shelling upon their open trenches; and men were buried alive as trenches collapsed under such bombardments.

C.E.W. Bean (Australia's famous war-historian) says: — "The area around the old windmill at POZIERES is more densely-sown with Australian sacrifice than any other place on earth." However, POZIERES WINDMILL was captured on August 4, after two heavy fights.

MOUQUET FARM, about one mile away from POZIERES, was the next stage in the Diggers' fighting on the Somme.

SIGNALLER MATT HOGAN
July, 1916.

OUR BRAVE INFANTRY

Dear Mother,

I am O.K. so far, although we have had a big bombardment here again. Our guns put in three shots to the Germans one. I had to ride out to the trenches with an urgent despatch while their guns played up Old Harry with the parapets; but so did ours to theirs.

I was just pleased to get away from the trenches, as shells were rooting up the ground and burying men, and others were busy digging them out; but this is only a trifle to what is coming very shortly when the big offensive starts. The enemy trenches here are only about 150 yards from ours.

I often see J. Kirk and F. Fraser who are in the Artillery. I also see R Barry and Martin Noonan from Birchip.

But I am satisfied we should all take our hats off to the Infantry. They deserve <u>all</u> our praise, as they are the backbone of the army all right.

I hear that we are not allowed to send mail away for six weeks, so that's proof that something BIG is going to happen — and the sooner the better. If a man survives the next five months he will get home alright (which I am hopeful of doing) but you know a lot of things can happen in a day.

At present, things are fairly quiet here, but that is only the lull before the storm.

The Russians are playing blazes with the Austrians, but I have expected that, and a lot more. That must please the Italians. In my opinion, the Russians will win the war. The French are sure to hold <u>Verdun</u>, as everything depends on it. Then it will be left to the British to hold <u>Ypres</u>, which could be another fight like <u>Verdun</u> — or perhaps worse.

The Germans have a great hatred of the British, but I am confident the British will hold <u>Ypres</u>. The Austrians now will be easily controlled, and I cannot see that the Germans are doing anything successful along their lines. Yet I think the war will not end until Autumn, 1917.

The only thing the Germans are superior to us is in big guns; but by this time next year we will be superior in everything, and what an awful time the enemy will get then.

All the same, we shall drive them back this year a good way. The sea-blockade must be starving Germany and that is why the Germans brought out their fleet at Jutland — and didn't they got an awful hiding from the Grand Fleet led by Admiral Jellicoe? The British are still in command of the seas.

It was bad luck to lose Lord Kitchener, who was drowned at sea, and just as the Russians are having the great success he predicted. The Russians have unlimited supplies of men, so they will have no more failures.

In our Company we have two men who keep our bikes in good working-order for despatch-riding. Lately, it has been very wet and cold here, so I dread what it will be like when winter arrives.

I suppose the newly-formed division will be over here soon from Australia. We read in the papers that the 38th. Battalion is training at Bendigo, and the 40th. in Tasmania.

They tell us that Australia is in favour of Conscription, and we certainly want all the men we can get for the big offensive.

I have got so used to shells flying around me that it would seem strange to be without them. One thing I do not fancy and that is being at sea against those submarines, as they really have me scared, I shall never forget the night on the bridge of our transport.

We were near Malta where some ships had been sunk by German U-Boats. We had two battalions on board, so it would have been a disaster to have had a torpedo sent into our ship that night.

There is no cowardice when face to face with the enemy, but an unseen foe is a different matter.

It will be a God-send when it is all over, but thousands of people will have sad news waiting for them before long. As I told you before — **the Infantry heroes, every one of them.**

"None but the brave deserve the fair."

LORD KITCHENER ON A VISIT TO THE FRONT
He was drowned on 5th. June, 1916.

*Pozieres: The machine-gunners coming out
pass the pioneers going in*

Private W. Davison who was severely wounded at Armentieres Brancepeth Castle, ENGLAND.

THE HORRORS OF WAR

<u>26th. July, 1916.</u>

"Just a few lines to let you know I am still alive and fairly well at present. I suppose you will have seen by the paper that I got smacked. I am just beginning to be able to use my right arm again. An Army Chaplain came to me when I was in the hospital in France, and wanted to know if he could write to anybody for me, so I got him to write to mother.

Well, Jim, I had a narrow escape. I was on the firing-step looking over the parapet at about 11 o'clock at night. The Germans were slinging over a good few bombs and one just missed me, but burst on the paradox behind me, killing a chap alongside me. He was sitting on the firing-step at my feet, He fell over dead, and I fell on top of him.

I got a piece of shrapnel through the right fore-arm which struck the bone. All my right hand was skinned, and a piece went in behind each shoulder, another piece at the top of my head, another under the short-rib (more to the back on the left side), and a piece of wood pierced my right thigh.

The shrapnel is still in, but the doctor is going to take it out. That same bomb also wounded another chap in the back, so I consider I was lucky. I just missed the big advance at Pozieres through getting hit.

The night before I got hit, the Germans made a raid on us. They sneaked over in die dark with bombs and tried to surprise us. Two of them jumped up in front of our barbed-wire, about a chain-and-a-half off. We shot both of them, and then got five more as they came along. You could not tell who actually shot them as so many of us were firing our rifles.

The flares they shoot across No-man's Land, light up the place like day. We went out and brought in one of the dead Germans. They were all fine, big, young fellows. We left the others out in No-Man's Land. It seems a pity to shoot them, but it is "KILL OR BE KILLED". War is awful. You have got no idea what it is like and it is hard to describe to you folks at home.

We were heavily-bombarded the night we went into the trenches at Armentieres. The sides of the trenches rocked with the concussion from the shells and trench-mortars. The Germans send over trench-mortars the size of an oil drum. One landed half-a-chain in front of our trench and the concussion blew the sergeant and I to the bottom of the trench.

You can see trench-mortars coming, and when they are falling, you can hear them "Swish! Swish!" through the air. I like the shells best — quick and lively — no suspense about them. But when the trench-mortars are coming you have to guess whether they are going to fall on you or not.

The machine-grins are terrors. They sweep along the top of the trenches, and it is "God Help You" if you happen to have your 'napper' over the parapet at that particular spot. You ought to see some of those chaps who get hit with pieces of shell. They are chopped about in all directions. You would wonder how some of them live after such horrific injuries.

I will not dwell longer on the horrors of war. I have not had word from home for a long time. I hope you can manage to read this, as my arm is not too good yet for letter-writing."

Convalescing

Private Cyril Grogan tells his parents (of "Olinda", Donald) what he thinks about the war.

MONGREL CURS!

July, 1916.

"Take it right through, this is a glorious life. It is a series of feasts and fasts — comforts and discomforts. One week, a full belly with all a man could desire; and the next week, a half-tin of bully beef and four biscuits per man. One week, a warm bed and enjoyment in town; and the next week, bitter-cold, rain and a muddy bed in a leaky dug-out in the trenches. But with fine men and good mates, we can still have a laugh and a jest when things seem at their worst.

For Heaven's sake, don't expect me to tell you anything about the war. Damn the war! I know this much — if I return home and see a man I know who has not got his colours up, he can expect no recognition from me. Such a man has deserted his country.

When we see around us the pitiful wrecks of homes, and the bodies of little children killed by shell and gas, we realise what would happen to Australia if we are beaten here. We must win — and we shall win!

Whether we go under in the struggle is a secondary consideration; because, if we lose, I look to the enemy to see to the punishment of those few mongrel curs who, by their inactivity, proved themselves to be traitors to Australia.

What has really made me mad is a letter from a 'one-time friend'. In his letter, he tells me of the good times he is having at home with the girls, cricket, picnics, dances, rows on the river etc. He winds up by saying, *"Australia is good enough for me"*, and calls me a "mug" for enlisting.

Yes, Australia is good enough for him, but it is we (the poor mugs) who are keeping him safe there. That is the part that hurts me most."

The 24th. Battalion moved out from Albert on the 26th. July. His Second Division was sent to relieve the First Division which had suffered heavy losses. The notebook of Arthur Clifford continues to tell us an amazing story of courage in the face of HELL?]

THE WESTERN FRONT   1916

POZIERES

<u>July 26th.</u> At 3 o'clock, we were roused out of bed to pack our kitbags, had breakfast, and got going. We marched to <u>Albert</u>, six or seven miles away, and rested there for a few hours. We put everything into our packs, except rations, mess-tins, waterproof and overcoat. We left our packs and moved off to <u>Sausage Gully</u>, and thence up to the Front-line.

It was dark before we got properly into <u>Sausage Gully</u> and we had some bother finding our way through the crowds. We battled through the traffic alright in the end, and then marched along the road to the Firing-line. At one point a machine-gun played upon us, wounding a few. Some shrapnel also knocked a few out. More news about this particularly awful road later.

We then got into a Communication-Trench, a very narrow one and shallow, too. In this trench were some of the First

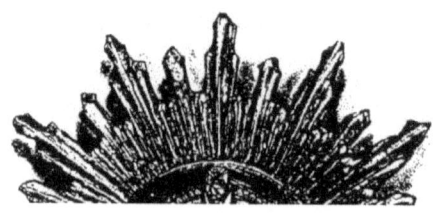

Division, acting as supports to the Front-line. It was hard work moving along here, owing to the narrowness of the trench and so many men crowded into it

After passing through the support-lines, the trench became more like a succession of shell-holes than anything else, as it was very much blown-in. After half-a-mile of this, we climbed out of the trench on to the level ground and walked across open country to the Front-line. We walked along the rear of the Front-line trench and lay down on the parapet until the men in the trench got out; and then we got in.

The men of this trench (known as Kay Trench) had only that very day chased the Germans out of the woods to their rear and dug in out in the open. They were very glad to be relieved as they had had a very bad time.

We could plainly see that they were nerve-shattered and very shaky from the effects of heavy bombardments. These men had been under continuous shell-fire for the last three days. We were to experience that same horror very soon.

* * * * * * * * *

<u>July. 27th.</u> It was 2 a.m. on Thursday morning before we, the 6th. Brigade, got into the line; so you can imagine we were fairly tired after marching all day from the Brickfields, west of <u>Albert.</u>

As soon as we got into our positions, we got to work to deepen the trench, which in a lot of places was only about 18–inches deep and could therefore afford us little protection. We worked like natives, and by daylight had it down to about 3 feet 6 inches. Then the trouble commenced.

At 9 a.m. on July 27th. a heavy bombardment began. The Germans did not spare us once daylight revealed our whereabouts. Fritz started shelling us and kept up a withering fire for the next 36 hours.

All day long, the big 5.9 shells killed, buried, or wounded our troops. By evening, half of my Company had gone. Some had shell-shock, some had slight wounds, some had bad wounds, and many were killed.

Lieutenant Kerr and Corporal Jaggers were blown right up with that first shell to fall on us. Nothing of Lieutenant Kerr was ever found. All day long men were buried alive and had to be dug out by their comrades. Kay Trench was murderously hit all day, both by trench-mortar bombs and shells bursting upon it frequently. We had no deep dugouts, and could only shelter in small recesses in the sides of the trench.

[*This was among the worst fighting of World War 1. The shellfire from the German artillery was so horrendous, that POZIERES is the most notorious name of all upon the Western Front.*]

After dinner, several fatigue-parties were detailed to go down to Sausage Valley. I was in the first party to go and get Mills bombs, and 23 of us went for them.

The Germans spotted us and started humping shells into us, right and left. The Communication-Trench being so open, it was a job for us to find any cover. A few of us got slightly-wounded on this fatigue and we lost plenty of sweat running for it.

We went down to the "kitchen-cookers" in the valley, and got some tea; then we ducked off, back up the trench, each of us carrying 24 bombs. We got back safely at dusk.

While we were away a good many more of my Company had

got wounded, including Smith and Beckwith, two of my cobbers. <u>Fenotti, who was in my fatigue-party, was running across the open ground in front of me when a shell landed under his feet, and only his head and shoulders were left behind.</u>

Before going further, I must tell you about that awful road from the advanced Dressing-Station. It is nicknamed, "Dead Man's Road" because both sides of this road are lined with dead Tommies and Australians. It is awful to see the way their bodies are mangled about, but the worse part is to see the gun-teams driving over the bodies of the dead and the wheels of the wagons crushing them up.

In the Support-trenches of the 22nd. Battalion, we had to walk over dead men, and occasionally bits of men. There were whole lines of dead men, half-buried, and it was an awful sight. But we had to keep going and take no notice of them.

Everywhere there were blackened men, torn or whole, who had been lying there dead for days.

After delivering the bombs, I got down into the trench again while 5.9's were still lobbing round us; but very few shells caught the trench and most fell just in front or behind us.

The shock of the explosion of these shells is terrific. Dirt, stones and pieces of metal were falling on us all day; and all we could do was crowd against the sides of the trench while the earth-shaking explosives fell fast around us.

We <u>waited</u>, which is much harder than "hopping the parapet". Men were buried alive, and others went mad.

We sat there in Kay Trench, hour after hour, waiting to be killed, or buried, by the collapsing banks. Men were dug out, only to be buried again. Some brave men played a game of cards while they waited for Death to arrive.

At midnight, our Sergeant came along and asked me if I would give Rolf a hand to take our badly-wounded Corporal Couch down to the Dressing-Station. Couch was at "B" Company's dugout so I ducked over, but Rolf was not there. He was away looking for a stretcher; therefore I decided to carry Couch immediately to the First-Aid Station on my own back.

I was just carrying him outside when shells began to burst all around the dugout entrance. They called out, "Take Couch back down the dugout or you'll both be killed!" Well, I carried him by the shoulders and another mate got hold of him by the feet. We were just starting down the steps when a shell exploded right behind us. Three machine-gunners near me were killed instantly, but I only got some shell-splinters in my back.

We fixed up Couch and the other wounded men, then I carried some S.O.S. flares back to our trench. About an hour afterwards a stretcher-bearer came along and told me to go down to the Dressing-Station and get my back seen to.

I started off and caught up with two squads of Stretcher-bearers who were completely worn-out as they had been going all day long. I took their two "walking-cases" on ahead and so hurried them along a little.

[*A battalion always went into action with* 16 stretcher-bearers, *but on this day not even a 100 bearers to each battalion would have been sufficient to cope with all the wounded.*]

There were some shell-splinters in my back, so the doctor fixed me up, painting my back with iodine. I had about two hours' rest in a corner of the Dressing-Station before returning to my Company.

* * * * * * * * * *

<u>28th. July</u>. There is a ridge in front of us called <u>Pozieres Heights</u>. We have been ordered to take that position, as well as the second line of German trenches — so that is our objective.

My 6th. Brigade intended doing it alone. However, with the great loss of men we have had, and the weakness of the ones left behind, and owing to the strain of the last few days, we are not fit.

The heavy bombardment which filled Kay Trench wth our dead men occurred on <u>July 27th.</u> — just after we, the 6th. Brigade, had entered the line.

[*Our war-historian, Charles Bean, writes, "So great was the carnage in the 24th. Battalion that for months afterwards, even when "K" Trench had been obliterated by constant shelling, its outline could be easily traced by the half-buried bodies which bore the red and white diamond colour-patch on their arms protruding above the mud".*]

So at dusk tonight the 7th. Brigade came in to replace us, and we were glad to get away out of this HELL. Sadly, on the way out we had some more casualties. We had just got into <u>Sausage Valley</u> when our own guns opened up with a vengeance. Hundreds of guns, from big 9.2 and 12 ins. down to .75's and 18 pounders, stuck it into the Germans for all they were worth, and our men were caught in the cross-fire.

It was a pitch-dark night, but the quick flashes of the guns lit up all the valley, and the cracking and roaring almost deafened us. We got down into the saps and trenches and got the first sound sleep we had had for about 72 hours. We were all completely fagged out and weary; not only from want of sleep, but from the strain that is placed upon men when under a continual bombardment.

We were hoping to get away from the Front-line for a while, but were disappointed to hear that the charge of the 7th. Brigade was a rotten failure. They didn't know their objective properly and got mixed up through lack of organisation.

But our comrades of the red and brown (the colour patch of the 23rd. Battalion) successfully advanced and dug themselves in — thus keeping up the fine reputation of the Victorian 6th. Brigade.

They were sorry that we (the 24th.) had not gone on with our sister battalion (the 23rd.) in place of the 7th. Brigade, as then the attack would have been a success! Now the attack upon the German positions has to be done all over again and that means more loss of life. However, it could not be helped.

* *

We camped in Sausage Gully for several days until 200 reinforcements were drafted in to strengthen our numbers. Each night we expected to go up and take the ridge, but they kept on postponing it.

We often went up to the Front-line, carrying rations to the lads who were holding it; and unfortunately sustained a lot more casualties doing this necessary duty.

On three successive nights, the "A" Company of the 23rd. Battalion went up and dug a "Jumping-Off Trench" (J.O.T.) about 300 yards out in front of our Line. So when the charge upon the ridge does come off, we will have that much advantage.

* *

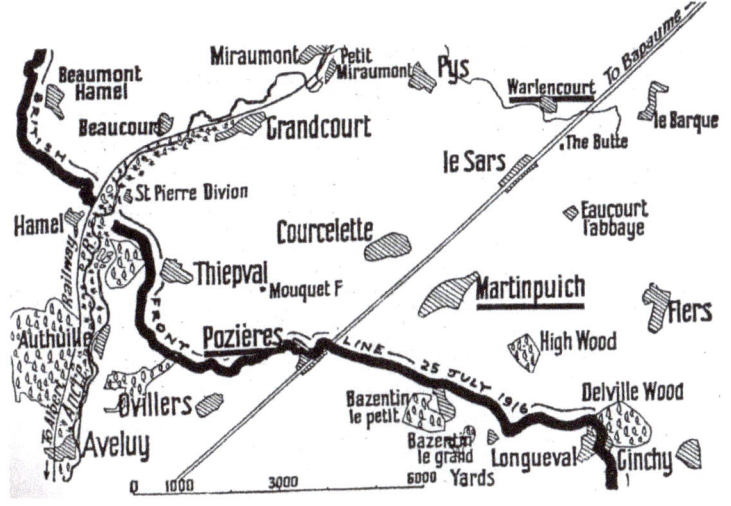

CARDS FROM FRANCE

Remembrance to Mother

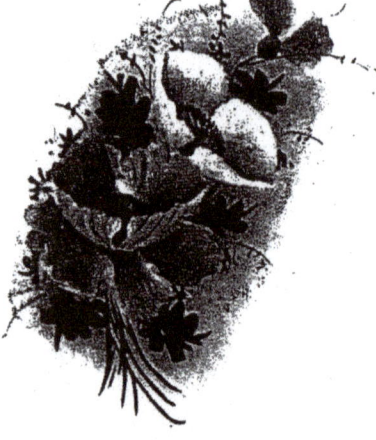

Mother o' mine, have no fear
Now that the time is drawing near,
For us to go to the firing line
To help the Boys to cross the Rhine.

Mother o' mine, keep up your heart,
God will not keep us long apart.
Mem'ries of home locked in my breast,
Thoughts that will make me fight my best.

Mother o' mine, I shall soon return,
And ever for thee my heart shall yearn.
Safe in your prayers I'll always be,
God give us quickly, Peace and Victory.

Mother o' mine, I can say no more,
But to bid you a tender au revoir.
God keep you free from this parting's pain,
And hope that we soon shall meet again.

A man should at all times and at any cost stand by his mate."
We know that this was the philosophy of the ordinary soldier as he faced the prospect of death on the battlefield — but the Australian soldier also possessed a sense of humour and in this anonymous poem we see an amazing wit in the face of hardship and danger — and also a fierce hatred of the Kaiser Wilhelm II who started that terrible war.

FOVANT TRAINING CAMP – ON SALISBURY PLAIN, ENGLAND -1916

There's an isolated, desolated spot I'd like to mention,
Where all you hear is, "Stand at ease", "Slope Arms", "Quick March", "Attention".
It's miles away from anywhere, by gad it is a rum 'un.
Chaps could live here for forty years and never see a woman.

There are lots of little huts, all dotted here and there,
For those who have to live inside, I've offered many a prayer.
Inside the huts there's RATS as big as any nanny goat,
Last night a soldier saw one trying on his overcoat.

It's mud up to the eyebrows, you get it in your ear,
But into it you've got to go without a sign of fear.
And when you've had a bath of mud you just set to and groom,
And get cleaned up for next Parade, or else it's "Orderly Room".

Week in, week out, from morn till night, with full Pack and a Rifle,
Like Jack and Jill you climb the hill, of course that's just a trifle.
"Slope Arms", "Fix Bayonets", then "Present", they fairly put you through it, And as you stagger to your Hut, the Sergeant shouts, "Jump to it".

With tunics, boots and putties off, you quickly get the habit,
You gallop up and down the hills just like a blooming rabbit.
"Heads backward bend", "Arms stretch", "Heels raise", "All change places".
And later on they make you put your kneecaps where your face is.

Now when this War is over and we've captured Kaiser Billy,
To shoot him would be merciful and absolutely silly.
Just send him down to Fovant Camp among the Rats and Clay,
I bet it wouldn't be long before he droops and fades away.

Anon.

On Salisbury Plain (photo: sgt. A. Walder)

PRIVATE ROBERT DICKIE (8TH. Btn.) was the son of Agnes and Thomas Dickie of Watchem. He was born at Watchem on the 27th. February, 1887 and educated at the local school. He later worked on the family farm and then enlisted for the war in 1915 at the age of 28. He fought in Egypt before taking part in the historic landing at Gallipoli on April 25th. He was slightly wounded on May 8th when his battalion, as part of the 2nd. Infantry Brigade, advanced against the village of Krithia, at Cape Helles. On the 12th. May he was wounded again during the fighting in Monash Valley and was taken to Egypt on board a hospital ship. He accompanied the Anzacs to France and went through all the earlier fighting up to the great Somme offensive when he fell during the fight for the village of Pozieres on 25th. July, 1916. (That was the first big conflict between Anzac and German troops.) Robert was killed whilst helping to place a wounded comrade onto a stretcher. (He was buried at the edge of Pozieres village.) His death was keenly regretted by all his battalion for he was noted for his soldierly qualities and devotion to duty.

Royal Horse Artillery Face the German Guns

ATTACK ON POZIERES RIDGE

(by Private A. Clifford)

At last, it is the night of <u>August 4th</u>. Tonight we go up. Every preparation is made. Our Battalion is not to make the charge because the 22nd. Battalion is to do that.

The "Heads" think the "Red and White Diamonds" (24th.) have had their share of honour and glory and the other battalions want to catch up with us a little. So we are to act as Supports and to reinforce the other battalions when necessary.

The 22nd. Battalion are going up and will get into the "Jumping-Off Trench (J.O.T.) at dusk. We follow and will get into that same trench as soon as they vacate it.

A terrific bombardment is to start at 9 o'clock and last for ten minutes to prepare the way. Our orders are, that even if we have to go through Hell, we must take that position. <u>We had to go through Hell, too!</u>

The Germans had an intense barrage of fire on our Communication-Trench all the afternoon and we had to pass through it. As we passed along, in some places the trenches were full of dead and wounded.

The Stretcher-bearers were doing their best to keep the way clear, but they had a hard job and did their damnedest. Each one deserves a V.C. What heroic work they do — dressing the wounded under Hellish-fire and then carrying them away with all possible care.

This affair resembles nothing on earth — just heaps of corpses and a horrible stench.

The 22nd. Battalion hopped over under our artillery fire. We passed into our old Front line and then into the "Jumping-Off position. One wave of our chaps went straight across and helped the 22nd. to dig in and strengthen their position; while the rest of us stopped in the "Jumping-Off Trench" (JOT).

Our chaps swarmed all over the Germans and brought back three batches of prisoners. In one batch there were more than sixty.

When daylight came, the Stretcher-Bearers were hard at it, hunting out the wounded and also bringing them in from the Front-line. All the time, big shells and "Whizz Bangs" were flying about, and knocking out some poor devils.

At daylight, our men who had gone forward to help the 22nd. dig in, were forced to return to their Support Lines because there were too many men crowded into the front trenches. The Commander of the 22nd. had sent back our re-inforcing troops in order to avoid over-crowding the Old German Lines.

I went down to the cooker-fires and took back two dixies of tea. It was a long trip and I was flat out when I got back to the line.

About an hour before sun-down, my Company was recalled to the Firing-line over the ridge, to relieve the 22nd. Battalion — or rather what was left of them, for they had been cut about a lot. There were dead Germans and our dead chaps everywhere.

Some of us were waiting in a shell-hole to move forward into our position, when Lieutenant Hughes (22nd.) came along and told me to go round to Captain Nicholas (24th.) with a message. Arthur Crook, who was sitting next to me, offered to go with the message, but I knew the way so I told Lieutenant Hughes I would go instead. Having safely delivered the message, I came back through a narrow trench.

I walked over a lot of dead men and heard a moan and discovered one of them was still alive. His legs and arms were buried and also part of his head. He was lying face down, with rifles and equipment on top of him so it was impossible for him to get up.

I set to and dug him out, but he was too far gone and I don't think he could possibly live, so I sat him up against the parapet and left him. I could do nothing else for the poor chap.

When I got back to Arthur Crook I found he had been severely-wounded. A shell had lobbed into our hole while I was away. One eye was gone, and all the flesh was blown off his hand and arm. It was awful. Another chap near him was killed, and another wounded badly.

It was our Captain Nicholas (24th.) and Lieutenant Hughes who later that day located the German machine-gun post which had killed so many of the 22nd. Battalion. Captain Nicholas captured the Germans and brought back their gun.

* *

I had been trained for bombing, and now all bombers were ordered to go on to the extreme left flank, about 10 yards further along the line than had been held before. As soon as we got into our position we went to work like natives — digging out the trench in which we could not even stand up at first without being seen.

We filled all the sandbags we had available and made a

fairly respectable job of it. Corporal Ernie White, J. Bickley, J. Rowlands and myself were on duty at this out-post. We ate some bully-beef and hard biscuits.

It was the first food we had had for many hours, but no one cared to eat. I had to force it down. But — <u>water</u>. We could have drunk gallons and gallons of it; but we only had our water-bottles and didn't know how long they would have to last us, so I could only take a few mouthfuls very occasionally.

It was now about midnight. A couple of us went on post-duty while the other two tried to get a little sleep. This, however, was almost impossible as it was so very cold; and with shells crashing, whistling and screaming all around us, it was not at all a pleasant night.

Daylight broke on Sunday morning. Private J. Rowlands was on post-duty and gave the alarm to send a bomb along the sap. We rushed down to the corner with our bombs and rifles. I threw a few bombs down the trench, which made one German hop over the parapet and run across country at about 40 miles an hour.

J. Rowlands and Corporal White aimed after him with rifle-fire. Jim Bickley was standing right alongside me, jamming a cartridge into his rifle, and I was just about to throw another bomb, when poor Jim got a stray bullet through his head. He died shortly afterwards.

When we started to attack, the enemy was out in front of us. Suddenly, several hundred yards away, Germans rose up in their thousands and commenced retreating across the Plain. Whether they meant to counter-attack us, or were just hiding there, we don't know; but at any rate they didn't seem to have the heart to attack us.

The morning was very misty and in some places we could not see Fritz too well, but we potted at him until we were tired of it. They seemed to be crossing that Plain for hours; and if only our Artillery could have got on to their position, they would have mowed down heaps of them. But we had no means of communication with the Artillery and it was too misty for our reconnaissance planes to spot the enemy troops.

Just to our left, the Artillery were dropping some very big shells every few minutes. This was to stop the Germans from coming along the trench to where we occupied it. Word was sent down to us that we could bomb our way along this trench and take possession of it; but our guns did not cease playing on it so we could not move.

As soon as it got light enough I worked my way down the first traverse, but could see no sign of any Germans. I then came back, and a little later Corporal White suggested that we go further along the trench.

He went ahead with his bayonet and I followed him with my Mills bombs. In the second traverse he picked up a lovely automatic-revolver. Here we found plenty of German equipment such as water-bottles, helmets and caps, also biscuits and other odds and ends. We again came back, but afterwards took another trip still further along the same trench.

We looked around the traverse where our shells were landing. The trench was knocked out of shape altogether, being nothing now but shell-holes.

We could not move further along the trench, as at any moment we might get cracked with our own shells. A big one did land nearby and we got the benefit of a shower of stones and dirt.

About 1000 yards in front of us the Germans seem to have a trench. We can see them walking up and down it, and also we see their parties coming and going from it.

There is also a battery of Whizz-bangs out there. We can see them every time they fire. They sent some Whizz-bangs on to us, knocking sandbags on top of us, but then they stopped for a while.

Jim Rowlands and I were sitting on a ledge, cleaning our rifles, when a Whizz-Bang came along and wounded Jim on the face, cutting it rather badly.

A big piece buried itself in the ground near me. If I had been sitting six inches further to the right, I would have had it right through me. We got field-dressings on Jim and he was sent away.

Then we dug out a hole in the side of the trench and buried poor Jim Bickley, covering him up with some waterproofs. We put a little cross of wood over him.

At about 2 p.m. some Germans came along the trench. Corporal White put a bullet into one, and we sent bombs after the rest. They wasted no time about getting away.

After this we had things in readiness for them. If any more appeared, we intended following them along the Sap, bombing them as we went. But that opportunity did not come as we got relieved about 5 p.m.

All this time the Germans kept up their barrage of fire on our trenches leading up to the Front-line. Being high up on the ridge of Pozieres Heights, we could look down and see our chaps coming along the Communication-trench, and see the enemy shells bursting along it, sending up great clouds of dust, smoke and stones.

All this ground around us is torn up with shells. I do not think there is one inch of earth that has not been shifted, and some earth has been rooted up many dozens of times.

About 5 o'clock, word came along the trench that the 4th. Division was relieving us. We were jolly glad when we heard it. We did not like the idea of putting in another night there. I can tell you we were not sorry to be withdrawn from <u>Pozieres.</u>

* *

We left there in two's and three's, straight from the trench across country to the saps. Fritz sent a few shrapnels after us, but most of us got out safely. We left <u>Sausage Gully</u> and camped for the night near <u>Albert</u>. But we were not yet out of danger, for all night long the Germans sent over big shells.

During the night of August 7th. while <u>Tara Hill</u> was being shelled, we were bivouacking there. One shell burst in the dugout — which had been an old gun-pit — where all the Heads of our 24th. Battalion were gathered. It killed Major Manning, (Second-in-Command) Captain Tatnall, (Adjutant) Captain Plant, (doctor) and Lieutenant Carvick. Colonel Watson got off with just shock, although he was rescued from the dugout in a state of collapse.

This terrible loss was a hard knock to all of us and had a depressing effect. We thought that, having just withdrawn from <u>Pozieres</u>, we were well out of danger. It was a great blow, coming straight after our heavy losses at the Front-line.

About 9 a.m. we got on the move again and in a few hours we were well away from the guns. We were all glad to get away from such a HELL — for you could call it nothing else.

They say it was the severest ordeal ever suffered by the A.I.F. I can tell you this — that all the time we were there, we had the smell about us of men who had been dead for days.

All that time at <u>Pozieres,</u> we had the sight of wounded men for whom we could do nothing. Hundreds of times we had to walk, or run, or crawl over dead men. More awful sights you could not wish to see.

We have left behind some of Australia's finest men buried in that earth. <u>Some are in hospitals, and they are the lucky ones.</u>

We are out of it now, for a while at any rate. I suppose some day we will be sent back to it, but there is not a man among us who wants to see more of it.

You read stories about men who are anxious to get well in order to go back and fight again. They are either awful liars, or else they have never been in the real, dinkum thing.

What I have written is a short account of the fortnight we spent in <u>Sausage Gully</u> and <u>Pozieres.</u> To describe the lot would fill a book — and then it would be only the half of it! But this little bit may give you a slight idea of what some of us have gone through, and what some of us have done, in all the fighting that has taken place.

To Arthur with love from Mother

EMBROIDERED CARDS FROM FRANCE

PRETTY COLOURFUL EMBROIDERED CARDS SENT TO LOVED ONES FROM FRANCE

PRIVATE R. T. ARUNDELL (OF CHARLTON) – 1916.

Dear Mother,

I got knocked in the "Big Push" at Pozieres, where they mowed us down like grass. Out of 1500 only 158 answered the Roll Call next morning, so you can form your own opinion about the way the Huns dealt with us. We got their trenches, however, and took 400 prisoners.

The Germans are a lot of cowards and curs; as soon as you get into close quarters with them, they will cry for mercy — which they never get! How could we show them mercy after they had fired at us for about two hours and knocked all our mates out of action?

I have been having a good time since I came to this English hospital. The people cannot do enough for us. They are always taking us out for motor-car rides, afternoon teas and concerts. It is good-oh!

My left arm is hurt and it will be some time before I am able to go back to the Firing-line again, as I would not be able to hold my rifle. There is a lot of shrapnel in the arm and it is fractured, so I am waiting for an operation to remove all the pellets of lead.

One piece hit me on the head and another on the right shoulder. But it is worth getting a good smack to have this rest in England.

I suppose cousin Donald is having a quiet time in Egypt. He wants to keep well away from France. It is murder here; but it is a bit exciting. The big guns roar all day and night.

We say the Dardanelles was child's play in comparison! More firing takes place in one day in France than was done on the Peninsula during the whole of the time we were there.

I suppose I will get over this wound and go back for more fight, because I do not think the war will be over this year. The Germans are losing a lot of men, and the Australians are getting cut up terribly."

* *

HERO OF POZIERES
– Private D. Ross – (of Charlton) 1916.

Dear Mother,

With the exception of my knee which troubles me, I am well. We are having very wet and miserable weather in France which does not make our position any better. I hope the war will soon be over and that I will get back home again.

Fritz I think is well on the move — backwards. Near where we were is what was known as Pozieres. Now the village is only a heap of brick dust, which just shows how thoroughly our Artillery did its part in driving Fritz out of his strongholds. He had grand dug-outs, some twenty feet deep, and large enough for a considerable number of troops. He evidently thought he was permanently there. But we drove Fritz out of his cosy nest and ruffled his feathers.

Today, General Birdwood presented me with my Military Medal ribbon, a piece of which I am sending to you. It was given me for work under heavy shell and machine-gun fire at Pozieres.

General Birdwood said he would present the actual medal later on when it arrives here.

Private D. Ross' citation reads: -

"Major-General Sir H. W. Cox, commanding 4th. Australian Division, congratulates <u>Private D. Ross</u>, 13th. Field Ambulance (4th. Division) on his gallant conduct and devotion to duty under heavy fire on Tuesday, July 25th. 1916, at Pozieres village, France."

POZIERES

Lance-Corporal Charles Alexander (St. Arnaud) writes about Pozieres.

Dear Mother,

<u>Delhi Hospital, TIDWORTH, England.</u>
<u>1916.</u>

I have had an attack of diphtheria, but am now making good progress towards recovering my health. When the good weather returns I hope to be able to get out again, that is if I can escape an eye-sight inspection.

Things have undergone a great change. The old army has gone, and it is a new force that is carrying on now. Gallipoli accounted for many of the finest and bravest lads that ever lived, and now the Western Front has completed the work of destruction — <u>and</u>

only here and there will you meet a soldier who has fought on both sides of Europe.

Men have fallen whose loss will never be repaired. I did not think that men of the present day could show such splendid qualities, but the war has revealed in our boys a high standard of self-sacrifice and devotion to duty. The best and bravest fall in the vanguard of battle.

I had better now give you a short summary of my experiences in France. We landed at Marseilles and proceeded northward to Bailleul, a little town within sound of the guns. We first went into action at Fleurbaix, where we were subjected to a tremendous bombardment.

After about a month in the trenches there, we went to Sailly where we had a rest. The people here were very nice and quite in love with Australians. The provincial French are a very homely and good-natured people. They will even sew your trousers-buttons on.

After a few days in Sailly, we marched across country to a little town in Belgium called Neuve Eglise. Then to Messines, in Belgium, where we suffered rather heavily and where we remained until our presence was required at the other end of the line. It was not long before we were en route for the Somme, as they always put the Aussies in the hardest fights.

We travelled a large portion of the way by rail. We detrained at Doullens, and from that place we marched by devious routes to Albert. The countryside was in all the glory of an early summer, and the weather was beautiful. Approaching Albert, the first sight to greet us was the colossal statue of the Blessed Virgin and Child — hanging head downwards from its pedestal on top of the church.

We rested at Albert for a couple of days, then one evening we moved off in the direction of the front. Soon we were crossing ground broken and furrowed by shell fire. The whole horizon to our front was red with fire. It seemed as though a great bush-fire was in progress. The roar of the guns was deafening. The earth shook beneath the bombardment of the British artillery.

Our battalion halted at a point not very far to the rear. Crouching in an old captured trench I gazed at the wonderful scene. We were quite content to remain spectators. All around us, and to our front, there extended a gigantic avenue of fire. It looked to me like the footlights of some vast theatre. Thousands of star-shells, rising and falling, added to this dramatic effect.

The British bombardment continued until early dawn, when, for a few minutes, the noise of the guns increased to a frightful intensity. Then all noise suddenly ceased, followed by the shrill crack of rifles and the tick-tack of machine-gun fire which denoted that an advance was in progress.

Two Australian Brigades had moved forward and captured POZIERES — no longer a town, but only a mere collection of bricks, dust and broken trees, but situated on rising ground of great military value.

Our brigade was in support — and so at about 4 a.m. we crept up closer to the captured position. The terrible aftermath of victory greeted our eyes. Rifles, equipment and bodies littered the ground. As we stood there, shells suddenly fell amongst us and a number of my mates were killed, or wounded.

We saw columns of prisoners passing by, walking stiffly, like dead men brought back to life. A soldier, with a wide grin on his face, escorted fifty German prisoners. A never-ending stream of our wounded was passing to the rear, but all were cheerful and greatly pleased with their success.

We occupied some of the German dug-outs. Very comfortable and cosy they were, too — deep down in the ground, with little tables, electric lights and mattressed beds. All day on the 23rd. July, we remained in that cover, about half-a-mile from our new Firing-line. The German shells beat harmlessly down, while we enjoyed the security of their underground dug-outs.

That night we moved up and crossed over the Firing-line into No Man's Land. We lay out in the craters and shell holes, waiting for the enemy's counter-attack. We had our bayonets fixed, and two bombs each to give the enemy a warm reception. Nothing occurred, so just when dawn was breaking we marched back to our place behind the lines.

It was on this return journey that I received my ticket for dear old England, and very glad I was to leave the place. At the first Dressing-Station I met Arch. Mills from Coonooer Bridge. He had a slight bayonet wound.

I was sent to Le Triport, a lovely little place on the French coast. It was the care and attention of Dr. Brown (a clever oculist from Sydney) that saved my sight. From there I was sent to dear old Blighty, and so spent a month in hospital at Chichester."

* *

(Lance-Corporal C. M. Alexander's *mother died suddenly not long after he was wounded. He spent the rest of the war in England, as his eyesight was not good enough now to allow him to return to the fight.*)

Private R. Griffin (of Charlton) describes his part in the attack on Pozieres Heights.

WOUNDED AT POZIERES
July, 1916.

"I was wounded in July. Our battalion went into the Firing-line one night to make a charge — and we did. It was shortly after midnight and the attack was a complicated one, but we successfully captured a big part of Pozieres.

After several days of steady bombardment, our Artillery (soon after dark) increased to a very heavy fire. This bombardment was spread over a fairly large front. I had never before seen such a spectacle, for the horizon was lit up, not by single flashes, but by a continuous line of quivering light.

You could catch the sweet scent of the tear shells which the Germans sent over in reply to our guns; and we had to pass through thick clouds of heavy gas from their gas shells.

We went over the parapet just after our Artillery fire was turned upon Pozieres village. Our men took the first German trench in front of the village — charging through the German shrapnel as if it were raindrops. Machine-guns were sweeping the ground in front of us, but we arrived and found few live Germans left in those trenches.

We swept on to their second trench, which was deep and well-built; but in places it had been smashed to pulp by our bombardment. It was here that a big shell lobbed over our heads and landed a few yards away. A piece of shrapnel caught me on the back of the head and knocked me to the floor. I was able to get back to my lines all right as it was only a slight wound, but enough to knock me out of the fight.

I told you last time that I was glad to get to Europe. None of the boys liked Egypt, because it is a dirty place, and too hot, and we were walking on sand all the time. The flies would nearly eat you alive! They would come into your tent like a swarm of bees. The heat there was too awful for words."

CAMPED IN EGYPT

The courage of our Australian troops at POZIERES HEIGHTS, is thrillingly described here by Corporal W. S. R. Campbell (of Charlton)

Dear Mother,

<u>1916.</u>

"We had received our orders and my battalion was to assist in taking two lines of trenches. Everyone was excited. Tea at 3-30 p.m. and march out at 4-0 p.m. Well, do you know we were trying to find our position for nearly <u>five</u> hours?

At last, to reach our destination in time for launching the assault, we made a bolt for it; but being so late, we caught the enemy's barrage and many of our men were killed before even getting there.

At the "Jumping-Off Trench" we had time to have a short spell after our exertions. Imagine how in the quietness every heart was beating loudly. We were only waiting for our guns to open up on the enemy's position. Suddenly, flashes appeared in the sky all around us, and the noise of the batteries close by told us that many of our guns had started their deadly work. The enemy's guns replied almost immediately. What an awful din! My poor mate got hit there, before we had even left our assembly trench.

"Fix bayonets and prepare to make the assault." There was not a sound in the trench except the clicks as each bayonet was pressed home. "Remember, boys, no retreat and no prisoners," were our last orders. Then, at the officer's command, we jumped out of our trench and made for the German lines.

It was impossible to run, as every second step we fell into the shell-holes. You should have seen the boys walking through that

Hellish fire. I knew we were getting close, for a hand-grenade passed by and exploded a few yards behind me. Then I was unfortunate, as a Hun bullet put daylight through my left thigh and I turned a 'sugar-doodle' into a shell-hole. It comes as a shock, though one expects it all the way.

I soon bound up my leg and turned to see the boys jump into the trench, and knew that things were right. I had charge of a fighting-section of ten men. Six, including myself, were hit; three severely. We were soon reinforced by our support troops, and word came down the line that we had gained our objective.

But what bad luck I had. Another six or seven yards would have taken me into the German trench. If we only had the German Artillery bluffed like we have their Infantry, then we would push the Huns out of France and out of Belgium in a fortnight. They're a crawling lot of worms! (I have a better name for them which I cannot write.)

They will fire at us right up to the time we hop into their trenches, and then they fling up their hands and cry, "Mercy, Comrade". I can assure you they get no mercy from the Australians, and they are very frightened of us. How can we give them any mercy after seeing them shoot down our cobbers?

Rumor has it that a Berlin newspaper said how some Australians captured a patrol of eight Germans, shot five of them, and <u>ate</u> three. I could write for hours about what we see, but some things I try to forget. French gunners say that this bombardment is worse than at Verdun.

I am in the base hospital at present and except for my nerves I am "Tip-Top", but it takes time to get the awful sights out of one's mind. How would you like to hold a trench against enemy attacks and all the time the dead and dying are lying thick around your feet? It is not the guns which unnerve, but the frightful sights. Very few of my battalion survived, and now I hate to go back there with all my mates gone.

Just fancy getting into nice clean white sheets again, and to have two pillows. Oh, the comfort of my cosy cot! Do you know that for two months we did not even have a blanket? But I must return to the line soon, to make Fritz pay for his nasty tricks."

LT.- COL. B. O. C. DUGGAN, D.S.O. commanded the 21st. Battalion at Pozieres Heights.

A REINFORCED CONCRETE ENTRANCE TO A CELLAR AND GERMAN DUGOUT

~ LIKE THE ROCK OF GIBRALTAR ~

Lieut.-Col. B. O. C. Duggan, commanded the 21st. Battalion at the attack on Pozieres Heights, and was awarded a D.S.O. for outstanding courage. (Before enlisting, he was a farmer at Sutherland, St. Arnaud.)

In both photos, he is posing in front of a captured German dugout which was now used as the 21st. Battalion's Headquarters. This huge "Cement-House" was nicknamed

GIBRALTAR by the Aussies because the Germans had built it with fibro-cement, and it looked as strong as a rock. Built over a dugout, the concrete observation — post contained a nest of enemy machine-guns. It was indeed strong for it was the only structure left standing after the heavy bombardment upon Pozieres village on the 24th. July. The rest of the country was just churned-up earth, smashed bricks, blasted tree-stumps,

Signaller Matt. Hogan
POZIERES AND MOQUET FARM

SAVED BY A WALLET

Weymouth Hospital. ------ 1916.

Dear Mother,
"I was sorry to hear about the death of poor Willie Barber, but mine was indeed a marvellous escape and could not have been closer. I believe my wallet saved my life as it was all shattered with a piece of the same shell, and only for that it may have killed me straight out. I got the wallet back and it contained letters and various articles.

I went under chloroform last Monday to get my leg straightened, and it was a painful thing. They had to break down every muscle in my leg, and when I came out of the chloroform the pain was frightful. The doctor thought I would only be able to stand it for one hour; but he asked me to stand it as long as possible. I stood it for six hours!

Then the doctor took all the old bandages off; but for two days and nights I never closed my eyes for the pain. My leg is much better now, but I cannot put my weight on it at all. I have been to a Medical Board consisting of three doctors, and I am returning home on six months' furlough. I feel sure I will be discharged when I get back to Victoria. I think I will be home in January sometime, but I would like to have a look around London before I leave England.

I cannot speak too highly of the sisters in this hospital; they are all splendid. There are about 5,000 wounded Australians here and we only have men-orderlies. The tucker is the best since I was wounded. Many of the poor fellows here are a lot worse than I am, so I ought to be thankful. I think in time my leg will be as good as ever it was, but for twelve months it is sure to be weak.

This English climate is horrible, always raining and cold; it is the same in France. I hope it will be hot when I get back to Australia. I had a long letter from Frank O'Donnell and heard about a few of the changes that had taken place in Birchip since I left. I will send a cable home before sailing.

I do not think my leg will ever be fit for active service again. I am getting it massaged daily, and I am now out of bed, hobbling about on my crutches. Nearly all my pals in the 7th. Battalion have been killed.

All the battalions got a terrible doing at Pozieres — yet the 3rd. Division is still in England enjoying itself.

I got a letter from the sergeant in my Signalling Section. He got his commission, and said it was awful where they were at present as it was mud and slush up to their knees. I saw Bob Barry's name on a wounded list some time back.

Although I have had a bad time, I am pleased I enlisted and came to the Front. I could have stayed in Egypt if I wanted to. I am glad I did not go into the 57th. Battalion, for the Germans gave the 5th. Division a bad time up at Armentieres; that is where we were for three months before we went to Pozieres.

One thing about Pozieres, our fellows gave the Germans something they will never forget there, although we also lost heavily. I do not think there will be much of a majority over here for Conscription as we would not wish to make anyone suffer like we have. But if it comes in, it will be a good job in one way so that some of the "old boys" can get a rest.

If our losses go on like this there will not be many of the 1st. Division boys left, and they have won the great Australian name at Gallipoli; but I think Pozieres was the greatest success of all. It was the 1st. Division that took it, but all the same, the 2nd. and 4th. Divisions fought splendidly round Mouquet Farm. The 5th. and 3rd. Divisions have <u>their</u> hard battles yet to come."

BEFORE A BATTLE

Lance Corporal Williams (of Charlton) writes movingly of his feelings before a battle.

1916.

"Abide with me, fast falls the eventide.
The darkness deepens, Lord with me abide.
When other helpers fail, and comforts flee,
Help of the helpless, oh, abide with me."

The last time I heard these words was in our church at home. Tomorrow we are going into the Firing-line, into the Valley of Death, and some of us will never hear that old, familiar hymn again.

In the fading light of that Sabbath evening, my ears eagerly drank in the sound of the ancient hymn. In the square of that little Belgian town, ravaged and looted months ago by the Germans, great crowds of our troops were billeted for the night, awaiting the battle of the coming day.

I stood and listened. Across the other side of the square stood an ancient church. Worn out and weary though I was, I walked over and entered. Standing at the altar of the church was the 'padre' and the pews were lined with our soldiers who stood with bowed heads singing in their youthful voices. I looked around at the faces of these Australian soldiers (some were mere boys) and I thought of their loved ones at home, waiting and watching for news of them.

These brave Australians stood and sang with all their heart and soul; and as soon as the hymn was finished, I heard the roar of the big guns, only a mile or two away, and it seemed strangely unreal. A few short, simple words of prayer from the old Padre, commending all of them to the great "GOD OF ALL BATTLES" and then another well-known hymn.

> "Lead, kindly light, amid the encircling gloom,
> Lead thou me on. The night is dark,
> And I am far from home, lead thou me on."

This was indeed a song of prayer, straight from the souls of these men who felt that, amid the dangers so real and so near, there was a "GREAT SENTRY" above who is sure to let them through the Gates of Heaven.

Writing a letter hom

Watchem Lads in Geelong Camp 1916

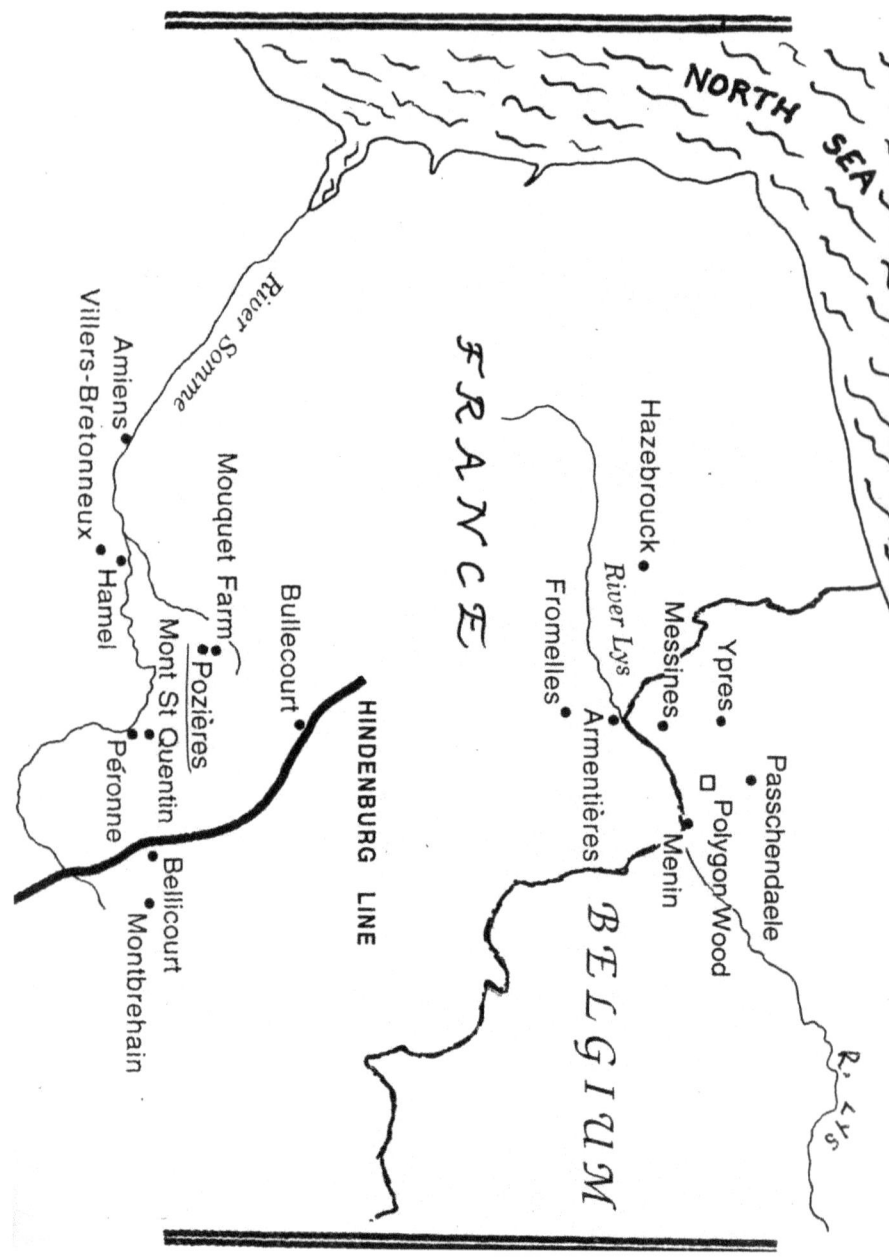

The following letter is from Private A. J. Smith, who was employed on the staff of the "Donald Mail" before he enlisted in 1915.

"Somewhere in France". — 1916.

Dear Mother,

I must be excused for not writing before, but we are not allowed to put much in a letter. I can't even tell you where I am in France, but you can guess; and I tell you things are humming some.

I am at present in a hospital at Staples (*Etaples*) with a slight wound in my arm, caused by a high explosive shell. It is what we term a "cushy" wound (it gives you a rest for a while). But I will be back at the Front again before you get this.

You can't imagine what a battlefield is like. You must be there to see it in reality. Fancy, the guns going their hardest for a couple of hours at the German trenches, the guns varying in size from what they term a "Grandmother" (which just sounds like a railway train rattling overhead) to a small gun that barks.

The first night we got into the trenches we got a lively all-night meeting, shrapnel coming over in galore. Twenty got buried, and only three were dug out alive. The first night my Battalion went "Over the Top" we had an easy victory as only a few Germans showed fight; but they were soon knocked out, and with only a few casualties on our side!

Just to show you what cowards they are. One of our fellows got his arm smashed to pulp in the German trench that we had just captured. Well, he was just crawling into a dug-out to rest for a minute when some Germans from inside sang out, "Mercy, Kamerades", and out they came and surrendered to him.

He walked them down the trench for about 50 yards to where some of us were standing; and imagine our surprise when we sighted him, leading the way to five Germans, and he was staggering and nearly unconscious with loss of blood. The Huns are nearly all like that; eager to get captured. They even sneak across to our trenches when they can and give themselves up."

**Private Dan O'Brien (of Charlton)
tells of his loss after Pozieres.**

WOUNDED AT POZIERES, ON 4TH. AUGUST, 1916.

"I am still alive, but have not been well enough to write before. I am now finished with war. They got me in the leg. My 20th. Battalion charged at Pozières on August 4 th. at 9-30 p.m. and I was in the first wave over the parapet. We advanced quickly and reached the German trenches before they were aware of our arrival.

I got hit just as I got to the enemy trench and I thought I was gone. But I crawled back 150 yards and stayed in a shell-hole all night. Next day two chaps carried me about two miles to the Dressing-Station where I was put in a Motor-Ambulance and taken away.

I was just on the point of death; and they kept injecting morphia to stop the pain. When I got to the Clearing-Station the doctor had a go to save the leg, but very nearly killed me.

There were two operations, and in the second one they took my leg off up near the thigh. So it will be "Old Uncle Dan and his Wooden Peg" when I come home. I am in England now and doing well, though lying on my back. When it heals they'll have to send me home to Australia.

Tell Jim we'll be able to have that long beer he was talking about. I was not sure once or twice that I'd ever get back, as it was FAIR HELL at Pozières."

(C.E.W. Bean writes: "The life expectancy of a young officer at Pozières was 24 hours.")

****

Lieutenant Les Simpson (of Birchip) tells his mother what happened to him in the Allies' "BIG PUSH" on the 8th. August.

A BLACK DAY FOR THE GERMANS

London General Hospital.
13th. August, 1916,

"I know that long ere this reaches you, you will be wondering what has happened to me. Well, my 5th. Battalion was right in the centre of the Allies' "BIG PUSH" on the 8th. August; but I did not actively co-operate until the 9th. after several of my platoon officers had been hit. I volunteered to take their place, with the result that I received this lot.

Before I got hit I had five machine-gun bullets pass <u>through</u> my tunic. The bullet that put me very close to Heaven came from the right front at about 50-yards range, and struck me low on the right side of the neck, just missing the main artery. From there it passed between the windpipe and the spine, just grazing the latter slightly, and came out at the rear of my left shoulder-blade. Now don't get the wind up, mother.

I thought it was all up with me at first, so I told my sergeant to write and tell you that I died without pain; but luckily there was no need. The sensation of the bullet was not painful, but awful. I had no feeling at all on account of the spine being grazed. You have seen a rabbit, when hit, suddenly stiffen and then lie still? Well, that is exactly what happened with me.

I knew nothing for at least 20 minutes; and then I found that instead of being in a "Higher World" I was still in the war. I collected my senses quickly but never moved, as movement meant certain death from enemy snipers.

Just then my sergeant said, "Sir, can you speak?" and I told him to leave me for dead. I thought this was the best plan — and it worked admirably.

When I gained control of my senses, I tried to crawl into a small depression two or three yards away, but a sniper let drive at me twice more and I had to stay still. Eventually I reached cover in a shell-hole, much fatigued.

Here, on investigation, I found that one of the shots which that sniper fired had, luckily for me, hit the service-revolver hanging at my right side. At this stage I thought it was time to make up my mind, so after a few words of prayer I told my sergeant to take over command of the platoon.

As I said before, I recovered my senses very quickly, and later on, when it got dark, I walked to the Dressing-Station. Now I am in London, and I have been joyfully singing all the time. But, as the doctors say, I am unnatural to have got off with my life.

Still, I don't think I shall be offered a trip home to Australia as I am too fresh, eating like a horse, and as good as gold. I can move both hands and walk anywhere I choose; though at present I am still rather stiff and slightly sore. LES."

Hand-embroidered card from France

SERGEANT ARTHUR CLIFFORD, M.M.

SGT. ARTHUR CLIFFORD
MOUQUET FARM

<u>1916.</u>

[*Somehow*, <u>Sergeant Arthur Clifford</u> *survived those dreadful days of relentless shelling in Kay trench at Pozieres. Now, he describes how his 24th. Battalion,* "<u>The Red and White Diamond</u>"*, took part in an advance upon Mouquet Farm.*]

"After a fortnight's rest at <u>Warloy</u>, and <u>Berteaucourt</u>, we heard reports that the Second Division was again needed at the Front. So, on the 22nd. August, our chaps of the 24th. Battalion went into the Fighting-line again — to <u>Mouquet Farm</u>, a place about three miles past <u>Pozieres</u>.

At that time I was in a rest-camp, having gone there a few days before to get a dental abscess attended to. In this respect I was very lucky, for my Company suffered heavy casualties when they reached the Front.

While I was in hospital, my 6th. Brigade relieved the 3rd. Brigade on the late afternoon of August 22nd. Unfortunately, their movements were detected by enemy aeroplanes; and consequently at 6 p.m. a heavy barrage of shrapnel and high explosive was thrown by the Germans upon that whole area, from <u>Mouquet Farm</u> to <u>Pozieres.</u>

My 24th. Battalion, which had lost so heavily in Kay Trench only four weeks earlier, was again caught badly. The Quarry was crowded with our wounded and this enemy barrage lasted for over six hours; so you can see why I was lucky to have missed that terrible experience.

It was a day later, on the Wednesday morning of the 23rd. of August, that I left the rest camp and joined some chaps who had come from <u>Etaples</u> and marched with them to <u>Albert</u>. We stopped there that night and on Thursday we marched up to <u>Sausage Gully</u>, picking up some chaps who had come out of the trenches. Then we went through to join our various Companies.

When I arrived, the 24th. were just changing over (in broad daylight) with the 21st. and moving forward into the Front line on their right. When two battalions change places with each other it is rather like the shunting of trucks in a crowded railway yard. We waited in the Support-lines until our chaps were in the Front-line, and then we went to join them.

The Front trench was a very poor one, being more or less a succession of shell-holes joined up. I took up a position alongside a stretch that had been blown in a few days before, and as soon as it got dark I dug it down deeper. This trench was so shallow that, unless you crawled around on your hands and knees, you were in full view of the Germans. Our Sergeant-Major put some men on the other end, and in a few hours we had dug it down.

About midnight our Corporal had a working-party out in front, digging a new trench. So I, with others, went out with bombs as a covering-party to protect them from any German patrols. Nothing much happened. We saw several parties of Germans but they were well out in No Man's Land.

When we came back at daylight, I began to deepen my part of the trench before it got too light. But while I was digging I suddenly came upon several men who had been buried by shells, so I had to stop as the smell wasn't too good.

The Germans sent a lot of Whizz-Bangs along our part of

the trench. We were in a very bad position, as Fritz could easily enfilade us with his machine-guns.

One bullet killed Sergeant Bevett and another bullet got Stagg. Alan Cooper was killed. Sergeant A. B. Arnel, M.M., had been killed the night before, and Corporals Harris and Beckwith were also killed — along with many others.

On Friday night a party went out to dig a bomb-pit in the vicinity of Mouquet Farm. So Corporal McLachlan, Private Bruce and myself went out as a covering-party for them. We were lying in the middle of No-Man's Land, and it was the coldest night I had ever experienced.

Two German patrols came along. One party of half-a-dozen could hear our fellows working and were trying to find out the position of them. I thought it would be a case of sticking a bomb into them, but they cleared off without coming any closer.

We could see them repairing their barbed-wire, and then one of our machine-guns hit them. By 3-30 a.m. the job was done and we returned to our trench, but our bombers stopped in that pit to man it during the daylight-hours.

The Corporal in charge got us an issue of Rum, and I swallowed it for I was as cold as ice and could hardly speak. After daylight, the Germans started rocking in their Minenwerfer bombs, and I suppose they had their work cut out for just at daybreak our guns gave them a hot time.

The 21st. went across and took some trenches. It had been a successful advance, with the exception of Mouquet Farm.

Mouquet Farm was undermined with big dugouts and the Germans had a pretty strong hold on it. At noon, the old

Sergeant-Major came along to ask for 12 volunteers from my Company to go and bomb <u>Mouquet Farm.</u>

I was among the 24 volunteers chosen — as well as some men from "C" Company. We got our bombs ready to move off. We knew that some of us (perhaps a good many of us) would never come back, so I gave my diaries and things to the Sergeant-Major in case anything happened to me; and many of the other lads did the same.

We went forward to a dugout just a few hundred yards from the farm and waited there for further orders. But, as it happened, we did not go on with the job, owing to the officer-in-charge, Lieutenant E. V. Smythe, not being able to get enough artillery support.

It was lucky for us the job was cancelled, as many considered it a suicidal effort. We knew that this daylight attack against Fritz in his strong dugouts at <u>Mouquet Farm</u> would have meant a desperate fight.

* *

<u>August 27th.</u> On Sunday morning, just about daybreak, we got orders to leave the trenches as the 4th. Division were taking over from us. It had rained a lot during the night and it was a wet and slippery job getting back. But we were so glad to get out we would have swam all the way if necessary.

We heard more about <u>Mouquet Farm</u> later. The 4th. Brigade were doomed to failure in their attempt to take it; but still another attempt had to be made. So it's quite probable that not one of us 24 volunteers who were going to try it would have returned alive.

Still, we may have succeeded and it certainly would have been more satisfactory if we had attempted the job; but I admit that we were glad to get away from that awful place. When we arrived at the kitchen-cookers, we were tired, muddy, wet and exhausted.

We got a big feed of the best stew we had tasted for many a day; and, as it was still raining, the remnants of us got into billets in <u>Albert</u> and had a good rest."

[*It was here, a few days' later, on 31st. August, 1916, that General Birdwood presented ribbons and decorations to men of the Sixth Brigade who had shown such outstanding gallantry at* POZIERES *and* MOUQUET FARM. *It is possible that* <u>Sergeant Arthur Clifford</u> *was awarded his M.M. (Military Medal) at this special ceremony.*]

TRAVELLING KITCHEN

A CHARGE AT MOUQUET FARM

AUG/SEPT. 1916.

[A Charlton soldier, in a letter to his father from an English hospital, describes his Infantry charge as "A Storm in Hell".]

<u>1916</u>.

We got up at 3-20 a.m. and left our billets at 5 a.m. We marched for four hours before reaching the Firing-line. That night we went into the reserve trenches and slept, where and how we could. The night was cold and we had no overcoats. The big guns were roaring and bellowing, without stopping, all night — there were two thousand of them.

The noise of the Artillery was enough to drive us silly, although we are used to a good bit of big gun fire. We saw a number of other battalions that had just come out of the Firing-line — at least, we saw the survivors, and they walked like men in a nightmare.

The shells were terrific, and the thought of a 10-inch shell conveys little to anyone who has not seen them burst at close quarters. But to anyone who has been under the big gunfire, a 10-inch shell means a bottled volcano and earthquake combined.

At 6 o'clock the next night we were told off in charging formation, and I was ordered to lead a bombing party that had to clear a German trench out. Everyone else made grimaces and bade us Goodbye — but they need not have done so because they all got jobs just as bad as ours.

At 8 o'clock off we went into the first line with shrapnel and high explosives bursting all around us. One of the other battalions had 15 men killed with one shell on the way up. I can tell you, we were all loaded like packhorses — rifle and bayonets, 220 rounds of ammunition, four bombs, two sandbags, waterproof sheet and haversack containing two days' rations.

Four battalions were to assault and take the enemy trenches. We had the left side, with orders to clear the German trench and block it. Then, we had to advance over 1300 yards of No-Man's Land to reach the German lines.

We got into position and lay down in the open. It was a frightful place with no trenches — only shell holes. On every inch of this ground a shell had burst and turned the earth up and the whole area was just a sea of brown craters. Our guns were roaring and belching; and so were the German guns. Machine-guns and star-shells were bursting — and as the assault time approached the bombardment swelled out to unbelievable proportions.

The ground rocked and reeled under the awful rain of shells as 2000 shells bellowed out from the German positions. It was like the climax of a thunderstorm in Hell. Suddenly the order came, "FIRST WAVE GET READY!" Up we got. "FIX BAYONETS!" — "ADVANCE!"

As our long line swept forward, something happened to wreck the advance — it was German machine-guns spitting from the German trenches right in front of us. I don't think a fly could have lived through it, and you might think there was no humour in such a sight — but there was.

We looked ludicrous as we waddled forward, falling into shell-holes, and the Major roaring at us, "Get off the b------ road!" I ran up one bank and fell into a shell-hole. I got up and promptly fell into another one and rolled to the bottom. I began to go mad and 'see red', but then a kind of deadly coolness came over me and I suddenly did not care what happened to me.

On and on we rushed, it seemed for miles. The bullets whistled past us, and our men were falling everywhere. But I took no notice for they seemed to be in another world. A fellow I knew went down next to me with a despairing yell, which made me turn my head and look at him. I met him afterwards at the Dressing-Station and he was not hurt very badly.

Out of the 200 who set off in the first wave only about 40 were now left. Our major was ahead, roaring out, "COME ON, BOYS!" although we did not need telling, for we were moving along as fast as our heavy loads would let us.

Suddenly we saw the Germans — my first chance to get at them in five months. The few of us who were let loose, bolted onwards, for we felt equal to attacking several battalions of Germans. They waited until we got within twenty yards of them and then they threw a battalion of bombs at us, which exploded in a wall of flame.

In fact, one burst under my feet, but did not hurt me. Still we ran on. A young man next to me roared out, "There they are, Fred." He was as mad as a bull and shook his head like a great dog. "Right," I said. The Germans ran away like rabbits, and tore across to their other trench. My greatest desire in life was to kill them, so I set off after them.

Then "BIFF!" and I was lying on the ground. The machine-guns were crackling again and thousands of bullets screeched above my head. Had I been standing, I would certainly have been riddled with holes.

I would like to have a talk with those people who say a bullet does not hurt when it first hits you. I lay on the ground and stuck my fingers into it and literally bit the dust for about five minutes. After that it seemed to go red-hot and then numb. It was spurting blood and I thought, "I'm done for." But at two o'clock a stretcher-bearer bound up my leg and assisted me back to our lines. Stretcher-bearers are the men who should get all the praise, for they worked splendidly under fire and were shot down right and left."

Corporal Sherrin sent the following poem to his uncle, Mr. W. D. Hart, of Watchem. It expresses heartache, disappointment and despair at the negative result of Australia's Conscription Referendum in 1916.

I'm tired with two years of fighting, I'm weary and long for a spell;
But none can be spared to relieve me, though this war is a living Hell.
I went with the boys at the Landing, and happened to pull safely through;
And I stuck it right out from that morning, till now, when I'm writing to you.
And here, in the trenches in Flanders, I've read all the papers you've sent;
And I'm glad that Conscription is talked of by the men in our Government.
It is not before it is needed, it should have been here from the first;
If we'd had more men at the landing, Johnny Turk would have got it worst.
I see that Australians are voting, as to what shall be done in the war;
And I'm sure they will vote <u>FOR</u> Conscription, it was certainly needed before.
They talked in the pubs all about it and said it was FAIR, EQUAL, JUST,
That if men would not share in our burden, Australia will say they MUST.
We are sure that the vote on Conscription will cause us our country to bless,
As help, badly needed, is coming when Australia has answered us, "YES".
We've just got a cable to tell us the news of your vote on this war,
And, by Jove, if I thought it was 'dinkum' I'd never go home any more.
There must be an error, or something, such news could never be true;
Australia go back on her soldiers? That's more than the Germans would do.
But here in the wet, muddy trenches, within a few yards of the foe,
We've learnt that Australia has answered our asking for help with a "NO".
We're tired, we're weary, we're wounded, with death up above and below;

But I'd rather die here with the Heroes, than go back to the Crowd who said, "NO".

Life in the muddy trenches.

A WAR HOSPITAL — LONDON

HIS MAJESTY, KING GEORGE V, REVIEWS AUSTRALIAN TROOPS ON SALISBURY PLAIN – 27th. September, 1916.

"We have just returned from the greatest parade of Australian troops that has ever taken place in England — or elsewhere for that matter! This morning nearly 40,000 Anzacs were reviewed by the King on Salisbury Plain," *writes a Charlton soldier to the paper.*

"Our soldiers had very little warning, or preparation, for this great honour paid to them. Reveille sounded at 5-30 a.m. at my camp on Lark Hill — which is only a small area of this immense and historic Salisbury Plain. Two hours later we marched out from our lines towards the ground where the review was to take place — about 4 miles.

Arriving there, our brigades formed up in pre-arranged positions as part of the great assembly. For two hours we waited while troops continued to arrive from all points of the compass. "Cripes, will they never stop coming?" was the remark heard on all sides.

Every branch of the A.I.F. was represented; and practically all companies were fully-trained and equipped to take the field. Infantry, of course, predominated. But infantry nowadays is required to know a lot more than it did before this war. Practically every soldier is a specialist in some particular aspect of fighting.

A large percentage of the infantry is trained in the use of various types of machine-guns. A great number become skilled grenadiers or bombers. Others are trained as scouts, observers, or snipers — and for all those other enterprises of war, according to individual capability and temperament.

Our field of artillery was very well-represented, with a long train of guns and limber-waggons that showed what a wealth of potential fighting force we have. The Light Horse — or "Australian Cavalry" as they are called in England — superbly-mounted and resplendent in gaily-waving emu plumes, looked magnificent. They were armed with sabres as well as rifles.

Signallers (because of the elaborate system of communication in vogue) formed a big percentage of this great assembly. Engineers, Army Service, Army Transport, Pioneer and Medical Corps were all represented in full war strength.

But it was the infantry which surprised us most, as hitherto we had not realised that there was anything like this great number camped hereabouts. You need to realise that Salisbury Plain covers an immense area — and camps, ten times the size of Broadmeadows, are scattered all over the place, only five or six miles apart.

It was a typical English autumn morning. Mists filled the valleys and shrouded the patches of trees that dotted the landscape. Thick clouds drifted low overhead; but occasionally the sun shone through, revealing the delightful autumn tints in the foliage of nearby lime trees. It seemed as though our special occasion would be spoilt by rain, but luckily this kept off till after the march was over.

At 11-15 we all "Stood-To". King George was due to arrive at 11-30. We stood, sixteen lines deep, in a line that stretched for over a mile; and when I tell you that one man occupies only 27 inches you will have some idea of the number in that vast assembly.

Then the Royal Standard was hoisted above the saluting-platform, and words of command were given simultaneously along the lines as 30,000 rifles clicked to the "PRESENT ARMS!" while the strains of the National Anthem blared forth from 30 massed bands.

His Majesty rode a magnificent, black charger and was followed by a retinue of about twenty. Accompanied by two Australian Generals, he rode along our lines at a walking pace and as he passed me I heard him questioning the General as to which State our battalion came from.

The Anzacs all looked soldiers, every inch of them. They stood like blocks of wood in the most approved military-fashion. After this inspection came the March-Past. It was carried out in double lines of thirty men, but with only twelve paces between the platoons.

The actual march past the saluting-base took nearly two hours; and I should think the king must have been rather tired of saluting by the time the last regiment went by. After the March-Past, we lined the road along which the king would drive when leaving the assembly-ground. We had a long wait, but our fellows were in fine form to give His Majesty a right royal cheering as he rode away.

I must add that near the end of the review our Australian airmen gave an amazing display of aviation skills; and one daring fellow looped the loop, over and over again. The figures he cut in the air were amazingly skilful. It came on to rain heavily just as we moved off; but snug and dry under our waterproof sheets, all the lads sang cheerily as we trudged back to camp."

THE CONSCRIPTION REFERENDUM
in 1916 – Majority votes for 'NO' was 72,476.

KRUPP'S FACTORY IN ESSEN *The Krupp family of German industrialists has always been associated with the manufacture of iron and steel, especially in producing war armaments during the 19th and 20th Centuries. Its factory employed only 74 men when founded in 1848, but 60,110 were employed to make death-dealing instruments of war for that great European War.*

Captain Bert Loel (Veterinary Corps) writes a very interesting letter to the "Birchip Advertiser" which describes how horses, too, were doomed to a violent death

"In the Field." 9th. August. 1916.

BLOWN IN HALVES

Several times I have made attempts to write to you, but each time I have been called away. But this time I have made up my mind to finish a letter to you, even if it takes me a whole week! I am sending this along so that you may show it to the people of Birchip and district who still spare a thought for their friends overseas.

To appreciate the war thoroughly, one wants to be planted in this God-forsaken place, month after month. But to start at the beginning.

The day after I landed in London, I reported to the War Office and was immediately sent to Aldershot (the main British Military Barracks) where I stopped a week. I was then sent to Woolwich (East London) to help form the 19th. British Veterinary Hospital.

After spending some time at Woolwich, we entrained for Southampton Docks. Our complement consisted of 5 officers, 500 men, 80 horses, 15 waggons and all the necessary equipment of a modern soldier.

We detrained and embarked at Southampton; and after a beautiful trip which included a voyage of over 70 miles up the River Seine — with the most glorious scenery on both sides — we landed "Somewhere in France".

We were then escorted to a barren place where we were told to organise our hospital. They gave us an uncultivated piece of rough ground and said, "There is your site, do the best you can with it"; and I tell you we have turned it into a great hospital. Sir Douglas Haig congratulated our Commanding Officer after he had inspected it, saying it was one of the best hospitals in France.

To give you some idea of the work entailed in its formation, the main road running through the hospital took just on 1000 yards of stone. It rather amused me to hear the remark of a Frenchman, residing in the locality, who on seeing the work we were doing said, "Yes, this is all very well, but I can see after we have got rid of the Germans we will have to dig you people out of here."

I might tell you that all the time we were building the place, the authorities were sending us sick and wounded animals from the Somme battlefields for us to treat, so we had our hands pretty full. Then, a week after we landed in France, one of our officers was posted to another unit up the line and shortly afterwards another officer got invalided with "Trench Nephritis". This left the Commanding Officer, a Quartermaster and myself to look after 500 men and 900 sick animals.

Well, I did this on my own for three months before another officer arrived; and in a short time there were 5 subalterns doing the work I was previously doing alone. I used to be at work by six in the morning and never got to bed until eleven in the night. I don't mind telling you I never worked so hard in all my life.

After seven months of hospital work I applied to go up to the Front and was posted to the 56th. Division; and it was whilst I was with this Division that I met with an accident which entailed my spending two weeks in hospital.

I was riding along to visit one of my sick animals when all of a sudden a shell burst about 20 yards in front of me. I don't know who got the bigger fright, the horse or I. Anyway, he started to perform.

He reared up and bucked a few times, and as the reins were hanging loosely on his neck, I had no control of him: so off I went over his neck.

Unfortunately my left foot got caught in the stirrup; and I expect the fact of him seeing me upside down gave him a fright and he immediately bolted with me hanging upside down at his side.

They told me afterwards that he dragged me about 200 yards. All I know is that he seemed to gallop all over me, and I thought every bone in my body was broken. The brave soldier who stopped that horse certainly saved my life.

The next thing I remember was a doctor at a Dressing-Station asking me to lift my head a little higher. From there I was taken to a Casualty-Clearing Station, then to a Red-Cross Train, and afterwards to a Base Hospital.

A strange thing happened on that journey down to the base. We pulled up opposite a trainload of Australians on their way from Marseilles to the Northern Front One of their officers came into our train and I asked him did he have anybody from the Mallee, Victoria. He said, "There is a Corporal Spittle. Will I send him along?"

You can imagine my excitement at the thought of seeing somebody from home after nearly twelve months. Anyway, in walked Jim as large as life and as fit as a fiddle. He was dressed in shorts, puttees and shirt, and looked very well.

We had quite a long talk of home and of the boys we knew, and Jim told me where most of them were now. When he had gone, one of the English officers said, "That is a fine stamp of a lad." And he was, too.

Jim's visit bucked me up for days, and after I left hospital I was posted back to my British Unit — the one I came out to France with. One day, while walking down the street of a nearby town, an Australian sergeant came up to me and said, "Bert Loel." I looked up at him and said, "George Puddicombe." We had recognised each other immediately.

He told me that he was camped a short way from where I was, and that some other Birchip boys were with him — Jack Hancock, Charlie Lefevre and Max Nonmus. I went to see them and it was quite a a merry meeting. Shortly afterwards, I had the satisfaction of being at the Front-line."

MUD ON THE FLERS BATTLE-FIELDS – NOVEMBER. 1916

**Corporal H. Willey (of Donald)
describes his work near Flers.**

"For a few days I was busy at Dernancourt, in the Royal Engineer yards, building sledges for transporting the wounded over the thick mud; and then on 12th. November, we did a 10-mile march to rejoin our company.

We passed through Fricourt, Montauban, Marmetz Wood

and Bernafay Wood. All these places have been battered about and look as bad as La Bassee.

Our next camp was at Longueval and it was a fairly tough old place as Fritz used to shell us regularly. We had to travel three miles to our work, and used to leave camp about 3 p.m. and return about 3 a.m. We would pass through Delville Wood and Flers, to work near Gueudecourt Wood — not far from the Front-line.

We were there for a month and I was not sorry when we were relieved. All the time at Flers IT WAS BITTERLY COLD WITH MUD AND SLUSH UP TO YOUR KNEES.

The only time we were troubled with enemy-shells was while moving up from our 2nd. Support Trenches to our 1st Support Trenches. This was about a quarter-of-a-mile over open ground, and as soon as Fritz saw us he would give us "What Oh!" with his shrapnel and high-explosives.

No doubt you have heard much about Britain's secret weapon — the "tank" — and on our way to work we used to pass three of them. They had been put out of action on account of getting stuck in the heavy ground.

Rain throughout November had made the ground water-logged and we had appalling conditions, with mud everywhere. Near Delville Wood was a fourth derelict tank — and it was this one that I had a good look at, both inside and outside. I was surprised how clever were the inside workings.

It is hard to describe tanks. They are egg-shaped, with caterpillars on each side, and these revolve right over the body. Inside, they carry two eight-pounder guns: these work on a turret which enables them to fire in any direction. As well as these big guns, they also carry six machine-guns.

Pockets are inside to carry the shells; and racks hold the machine-gun belts. The driving is done from the front, and the steering by two small wheels at the rear. Loop (spy) holes are all around and these can be closed when not needed.

I would have liked to take a snap of it, but the day was too dull. Getting back to camp we found the majority of the boys were sleeping in tiny dug-outs built on the surface of the ground, as the trenches were too wet.

Conditions were abominable with snow and mud and lack of sunlight. We were glad to go back for a rest, and left the line on the 8th. December; but what a circus we had getting away as it was just about Fritz's time to send over his daily iron rations.

On the way back, we stopped at the Sydney camp (which is just in the making) and had a good, hot bath, and I can tell you we needed it AS WE WERE MUD FROM HEAD TO FOOT.

We then had a 12-mile motor-bus ride to a place called Franvillers, and then left there next morning in motor-buses to Vignacourt. Brother Vic has gone into hospital — but nothing serious, only a touch of Trench-Feet.

We have just finished tea and what a good "blow-out" — 2 lb. rump steak, 1 dozen eggs, bread, butter and jam between the three of us. You know, fill the "Inner Man" and you feel alright. We have plenty of dry straw to lie on, and a bonny coal-fire going — the coal we pinched from the railway yard — so we are real cosy and happy."

Britain's secret weapon, the TANK, first appeared in July, 1916. (But I think her most effective Weapon against the Germans was the Australian Digger.)

Private J. Leak runs under heavy machine-gun fire to bomb an enemy trench. He was awarded the V.C. for several similar acts of gallantry

Private Martin O'Meara, AIF, carries up ammunition many times to the trenches through heavy shellfire, showing utter contempt for the danger. He was awarded the V.C.

PRIVATE ROGER HOGAN DESCRIBES A MARCH TO THE TRENCHES

"Next morning we were up at 3-30, breakfast a little after 4 and after 5 we were on our way to the station. We weren't very long on getting aboard the train and we soon settled down for a long, tiring journey. We arrived at our detraining place about 5 in the afternoon and from there we had 12 miles to march to where we could camp for the night. It rained nearly all the way and we were both wet and weary when we arrived there about midnight; and within the next few days we had three good long marches.

We saw some very pitiful sights — refugees along the road, old people hardly capable of walking and carrying all their belongings with them, others were more fortunate having their luggage on some kind of vehicle. Well, just as we thought that we were going to be in the big shoot an order came for us to pack up and be ready to move at a moment's notice. So one evening at 5 o'clock found us moving back along one of the roads that we had come along the day previous. About midnight we were getting on a train at a station that the Hun was shelling, so I didn't feel safe till we had left that place behind us.

Next day we passed a lot of civilians hurrying back along the road for their very lives, going in the opposite direction from us. About 4 p.m. we marched through a town that the Hun was shelling. We halted in a field and only had time for a quick wash when we got orders to move up to the front line in 20 minutes. After marching about three miles we halted in a wood and had tea and waited there till it got dark enough for us to proceed to the front line. Then we had to cross a creek which was wide enough for some of the chaps to fall in and get wet up to their waist.

We got to the front position about midnight and dug in straight away, but we had only dug down about two feet when we struck water and there's not much cover from shell fire at that depth. We had some very severe shelling to put up with, but luckily nobody was hurt, although we were covered with dirt once or twice. We intended to live in a house that was close by and unoccupied, but on the second day we were shelled out of it.

- Lance Cpl. Les Harrison

A distribution by the Australian Comforts Fund. Unpacking the gifts.

Sapper Harold Willey
LIVING WITH THE PIGS

<u>August, 1916.</u>

"We are now out of the line, resting. We came out of the trenches yesterday morning, and marched eight miles to here. This is only a small village, and we are billeted at a house in the town. Our quarters are not the best, but are much more preferable than the trenches.

Two mates and myself are living in an old pig-sty (8ft. by 5ft) On the other side of us, brother Vic and six others are camped in an old hay barn. Alongside our quarters, three "Dinnies" (pigs) are living, and I might tell you at times they hum some.

Well, dear parents, since my last letter I have again seen the real horrors of war as we were in the trenches for nine days without a break; and in that time I saw sights that are too awful to relate. Without a doubt, Australia has some bonny lads, and it was just lovely to see them marching up through the communication trenches to the firing line, and all so lighthearted and jolly.

But the return scene is a different picture when the nerve-shattered remnants of a Company come back from the firing line.

Some of the poor fellows looked real haggard and worn-out, but even the worst cases are always ready for some fun. Then the walking-wounded pass by, and these, too, always had a smile on their faces. I have heard it said that an Australian's heart could not be broken, and I am satisfied now that the saying is quite true.

I must not forget to mention the stretcher-bearers, as these lads deserve great praise, and I feel sure that there is not another unit in the army that has a more dangerous and trying time. Every one of them deserves a V.C. I might also tell you that some of us were not sorry to get out of the trenches for a spell, as being there nine days, practically without sleep, we

Now I suppose you have been wondering what part of the Front we were on, and what work we were doing? Our first night out we were doing repairs to an old German mine near Pozieres. This was pretty dangerous work, as Fritz had our range to a nicety and he was giving us a fair share of high explosives and shrapnel. I was not in the trench long, as I had to go with the Captain of another company up to Contalmaison to see where the Royal Engineers' dumps were situated.

Contalmaison was at one time a very pretty village, but it is now just a heap of ruins with not a single wall left standing. This is still a very warm spot and is still being shelled by Fritz.

Our next night out we put in a new trench, and I might tell you it was a case of "DIG FOR YOUR LIVES" as Fritz was still very liberal with his iron-rations. We put in a 200 yards sap that was 4 feet deep, in only an hour-and-a-half. So you can see we did not waste any time.

Then, we deepened it to 7 feet and have been complimented by officers of all units as to it being one of the best saps around

Pozieres. We have built strongholds a few yards behind the firing-line, and also erected a shelter for an advanced Dressing-Station.

We have been a very lucky Company, only having 5 killed, 6 wounded, 5 shell-shocked, and several sent away sick. I asked brother Vic. if he would rather be here than on the Gallipoli Peninsula; and he stated that at the Peninsula, at times, things were quiet, <u>but here there is not one moment's quietness.</u>

You just imagine, dear parents, hundreds of guns of all sizes barking for all they are worth, and the screams of our own shells passing overhead; and, in return, the bursting of high explosives and shrapnel from Fritz. It makes the place a "LIVING HELL".

I have got a few German souvenirs, consisting of a rifle, mess-tin, machine-gun belt clips of cartridges, and a couple of tunic buttons which I cut off prisoners as they were coming down the saps at Pozieres. These I am going to try and hang on to, till I can find a safe way to send them home.

Dear parents, now to answer your dear letters of 24th/25th. June which I received yesterday on arriving here. I must say it was just lovely to receive them. At the time we were feeling very tired after our work in the trenches and the march to here; so they cheered a fellow up grand and made him forget all about his tiredness.

We also got several letters from dear old Donald and Melbourne friends; also a parcel containing smokes, chocolates and a box of Butter Scotch. These were exceedingly acceptable, as there is no chance of buying such luxuries in this part of the world.

After a good night's sleep, Good Oh! But I am sorry to say poor Vic's nerves are very much shattered; and it is no wonder as he has been through almost every engagement from the beginning of hostilities at the Gallipoli Peninsula and he ought now to be taken out of the ranks and given a well-earned rest.

With this exception we are in good spirits; and as we are just now advised of a further move immediately I must draw this letter to a close. With our fondest love and remembrance to you all."

A TRENCH ON THE WESTERN FRONT

Sapper Victor Willey. 12th. Coy. Field Engineers
'Somewhere in France'. SENLIS

"PLEASE PASS CONSCRIPTION."

<u>19th. August. 1916.</u>

Just a few lines, dear parents, to let you know that I am still in the land of the living; but at this time of writing my nerves are terribly unstrung and this is no wonder after the experiences I have gone through since the landing at Gallipoli on that memorable <u>25th. of April. 1915.</u>

Since then I have been in practically all the big engagements, including Quinn's Post, Dead Man's Gully, Lone Pine, Krithia Heights, Ypres, Courcelette, and the Somme and Ancre battles. Taking the engagements all through, the Battle of the Somme is the worst engagement I have been in. Yet, on the Gallipolian-Coast we were hard-pressed and lost hundreds of our brave comrades — and for what purpose? No doubt we held Johnny Turk in check and so prevented him from sending a large army to assist the Germans in their advance on the Russians, but our poor lads paid dearly.

You will see that I am out at <u>Senlis,</u> a few miles away from the firing-line, but long before this letter reaches you I will be back in the firing-line again, and <u>may</u> be fortunate enough to pull through. I can assure you I am sick and tired of the hardships and terrible sights of this awful war. Yet I suppose I should not complain as I am one of the lucky few of our old company left to continue the struggle. The majority of my company has been wiped out. Only just recently, the infantry supporting our company copped, What Oh! But my company only had three killed and twenty wounded.

A few days ago I received a letter and clippings from your local newspaper regarding the "WELCOME HOME" to Privates W. Allan and J. Cameron, and no doubt it was extremely kind of the Donald folk to show their appreciation of the services rendered to our country by these two Comrades-in-Arms. I do not wish any offence to dear old Donald friends, but my great ambition is just to return home safely, without any fuss, and see your dear kind faces once again. That is all the "WELCOME HOME" I pray for.

When Peace is coming, God only knows! Let us hope it will not be long before this terrible war is over; though by the way things are going over here, the end seems as far off as ever. We are gradually gaining ground, but have to fight stubbornly for every inch we gain.

Our Australian ranks are gradually being thinned, and it is to be hoped that <u>Australia will keep to her promise and send us more men at the earliest opportunity</u>. Otherwise, we will lose what prestige we have already gained for our native land; and, when our Battalions shrink to nothing, we shall be transferred into British regiments and lose our identity. This is the Gospel Truth! So we anxiously and sincerely hope the Nation of our Birth will not "turn us down" in this life-and-death struggle against our bitterest foe.

To give you some idea of the way we are pushed for more men, I will give you a recent example from my own experiences. I had been in the trenches for 15 days, and afterwards I came out for my 5 days' rest. But on the <u>third</u> day we were again ordered back into the trenches, and were there for another 6 days before we were relieved.

If sufficient reserves had been obtainable we could have had our deserved rest. So, surely, it is now up to many of our Australian lads to come over here, put their shoulders to the wheel, and help us remove the German Military Power from the face of this earth.

AUSTRALIA'S LIGHT HORSE BRIGADE

During the First World War (1914-1918) much of the fighting took place in the mud on the Western Front (Belgium and Northern France), yet there were equally important military actions by the British forces against Turkey in the Middle East.

Across the burning deserts of the Sinai Peninsula, Australia's Light Horse Brigade fought courageously against the Turks to stop them extending their Ottoman Empire. A Birchip man, Trooper Ernest Phelps, describes how they slowly but steadily advanced across the tortuous sands in June, 1916: -

"We are out in the desert fighting the Arabs and the Turks. It is the worst place I have ever been in . . . We had an aeroplane over our camp recently and it dropped five bombs right in amongst our horses, killing 28 horses and 14 men. There was a great mess — bits of horses and men scattered all over the camp. Before we arrived in this place, the British Yeomanry had a bad time and lost everything to the Turks — but we will revenge them. In our camp there are about 4,000 mounted men. Every day the weather is very hot and goes up to 120 degrees in the shade and we get some awful rides in the heat. The

last one we had was 20 miles in the saddle from 7 p.m. to 12 o'clock the next day, without any food or drink for our poor horses. It was a rough job for the horses and a lot of them "snuffed it" on the journey."

The Australian Light Horsemen came from farms and outback stations, so their horsemanship was superb and second to none in the world. Also, they had transported their own horses with them — a unique Australian breed called 'walers'.

ROMANI

A Charlton man, Trooper Thompson, writes about his part in the famous battle of Romani, in 1916: -

"On the morning of the 4th. August when the Turks made their attack, we were called out of bed at one in the morning and were saddled up and out of camp in ten minutes. It was quiet and peaceful all around us, so no one could have guessed that in less than two hours there would be such a Hell. We stopped the Turks as they advanced and held them up for three hours till everything was ready behind us for their reception — so then we galloped back and the Turks thought we were retreating. Of course, they rushed headlong into our ambush — and had a taste of Hell of their own. After an hour they had suffered enough, so it was their turn to retreat. Our own losses were pretty light, but our poor horses suffered severely as the shells bursting over our heads played havoc with their nerves. We followed the Turks next morning and made a second attack about 25 miles from our camp. We captured over 4,000 prisoners, hundreds of camels and a large amount of baggage, guns and ammunition. The Turks were heavily defeated with some 5,000 of them killed and wounded. Now the Turks have cleared right away from here — never to return, I hope!"

TROOPER NAIRN

On the 8th. December, the 8th. Light Horse attacked Magdhaba after a night march from El Arish and this is where one of St. Arnaud's heroes met his death. The parents of Trooper Alexander Nairn received the following letter: -

"Your son was admired for the conscientious way he always performed his duty. It was the strong determination to do all things well that led to his death. It was in the final charge on the Turkish position at Magdhaba that Alex went down. The order to charge was given and he rose with the others to fix bayonets. Unfortunately, his bayonet did not fit properly into its socket so he had to pause to adjust it — and those few seconds gave a Turkish sniper a chance. Alex was shot through the jaw and down the throat — and though he lived a short time he never spoke. He went through a storm of bullets all day, but it was in that final charge that he died."

With many others, Trooper Alex Nairn died like a hero. They were all brave men, fighting on behalf of righteousness and justice.

GAZA

By the beginning of 1917 the Sinai Peninsula was safely in British hands — and then the final invasion of Palestine began against the Turks who were strongly entrenched from Gaza to Beersheba. A Birchip man, Trooper Earl Neyland, describes the second attack at Gaza on 17th. April, which lasted for two days: -

"Brother Ted and I never got a scratch, though men were killed and wounded on both sides of us. It was the biggest battles we had been in. Our Brigadier-General Royston says he has never seen anything like it. Gallipoli was nothing compared to it! The air was thick with bombs, high explosives, shrapnel and bullets. I'll never forget it — and

young brother, Ted, was as brave as a lion. Now we have such a lot of empty saddles, so must wait for reinforcements. My word, it is very hard to lose your mates. Enemy aeroplanes flew all around and above us, dropping 100 lb bombs which knocked men and horses to pieces. It was murder!"

But in spite of the courage of those Light Horsemen, that second attack on Gaza was a failure.

BEERSHEBA

The next charge against the Turkish line was at Beersheba (just south of Jerusalem) and it was here that the 4th. Australian Light Horse Brigade rode into our history books on 31st. October, 1917.

It was 4-30 p.m. when eight hundred Light Horsemen mounted up and charged across open ground under a barrage of shells and bullets from the Turks. Bullets picked off horses and riders, yet whooping and yelling the Australians rode on until reaching the enemy's trenches. Then they jumped to the ground and fought hand to hand — and by using their bayonets they secured a major victory in the Middle East war.

A Watchem man, Trooper Jack Yetman, was badly wounded at Beersheba and had to be carried to a Cairo hospital for treatment of his wounds. He writes: -

"We had to put on our own dressings and then wait hours for the sand-cart to arrive. I have never suffered so much agony in my whole life, what with the pain of the wound, the jolting of the cart, and the long wait in the burning daytime and the bitterly-cold night. Because of the delay and the heat and the lack of water, poor Fred, my mate, died about an hour before reaching the First-Aid station. We survived everything they threw at us, but I never expected to come out of it alive. At the capture of Beersheba, our Colonel Meagur was killed, as well as Captain Watts, our C.O. We miss our old Colonel."

Of the 800 horses and horsemen who took part, 31 men were killed and 70 horses died. It was, indeed, the last great cavalry charge in history — and every bit as brave as the famous charge of the British Light Brigade against Russian cannons during the Crimean War (1854-6).

Light Horse on the march at Jifjafa

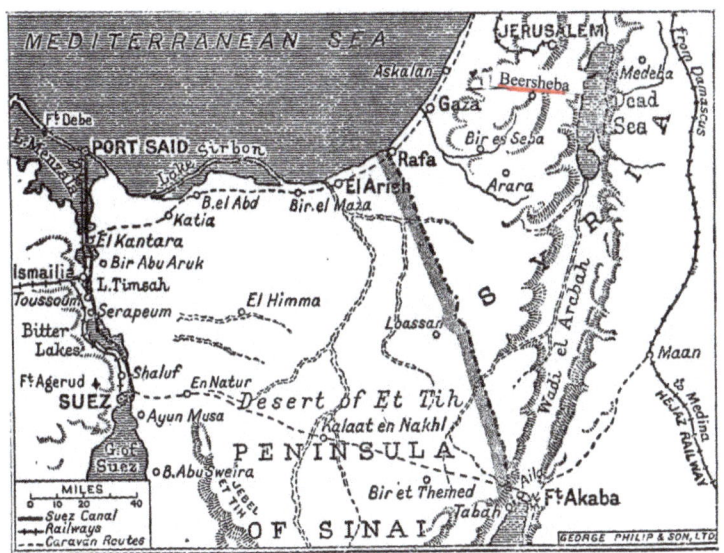

Map of The Suez Canal and Peninsula of Sinai

TROOPER NELSON LANGLEY — 13th. L.H. REGT — ENLISTED 31/12/14

THE HISTORIC CHARGE OF THE LIGHT HORSE AT BEERSHEBA

From a letter by Lieutenant Guy Haydon to his family and written from a Cairo hospital.

"At 4 p.m. orders came to mount and we marched along to within 3 miles of the town until we could go no further without being in full view — then we got the shock of our lives. The order came: 'All pack horses, excepting Hotchkiss rifle packs, fall out and remain behind'. Then followed a few minutes later the order: 'The 12th. and 14th. L. H. Regiments will charge Beersheba on horseback, the town is to be taken at all costs' — and five minutes later we were on our way.

We trotted for the first two miles, then the Turks opened fire on us from a line of redoubts *(small, enclosed fortifications)* about half a mile out from the town and we could hardly hear anything for the noise of their rifles and I never heard such awful war cries as our boys let out.

They never hesitated, or faltered for a moment. It was grand. Every now and again a rider would fall off, or a horse would drop, but the line swept on. I saw Major Fetherstonhaugh's horse go down, killed by a bullet to the head. The Major got up and ran for cover, only to fall again shot through both legs. A few seconds later a bullet hit me high up in the left buttock, just under the belt, dropping me sprawling on the ground. I rolled down into a (rifle) pit and into safety

But all this time the charge went on. Men raced their horses through and over the enemy trenches — and while some of us were still engaged in hand-to-hand fighting in the trenches, the remainder had charged through the town and to high ground beyond. The town was ours."

So that was how the Australian Light Horse captured the well-defended desert town of Beersheba on 31st. October, 1917, in one of the greatest charges in history — but the men were desperate for water and knew their horses would die unless they captured that water-rich desert town. Although a great victory it cost the lives of 31 men killed in action with another 36 wounded, but they enjoyed drinking the water — and, luckily, the Turks did not have time to poison those wells before they got there.

Colin Dunlop Donald (born 1879) was lucky because he survived the Great War after fighting in France (against the Germans) and then in Mesopotamia (against the Turks). He was an officer with the 30th. Lancers in the 1st. Cavalry Brigade and many of his war letters tell us about his exploits. At first, he went as a cavalryman to fight in France, guarding the flank of an Infantry Brigade. (British Cavalrymen bravely did the same at the Battle of Mons in August, 1914.) But Colin says in a letter dated August, 1915 to his sister-in-law: -

"We cavalrymen have become obsolete in France and, consequently, we have now entered the trenches to help the infantry. Today, I am sitting in the trenches, watching one of our aeroplanes being plugged by the Germans. Their shells are screaming over us and bursting just behind. These trenches are full of rats. I've had several hairbreadth escapes, but no one can realize the horrors of war until they spend time at the front and take part in several advances — or get into a trench after a heavy bombardment and hear the explosions of shells and the hissing and cracking of bullets — and see limbs severed by shells — and smell the rotting corpses lying all around — and watch flies by the million follow the food down your throat."

However, when Colin had his horse returned to him in the summer of 1916, he was happy to be sent to fight in Mesopotamia, a place of hot, dry desert regions. In April, 1917 after his Cavalry Brigade had advanced rapidly on Baghdad he writes; *"We went into Baghdad and found the place gutted. The Turks had burnt all the public buildings — and the Kurds and Arabs had looted the Bazaar and smashed everything. The city's vandals completed the enemy's destruction by setting fire to buildings and looting. We evidently got here just in time to avert a massacre of the Christians* and Armenians. The Bazaar was looted on the Saturday night and the massacre was to take place on the Sunday morning. We arrived on Sunday morning, just in time. The Christians were all waiting in their houses to be murdered and couldn't believe that our British troops were there to save them."

Eventually, Colin and his cavalrymen succeeded after all their hard desert fighting against the Turks and made a triumphal entry into Jerusalem, led by General Allenby, on the 11th. December, 1917. Thus ended the reign of the hated enemy. It was a memorable day in the history of Christendom because for centuries Turks had occupied the Holy City, but now, at last, a great British general had captured and occupied Jerusalem for the benefit of Jew and Christian alike.

Colin Dunlop Donald wrote, *"The most moving moment of the victory to me was when our great leader, General Allenby, refused to ride into the Holy City, but got off his horse and humbly walked through the gates of Jerusalem. Can you imagine the humility of such a great conqueror? The picture of that moment will always stay in my memory."*

Cavalrymen in France

General Allenby enters Jerusalem on foot

Cavalry ride into Baghdad

Stretcher-Bearers

The horrors of war.

PROOF OF A SOLDIER'S DEATH

Here is an example of the kind of information that was necessary to enter upon official war records — and especially essential for the next-of-kin. Eye-witnesses were vital because their description of events could avoid any possible confusion concerning the death of an individual soldier. Notice that there are <u>two</u> informants.

> "I saw Jack V. Jacobson killed by a bullet in the advance early in the morning of October 4th. He was quite close to me, but as he died instantly I could not do anything for him. He was buried at Zonnebeke and a cross with his name on it was erected quite recently, during the last two months. He and I were great friends and I always carried his address with me, but unfortunately I lost my pocket-book just at the time I most wanted it, so was unable to write and tell his people about him as I could not remember their address."
>
> (<u>Eye-Witness and Informant</u>: L/Cpl Thomas Malone, 665 — 24th. A.I.F.

Description: He was tall, well-built, nicknamed 'Jake' by his friends.)

"I was with L/Cpl. Jack V. Jacobson (24th. Btn. A.I.F. formerly C. Coy) when he was shot through the head by a sniper and killed instantaneously, during the advance at Zonnebeke on Oct. 4th. just before we reached our objective. We had to go straight on and leave him. I went back afterwards to get his things, but someone had picked him up. I think the stretcher-bearers must have taken him away and buried him. He was probably buried on Zonnebeke Ridge, but I have not seen his grave. I wrote to his people afterwards, but I do not know whether they received my letter. Jake came from Australia in May, 1915, and I joined him in Egypt a month later. He was my best friend all the time we were together."

(*Eye-witness and Informant*: L/Cpl Albert Pickering, 1810, 24th. A.I.F.

Description: Jake came from Macarthur, Victoria. He was single, a farm-labourer, and was made L/Cpl. the night before we went over the top.)

Private Joe Fraser (of Birchip) writes to friends about his experiences.

"SOMEWHERE IN FRANCE".

4th. October, 1916.

Just a short note to let you know that I am living, and well, and dodging the shells (which is more by good luck than good management).

We have been moving about a good bit lately and I have not had much opportunity of writing. I received your letter the other day (about five months behind time) and in it you stated that some newspapers had been sent, but I did not get them.

The weather is very wet and cold here now, but we are pretty cosy in our dugouts. If we ever have the luck to get out of this war and get back into civilian life again, a man won't trouble much about building brick or wooden houses while he can get sandbags.

It is surprising what a cosy home you can make out of them. When we get back, we won't be happy unless we are crawling into a dark hole.

We are making sure of what ground we are taking from the Germans now, as we have nearly half of France and a good lump of Belgium.

I thought last Christmas that there might be a chance of us being back home for this Xmas, but I am inclined to think that we will be lucky if we are back home for Xmas 1917. It will soon be 12 months since I left Port Melbourne (23rd. November). When I look back it seems like 12 years!

This time last year, we were playing soldiers at Melbourne Show Grounds, which was the pleasure-part of soldiering; and goodness only knows we thought it was bad enough in camp there.

It is marvellous where a man can live when he is hard put to it. A waterproof sheet, a blanket, wet clothes on his back, a tin of bully beef, a couple of hard biscuits, with five francs in his pocket — and a soldier is happy.

We were always anxious, when we were training in Egypt, to have a look at the Firing-line, but now we have had more than sufficient of it. I have been in action off and on since the 1st July, and am going good yet. A man has his ups and downs, but it is not too bad.

AN ENGLISH OPINION OF OUR SOLDIERS

"The streets of Central London are filled with soldiers from all parts of the British Empire, but I am bound to say that I have a very kindly feeling in my heart for the Australians — such bronzed, big, mighty men.

I look at them admiringly as they swagger along (I know of no other word to describe the way they walk) with their cowboy hats, their jolly faces, their laughing eyes and their open-hearted manner. They move as if born to rule and born to dominate others.

I love to talk to them, with their freedom from affectation, their heartiness, and their total absence of awkwardness or shyness. They seem to regard themselves as boys who have come home to their own folk; and certainly Britain is their home, for is it not the birthplace of their parents and grandparents?

They know their relations are glad to see them — as indeed we all are. They are determined to give themselves as happy a time as they can while they are among us. I have heard of their wonderful deeds at Gallipoli and I am proud to shake their hands; for such battle-fame will live for evermore in our History books."

DIGGERS ON LEAVE (29th. Battalion)

Like most Australians who visited England from France, Private Charles Bertie Gilchrist *(on right) found relatives in the 'Old Country'. He went north, to Pontefract in Yorkshire; but all over Britain, from Lands End to John O'Groats, young Australians were searching for*

COLONEL NEWSTEAD fought with the Suffolk Regiment in the war. He was a descendant of William Donald, an early squatter in the Wimmera (north west of Melbourne) after whom the rural Victorian town of DONALD was named.

Colonel Newstead *lost his life in France and a fellow officer who was present wrote the following words about him:* — "On March 4th. 1916, I was with the Advanced Guard, which the Colonel was commanding, and we came under a very hot fire; he, his

Adjutant and myself were all together for about half-an-hour. He then ordered me to take our Maxim gun back a little way and he came with me to select a new position for it. After this he left me and went forward to the right under very heavy fire to make further dispositions, and then I lost sight of him. About five minutes later his Adjutant ran past me and called out that he himself was hit in the face and that the Colonel had been shot in the side. Colonel Newstead was removed to the camp near Bare and carefully attended to by a doctor, but he died the next morning and was buried the same evening not far from the camp. He was a brave and gallant Officer — he did not know what fear was and his first thought was to look after the interests of others. He was the best and truest friend to me that anyone ever had, a friend who could never be replaced. He was 39."

Thousands of Scots fought and fell during the First World War and to commemorate the centenary of that war, a special Drumhead Service was held at Edinburgh Castle to remember the fallen. Musicians from the Band of the Royal Marines will construct and deconstruct the Drumhead that will be the centrepiece of this major commemorative event.

Drumhead Altars

On 28th. October, 1916, the hospital ship, Galeka, was entering Le Havre port when she struck a mine and sank. Fortunately there were no patients on board, but 19 Royal Army Medical Corps personnel died as a result.

Photo — Gunner Geddie Pearse

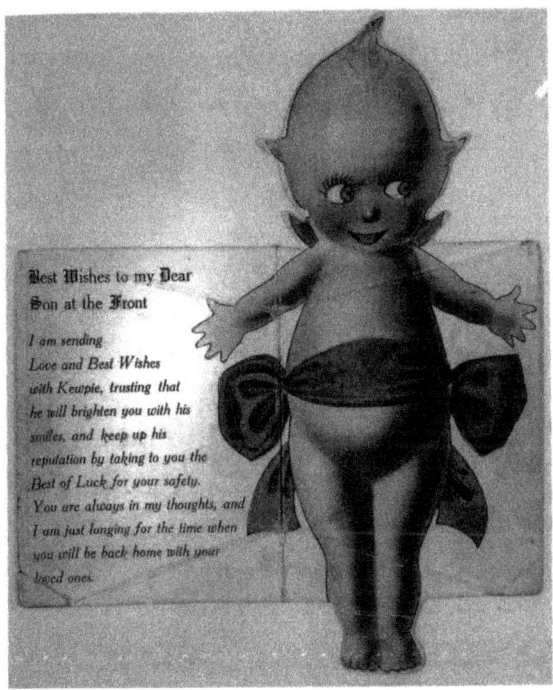

A LUCKY KEWPIE-DOLL CARD

The Somme Mud

The battlefield at Flers was like a dreadful nightmare to the men. The whole field was turned into a vast bog as cold rain and thick fogs I continued day after day. Men and animals floundered through the mire, sinking in the slush, and often unable to extricate themselves from the grip of the deadly quagmire. A man would do well if he made a hundred yards in one hour over this kind of terrain — and often he became hopelessly bogged down. Weapons at times were clogged with mud and useless; clothes were soaking wet and grimy; and bodies were utterly exhausted. Carrying supplies to the trenches was more than flesh and blood could stand — yet for the sake of their comrades who were relying on them, fatigue-parties struggled and ploughed onwards through the deep mud. The <u>real</u> battle was against the conditions of that terrible winter.

IN THE MUD AT FLERS – 5TH. NOVEMBER, 1916.

Private Roy Haase (of Wedderburn) paints a grim picture of his battalion's attack in the rain and mud at Flers.

Dear Mother,

I was in the leading Company of my battalion when we reached the Front-line on the evening of November 4th. Our objective was a sunken road near Gueudecourt. We had a tiring journey through the mud from Delville Wood, but arrived at the Front-line about sunset and filed into the Jumping-Off Trench before dark. Then the rain began to fall at midnight and drenched us.

Unfortunately, as our second company came up over the open ground they were seen by the Germans who at once sent over illuminating flares and a light barrage. We had to lie in the mud and rain and wait for the order to advance. At 12-30 our Artillery started a barrage fire upon No-Man's Land and we went over the parapet, but the rough muddy ground gripped our feet like quicksand.

We could not follow the barrage quickly enough, as the mud was like glue. Then our barrage lifted and let us through. But our advance over muddy No-Man's Land was too slow. It gave the Germans time to swarm up from their dugouts and use their machine-guns upon us. Many of our men fell, and the rest hesitated and were lost.

We went back to our trenches and re-organised. Our third Company joined us now, and with these reinforcements we launched another attack immediately. This time my party reached the German trench and we were holding it when I was wounded in the wrist.

I helped another chap with a broken leg, but the deep thick mud tugged like glue at the bottom of our boots and I had to wait for help from the stretcher-bearers.

I believe we were at a disadvantage on November 5th. as the moon was rising behind us and it showed us up to the enemy. Their machine-guns played havoc amongst our troops. The rain and mud just made fighting impossible.

SAPPER VICTOR WILLEY writes about CONDITIONS ON THE SOMME "FLERS" 28/10/16

"Well, dear Parents,
You will think me a fine one for keeping you waiting so long for a letter, but the way we get moved about from one place to another, we don't get any time for letter-writing.

We are never settled anywhere now, and are continually on the move from one place to another; and I can tell you it is very trying this cold weather, as a man gets wet through, day after day.

For a solid week I have never once had dry feet, so you will not be surprised to hear of me going into hospital with the "screws". In fact, I have rheumatism already in BOTH my shoulders.

For two days and two nights we were working in the trenches with water and slush above our knees; but we wore gum-boots reaching up to our thighs and these kept a chap from perishing. Yet after coming up out of the trenches it was many hours before you could get your blood back into proper circulation.

And the MUD is thick upon this water-logged ground. It is impossible to move about quickly, as the mud is as sticky as honey and as slippery as butter.

I don't think I told you in my last letter, that poor McMillan (my mate) was killed up in Boris-Baree Wood, in Belgium, as soon as we arrived there. He was among the first men to land on the Gallipoli Peninsula, and went through that Campaign with me.

He was also twice through battles on the Somme (which is a Living Hell), and then to meet his death on such a quiet Front seems bad luck. I will tell you how it happened.

He and I were lying up on the parapet of the trench, talking about how quiet it was around there. We could not sit <u>inside</u> the trench as on that day we had a big infantry party digging along to improve it.

It was just about time to knock off work, so I said to my mate I would go and fetch food for both of us from the other end of the trench. I was on my knees, ready to stand up, when an enemy-flare went up, and the next thing I heard was a big SMACK alongside of me.

Poor Mac was shot through the head by a sniper, I knew he was gone as soon as I looked at him; but he lingered for 12 hours and nothing could be done for the poor chap.

He was one of the finest mates I ever had. He neither drank nor smoked, and he never swore — and he was always ready to take the blame upon himself for anything that went wrong.

Later that same day, our section-officer was wounded in the

arm and got a bonza trip to Blighty. Oh, how I was wish it had been me! The next night I was working in no-Man's Land in charge of an Infantry party, when a comrade on each side of me was shot — one had his leg smashed and the other had his hand shattered.

We are about to leave for the Somme again; and God Help Us because that Front is a perfect Inferno. But I may be lucky enough to get through again, though I suppose my turn to "turn in my chips" will come one of these days.

Did you know that Hector Small and George Wardley had been slightly wounded? So, they are far better off than we are at this present time. May they both be out of action for months.

It will be Christmas by the time you get this letter, so I sincerely wish you all the Compliments of the Season, a Prosperous New Year to all Donald folk, and a bumper harvest to farmers — and may 1917 see this cruel and terrible war ended, and German Militarism crushed for ever."

PRIVATE STANLEY CANNARD is one of four brothers on active service. He describes conditions on the Somme in the winter of 1916-17.

FRANCE. 28/12/16.

"I received your letter, Dear Mother, after coining out of the line, where we had a pretty trying time as the mud and water was up to our knees. I have a bad case of Trench-Foot (left one) and cannot get any life into my toes. Lots of lads are suffering from Trench-Feet due to the appalling conditions in the wet trenches.

Mud, mud and more mud! You just cannot stand too long in one place without sinking up to your knees. Some men have to be <u>dug</u> out of the mud. One man had his back broken when they were pulling him out of the mud. Well, I'm not going to tell you much about the war, as it is no good, because you cannot realise what it is like from over there. It is just too awful. I don't know how I got through; but I think if one never stops to think about it, that helps.

We were in the muddy trenches for ten days and I was in the "Hop-Over" and it was funny really. You see, Fritz took it into his mind to attack us on the same morning and we met half-way; and as he couldn't get back for our barrage we had no trouble in taking his ridge.

But the difficult part is trying to hold the area until you dig in. The mud just slides back again. We suffered severely; but I am not allowed to tell you our losses. Anyhow, our Company is now very weak.

If you were sitting in a trench with 2,500 guns of all different sizes roaring night and day, and Fritz's machine-guns, too, you would be a bit nervous, I'm sure. We had nothing to eat or drink for 24 hours the last time we were in the Line, due to the mud stopping the movement of carrying-parties.

There is no doubt you cannot beat the Australians for fighting. Fritz just puts up his hands and runs for his life. We captured a lot of Germans with Red-Crosses on their arms, who were using machine-guns, so you can bet they got it."

CROSS THE SNOW, NEAR FLERS, JAN 1917.
DUCKBOARDS — *these long pathways were the first effective relief for the troops.*

CPL. I. H. HARRISON

"OVER THE TOP" INTO "NO-MAN'S LAND"

Miss Maggie Pope received this newsy letter from Private Herbert Lewis, of Donald.

MOO-COW FARM

"SOMEWHERE IN FRANCE" 1916

"I will endeavour to give you a brief account of our movements since going to France. I joined my battalion on the 14/8/16 after being five weeks in England; and then we were three weeks in a training camp at Etaples on the coast.

This battalion had just come out of the trenches at Pozieres — with pretty heavy casualties. It's no use my explaining what it was like, as you have already heard that kind of thing at least a dozen times. We were camped at Albert, which is now reduced to ruins; but this place marked the starting point of the Somme advance by the allies.

We marched back through villages, stopping at this village one night, and at another one for two nights, and so on; till in the course of about eight days we found ourselves back at Albert. We camped here for one night again, then marched into the trenches at Mouquet Farm — which you may remember cost us a lot of lives to take it. Mouquet Farm is linked up with Thiepval, — one chain distant, by an underground tunnel.

Mouquet Farm was a veritable network of deep dug-outs, ranging in depth from 20 to 30 feet. These dug-outs have two or three entrances by which the Germans gain access to their trenches. When our bombardment would start, the Germans would get into these dug-outs and hide; and then, when our boys went over and jumped into the German trenches, the enemy would swarm out upon them like bees. However, I managed to get out of this action with a whole skin.

In the course of the next few days we entrained for Ypres. We put in a few days at a camp, training and so on, and then we went out to the trenches once more. We found this Front-Line comparatively quiet after the Somme, and nothing of much importance happened whilst in there. We were for the most part, building new trenches behind the Front-Line to form a second line of defence.

This is where I wrote to you last from Belgium. You will notice that Ypres is just over the Belgian border (and not in France as most people seem to think). Whilst here I caught the "mumps" and went back to St. Omer Hospital for two weeks; but I just got back in time to move into the Front-Line again, immediately in front of Ypres. We could see the remnants of that town from our Front-Line.

I didn't go into Ypres myself, but the boys say it was a beautiful town. We had a fairly comfortable time here; although we always had a feeling of insecurity as it was a great place for springing mines, both by Fritz and by our own boys. In fact, one night the Tommies relieved us in the trenches and the very next night Fritz sprung a mine and blew them up sky-high; so our luck was in that time.

The cold was intense, winter arriving in earnest. We had a few casualties here, principally with Rum-Jars and Minenwerfers, which are two distinct types of German Trench Mortars.

After leaving there, we entrained for the Somme, this time going into action at <u>Flers</u>. Here we found conditions simply abominable. The roads were like thick, sticky porridge for miles; and when we got into the trenches we were up to our waists in <u>MUD</u>.

It may seem incredible, but you can guess what it is like with continuous rain and battalions of men going in and out of the trenches all the time. You can see the reason for this constant movement as it is impossible for men to stay in the trenches for more than four days at any one time under these awful conditions.

Heavy artillery-lorries often got bogged down in the mud and caused traffic blocks for miles and it was amazing that the German airmen missed such a great opportunity to bomb our congested roads. It was here that Ivan Harrison was killed, on the corner of <u>Delville Wood</u>.

We went out and marched back to <u>Rainneville,</u> a village six miles from <u>Amiens</u>. We had leave into <u>Amiens</u> which is a fine big town. We spent Xmas and New Year in <u>Rainneville</u> — and a pretty quiet time it was.

After a rest-spell of two weeks or so, we turned our heads again for the Somme, going into the line at <u>Flers</u>. I had only been in two days when a shell came over, and, as already stated in a previous letter, it killed 2 and wounded 14 of us — Ralph Harrison and I being among the wounded.

I have found out that Ralph is now in England and he is coming up to see me. If you see Mr. Harrison in Donald, you might tell him that Ralph is doing splendidly, as they will be worrying on account of their eldest son's recent death.

I am still waiting to have an operation for the removal of shrapnel, though I'm feeling pretty good. Jack Baker is still in England. I have been down the town in a wheelchair. One of the boys pushed me down and back. I consider myself very lucky, as a few days after I left France my battalion went over the top to capture a ridge of hills; and out of a Company of 200, only 20 came out alive."

(However, this brave soldier's luck eventually ran out. Gul. H. H. Lewis was wounded again the following year, and he died from his wounds on 1st. August, 1918.)

Ypres in ruins

Transport Ship at Capetown

A TRIP ACROSS THE WORLD

Trooper W. J. Phillips (St. Arnaud) left Melbourne on the 6th. September, 1916, as part of a little band of Light Horse reinforcements.

2,000 MORE ENGLAND. DECEMBER, 1916.
"As our ship moved off, the scene was most patriotic. The decks were lined with boys in khaki, holding on to streamers of red, white and blue, whilst the crowds on the pier were holding on to the other ends. Amidst ringing cheers, the vessel swung off at about 12 o'clock, making for the Heads. . Dinner was served shortly afterwards, and full justice was done to the roast beef and potatoes. The afternoon was occupied in letter-writing; whilst the huge vessel moved along towards a foreign destination and our unknown fate.

The next night I was strolling on deck, hoping to see someone from St. Arnaud, when I caught sight of Ernie Fithall from Beazley's Bridge, Jack Stewart from the Volcano, Bob Cossens from Traynor's Lagoon and Jim Gibney from Coonooer. They told me that Charlie Osborne and the Willoughby brothers were also on board, as well as Harry Churchill from Charlton. We all had a jolly time together.

After a few days at sea, most soldiers were on their feet again, forgetting about the fish they had occasionally been feeding.

Almost everything one requires can be bought on this ship, although the tariff is high. Two pence each for apples and oranges; one shilling for a pound of mixed biscuits; and sixpence for a shave or haircut from the ship's barber.

The most popular amusements on board are quoits, cards and boxing. We also have interesting lectures on various subjects by the officers. Books and newspapers are in constant demand, and in this respect the Y. M. C. A. proves a great boon to soldiers.

On Sundays we have a Church Parade, and that carries one's mind back to our loved ones at home who are praying for the safe return of husband, son, brother, relative or friend. For the time, we are separated from them by thousands of miles of sea. Some nights we have concerts held on the boat-deck.

Each morning the bugle awakes us from slumber, and soon the ship is alive with a moving mass of human beings; there are about 2,000 of us here. Mess-Orderlies parade at a quarter-past-six to collect the daily rations of sugar, tea, coffee, milk, butter and bread. Jam is served only once a week.

Sports are held occasionally, including foot-racing, tug-of-war and potato-races which create plenty of amusement; and the determination with which the various games are played indicates what the German can expect when he gets into close contact with the Australian soldier. Daily rifle-practice reminds us of the real purpose of this journey.

On the 26th. September there was a death on board — a New South Wales soldier died suddenly. At 10 o'clock the men of the different units were drawn up on parade and the vessel was slowed down, almost to a stand-still.

The band played the Dead March, and, the burial service having been read, the body was committed to the sea. After a volley from the firing-party, the bugle sounded the Last Post; and in a few minutes the throttles of the engines were opened and the vessel once more bounded forward, leaving behind one whom I cannot forget.

On the 28th. September, land was sighted for the first time since leaving Australia just three weeks ago. Everybody was delighted. We passed a lighthouse standing at the entrance to the harbour, adjoining which is the town of (*Durban*). We had to wait for a pilot, so in the meantime we had breakfast. At 9 o'clock our vessel dropped anchor alongside the pier.

Two hours later it was announced that General Leave had been granted to all troops as the vessel had to be coaled. By about 12 o'clock the troops had all disembarked, and after a route-march through the main street (a distance of about three miles) we were dismissed at the Town Hall and told to be back at the ship by 11 p.m.

The streets were soon alive with soldiers. The Y.M.CA. is just as prominent here as it is in Australia, and they had a spacious hall, with quite an army of helpers, including many ladies. There was seating accommodation for 300 in this hall and it was conducted on the lines of a big restaurant. Tables are available for soldiers to write letters (on Y.M.C.A. paper) and there is also a room where a wash could be enjoyed — which was greatly appreciated after our march through the dusty streets. The Y.M.C.A. does not charge us for all these comforts. Refreshments are supplied to us for a small fee (which would not pay for half the cost of the eatables). The charge for a good cup of tea is one penny; a large sandwich of bread and beef, one penny; a block of cake, one penny; and a good meal costs no more than sixpence.

One can eat as many oranges as one likes, and there is a good supply of free cigarettes. The Y. M. C. A. building is nearly always full of people and there is plenty of music. The building is named "The Y. M. C. A. Hut", but a more appropriate name would be "The Visiting Soldiers' Home From Home".

The buildings of this town are principally of stone, and can be compared with those in Melbourne. The streets are wide and very clean, and the trams (run by electricity) are double deckers, licensed to carry 60 passengers. They were placed at the disposal of the soldiers — FREE. There is a splendid museum here, and also zoological gardens. The cost of a tram ticket is only one penny per mile.

The shops are large and varied, but the prices of the goods are higher than in Australia, excepting tobacco and cigars. The hotels are on a par with those in Australia for prices; but are open longer hours, from 6 a.m to 10 p.m. I met an elderly gentleman in the street, and he gave me half-a-dozen choice cigars (similar to those Sir Peter used to smoke in St Arnaud).

During our conversation this gentleman expressed his admiration for the Australian soldiers; and also remarked on what a wonderful country Australia was in sending, what seemed to him to be, an endless chain of soldiers to assist Great Britain in the war. He added that they were a fine body of men who would apparently stop at nothing when facing the foe.

I asked him what was the population of that city; and the gentleman replied, "About 35 000 whites and 70,000 blacks". He explained that as a rule the black men were lazy and made their women do all the work. A friend of his had about 50 blacks working for him, and their wages were 2 pounds a month, besides a little overtime. These blacks never drew on their wages if they could help it, living on what they made by overtime. Then, as soon as they had saved enough money to buy three cows, they were in a position to get married. They settled the wife down, and then bought another wife, and so on, until they had well up to five wives. Then the wives had to work to keep the husband!

A milch cow in that country was worth about 7 pounds. There are numerous rickshaws in the streets, drawn by natives, who hire the rickshaws from the council.

Willoughby and I went by train and motor for a trip into the country, and we passed through some very rich land amongst the sugar cane. We halted at a hotel, licensed by a man who was originally a resident of Kerang, in Victoria, and he knew several St. Arnaud people. What a small world it is!

We returned to town and met Fithall and Churchill, and after tea we took a run down to the beach. We spent two days in (*Durban*) because the process of loading coal was very slow. About 50 coolies carry the coal in cornsacks on their backs up the gangway.

The next town we visited (*Cape Town*) had a population of about 29,000 whites and 40,000 blacks. It was situated along a beach and a railway line ran through the street for some distance; and, considering the heavy traffic, accidents were not frequent.

We visited the bay and found the place alive with soldiers. The ladies provided afternoon tea in a quaint-looking building.

In the evening, the Y.M.C.A. arranged a concert, which concluded with a coffee supper. We had a really good time. On returning to the ship we soon resumed the voyage, which, since leaving Australia, had been exceptionally good, particularly from the weather point of view.

It was somewhat hot passing through the Tropics, but during that part of the journey the decks were covered with tarpaulins to give plenty of shade. Our next stop was in a small harbour for a few hours at (*Dakar*) where they put off meat from our troopship to an English warship. I can tell you that the locals here caused no end of amusement.

As soon as it was daylight, the water in the immediate vicinity of our ship was alive with little boats, each containing from four to six young natives. They brought oranges, bananas, money-bags, postcards, photos etc., and we soon found out that they had a great liking for money. They asked for money to be thrown into the water and they would dive and secure it. They are certainly expert swimmers. At last the water became so thick with them that they got in each other's way, and to keep the fun going was too expensive. They then began to bargain for the fruit and other things they had for sale, but one could never get the best of the deal with them.

One of the soldiers passed down 4/6 in a bucket for different items, but as soon as the local got his hands on the money he made off with it. A box of potatoes which happened to be on the deck came in very handy; and the local was nearly killed with potatoes before he got out of throwing distance.

We left there about 11 o'clock that night, without getting a chance to land. We then got into waters which abounded with ships. Some consternation was caused when an object like a buoy appeared in the water ahead. It could have been a mine, so the vessel was immediately steered clear of it.

A fierce storm occurred in the Bay of Biscay, and amidst a state of confusion (amongst falling crockery and the like) the bugler sounded an alarm. Everybody immediately put on a lifebelt After about half-an-hour's suspense, the bugler sounded retire; and when we got on deck, a destroyer could be seen — happily one sent from British Headquarters to watch over and protect our troopship from the enemy U-Boats.

After breakfast the weather brightened up a bit, and most of the soldiers were on deck, when suddenly a great wave dashed against the ship with such force that an officer was washed overboard. The ship was stopped and a boat lowered. It was manned by a crew of soldiers who eventually rescued the officer. He was in the freezing water for 55 minutes; and if it had not been for a soldier who had the presence of mind to throw him a lifebelt immediately he fell overboard, I think he would have drowned.

Once more, the ship proceeded on its way; and although the journey was nearly over, those on board had an anxious time. At about 4 o'clock that afternoon everybody was ordered to put on a lifebelt. Throughout the whole night the ship glided along quietly, and on Sunday morning, as we went on deck, we saw land — good old England — the land of our forefathers and home of the Union Jack.

Around us were warships of various sizes, bristling with guns, great and small, spelling death and destruction to whoever and whatever they may be turned upon. Within the hour, there landed close upon 2000 more of Australia's sons who are sworn to do, or die, in upholding the traditions of the Great British Empire — and to keep the grand old flag flying.

I must close now, wishing everyone a Merry Xmas and a Prosperous 1917. Tell all my friends that if they want to write I shall be pleased to reply as promptly as time permits."

No. 2896, Trooper W. J. Phillips, 20/4 Light Horse, A. I. F. Abroad.

- STONEHENGE -

UPON SALISBURY PLAIN

While looking at it, I wondered if ever human sacrifices were offered there, for such things used to be done by worshippers in those days? All around the circle of stones can be traced the remains of an old moat, or trench, some 20 yards from the circle. Of course, the "Altar-Stone" is to the east of the structure. In another circle, half-a-mile from the main circle, are large mounds, 15 feet high and 30 yards in diameter. These are ancient burial places, and when searchers opened them they found gold and other ornaments. In many places they found stone mauls and wedges. The upright stones are 18 feet high, by 3 feet by 3 feet, and weigh from 40 to 60 tons. The cross stones on top are carefully-carved and fitted together on each column.

(<u>Cpl. A.F.C. Campbell)</u>

A SOLDIER'S DEATH

Mr. and Mrs. John Rowe, of St. Arnaud, received the following sad particulars concerning the death of their son, <u>Sergeant Percy Rowe.</u>

FRANCE. 10TH. DECEMBER. 1916.

"I am enclosing details of how Percy Rowe, the Collingwood crack-follower, got fatally wounded. I don't know where Percy lived, so I am sending this letter to the Collingwood Football Club in the hope that some-one there will forward it to his home.

I was with Percy in a bombing-post in one of the hottest corners of the Somme firing-line. It rains shells and bullets over here, and on that fateful day we had some very miraculous escapes from Fritz's iron rations. Fortunately, none of our boys was seriously hit until about half-an-hour before we were due to be relieved from the Front-line.

That was when Percy was injured. It was about 6 p.m. on Monday, December 4th. Percy was stooping down attending to his equipment, preparatory to leaving the line, when a shrapnel-shell burst on the parapet about three feet above our heads. Percy gripped his side and fell to the bottom of the trench. Turning to us he exclaimed, "I'm gone; good-bye, lads; shake hands."

He held out his hand, and as I gripped it he turned over and rolled in pain. I immediately sent for the stretcher-bearer. Then with the aid of another lad, I undid Percy's clothes and dressed his wound. It was a jagged wound, about three inches long, in the small of his back near the left kidney. Percy complained of a dull pain and said he felt something running in his stomach. (I suspect he had an internal haemorrhage.)

The stretcher-bearers carried him to the dressing-station, but I believe the doctor held out no hope from the first. Poor Percy died the same night. His remains are buried in a battlefield cemetery near Trones Wood. Percy was our Platoon-Sergeant, and I can tell you the boys of No. 11 Platoon feel his death very keenly; for he was an honest, straight-forward sport, a good and game soldier, and he had the fullest confidence of his men. I am writing these details as I reckon it is my duty, for the sake of his wife and family and friends."

Alf. Cohen. (29th. Battalion)

"DON'T WORRY" / "BE HAPPY"

The philosophy of a French soldier is quite an amusing one, for he insists that "everything might be worse than it is!" He explains what he means:- "Of two things one is certain — either you're mobilized, or you're not mobilized. If you're not mobilised, there is no need to worry. If you are mobilized, of two things one is certain — either you're behind the lines, or you're at the front. If you're behind the lines there is no need to worry. If you're at the front, of two things one is certain — either you're resting in a safe place, or you're exposed to danger. If you're resting in a safe place there is no need to worry. If you're exposed to danger, of two things one is certain — either you're wounded, or you're not wounded. If you're not wounded there is no need to worry. If you're wounded, of two things one is certain — either you're wounded seriously, or you're wounded slightly. If you're wounded slightly there is no need to worry. If you're wounded seriously, of two things one is certain — either you recover, or you die. If you recover there is no need to worry. If you die, you can't worry."

PRIVATE FRANCIS PHELPS (of Birchip)

A REAL BED

SALISBURY PLAIN. 25TH. APRIL. 1917.

"I have just returned from leave in London, and spent an enjoyable time there. Vin Stevens and myself went together, and after a rather sharp train journey arrived in "The Heart of the Empire" at 2-30 p.m. on Friday, 21st. of April. After considerable delay we were free to go to the War Chest Club, opposite A.I.F. Headquarters in Horseferry Road.

After an excellent tea, we started off to the Adelphi Theatre, where we saw a play called "High Jinks" (which was actually twice played in Melbourne while I was in camp there). Eleven-thirty found us back in the War Chest Club, and soon we were fast asleep in a real bed — a novelty after sleeping on boards with five blankets for months and months.

As there was no Reveille at 6-30 a.m. we slept until 8-30 when we thought it was about time for breakfast. This also was a novelty, as we had not used plates, or cups and saucers (to say nothing of a white tablecloth) since we left home in Australia.

At 9-45 a.m. we started off on a tour of London in a large party, going first down past Westminster Abbey to the street where enemy bombs fell in the first Zeppelin raid on London. The walls on each side of this street still bear the marks of the explosions.

Continuing down the Strand, we passed the Aldwych Y.M.C.A. Hut on our left, and reached Melbourne House where we waited for our guide. Driving slowly, we passed Somerset House, Queen Anne's Mansions (the highest buildings in London), Buckingham Palace, St. James' Park, Queen Victoria's Memorial, and on to the Tower of London.

Here we spent quite a long time, visiting the Crown Jewels, Armories, the Bloody Tower, the scaffold where two of King Henry VIII's wives were executed, and the Bell Tower (where King Richard III lived, and from which he sent his assassins to murder the little princes in the Tower).

St Paul's Cathedral was next visited, and its beauties and tombs thoroughly explained by our excellent guide, who then returned us for lunch.

On Sunday morning we visited Middlesex Street in East London — better known as Petticoat Lane — and here we found hundreds and hundreds of people who were buying from the stalls in the street.

Hyde Park, Picadilly, Leicester Square and Trafalgar Square completed a busy morning."

Gunners In Action Wearing Their Gas Helmets.

THANK GOD FOR THE Y.M.C.A.

MR. ALBANY BELL (a Y.M.C.A. worker) describes incidents on a troopship which departed from Australia at the beginning of 1917. His job was to look after the physical and spiritual needs of the troops.

"We went away from Dakar strongly-convoyed. One of the war boats (a doughty little fighter) had been in all the scraps outside Jutland, and carried the evidences in patched funnels and sides. She buzzed around us like a hen worrying over her brood of chickens. After sailing for days, from goodness knows where, we picked up other troopships and then we all settled down for the last lap home to Blighty.

On one occasion a strange vessel was sighted and she was ordered to come up close for inspection. When this was done, she was told to keep away from the transports, but as she sailed up too close again, a couple of shots and a warning shell fired across her bows soon sent her right about turn. The British Navy takes no risks when guarding us.

Later, a flotilla of topedo-boats took us over. They look like cheeky, little bulldogs, and can sail around us as fast as a streak of lightning. We entered on rough water in the Bay of Biscay and the boys began to feel sorry for the little torpedo-boats and suggested we should take them on board.

The wind increased to a gale until it was too rough for the

U-Boats to operate; and this weather continued till we reached port. As we had had beautifully-calm weather up to then, we could fairly call it a 'providential' voyage. We had some lively times with the rough weather; and the lads were just like a lot of schoolboys let out of school.

One mess-orderly lost his balance and capsized a dixie of soup over a man coming up the steps. Of course, the man took his soaking like a lamb (I don't think) and the deck was blue with his profanities, well-sustained for several minutes, while all the men on deck were screaming with laughter at the poor man's appearance.

It is astonishing how we can see the joke when misfortune happens to another fellow; but when the mess-orderly told them there was no more soup for them, the joke immediately lost its point. So then they started on the mess-orderly with forceful expressions of their opinions on his clumsiness.

When we reached calmer waters we received a wireless message from a British vessel, saying, 'Just about to be shelled' — so you can guess that we were not sorry to get safely into harbour."

Private F. A. Tyers writes to his parents in Birohip.

HARD NUTS

January, 1917.

"On our embarkation at Port Melbourne on the 25th. September, 1916, we put out to the Heads, where we anchored for the night. We got a wriggle on next morning, and in a short time there were more on board sick than otherwise.

We landed at Durban on 15th. October and had a good time. We had to sleep on the boats every night, but got leave on three afternoons. We left Durban amid showers of mandarins and yells from the locals. I tell you, they are hard nuts!

All went well until the 20th. October when we dropped anchor at Cape Town, and, as we could not get shore-leave, our only entertainment was watching the locals lumping bags of coal into the hold of the ship.

We left there next day and about a fortnight later crossed the Equator, when all the men got ducked under the shower-bath, clothes and all on, but it did not make much difference to us. I had to guard the freezing works, where water was being cooled so as we could get it to drink.

We arrived at Dakar on 2nd. November, and before the anchors were dropped about 30 boats were around us and the occupants were diving into the water for "trays" and "sprats" which we threw in. It was great fun for us.

A French warship came into port while we were there, and she looked splendid. After a four-hour stop in Dakar harbour we put out for the last lap, and none of us was sorry.

We struck rough seas between Dakar and England, the last week of the voyage being the worst of all. All of us had to wear lifebelts throughout the day, and sleep near them at night. But they do not make bad pillows, so in the latter period they were mostly used that way!

We arrived at Plymouth at 10 p.m. As our blankets were all stored away (and without any tea or beds) we had to make the best of it sleeping on board for the night, with only our overcoats for covering.

We got off the ship next morning and entrained for *London*.

Horses pulling burning wagon

A gully full of dead and dying

Corporal Herbert Storer (Carapooee West) writes home from a Reading Hospital to tell his parents about his injuries.

MUD – MUD – MUD

No. 1 War Hospital, Reading, Berkshire, England. February, 1917.

Just a line to let you know I am now in hospital in Reading, England, with trench feet. I sent you a cable, so I suppose you knew long ago. They are almost better now, and I may be going to an Auxiliary — Hospital any day.

Brother Sam was well when I left France. He never had to go up to the Front-line. I am pleased he never had to go up, as nearly all of us got bogged. It took us six hours to walk three quarters of a mile, through mud that was above our knees.

I suppose that only one third of us got there that night and I was the only Corporal that got there. I had to do such a lot that I got trench feet from standing in the mud for so long.

The other Sergeants were all sick or bogged, but I stuck at it for three days and nights, until my feet swelled so much that I was sent away. I am glad to say that I have now recovered and am in good health.

I was in Rouen hospital, in France, for four days, and it is a grand city. You might have read how the French capital was shifted there when the Germans were so dangerously close to Paris.

The papers are full of Peace-Talks today, but it will come to nothing, as usual. We get fourteen days' leave sifter we come out of the convalescent camp.

I read in an English newspaper that Uncle Bob Dennis had died. The paper said that while he was robbing bees, he was attacked by a swarm of them and dropped dead. I would not have known but for seeing the newspapers.

A WINTER'S RAID IN FEBRUARY, 1917.

Private Ned Mulquiny (of Charlton) describes to his father what it was like to be in a raid upon the German trenches.

1917.

It is not so cold now, but is much colder than Charltons. The French farmers are all busy sowing their crops. Tell Mrs. Churchill I saw Harry a few nights back and he is looking well.

I am writing this within 400 yards of the enemy trenches, as we came up to the Front-line two nights ago. The weather last week was terribly cold with driving winds and snow. Some weeks ago we carried out a raid on the enemy trenches, and in every way it was a great success — for over two weeks we were rehearsing it.

From aerial photographs we studied a sector of Fritz's trench until each of our men knew the exact place assigned to him. Then, one night after a short but very heavy bombardment, we went over. So heavy and accurate was our Artillery fire, that his barbed-wire was blown clean away and his trenches knocked to pieces; while part of his Front-line was changed into nothing but shell-holes.

We used to think that our trenches were wet and muddy, but

they were not nearly as bad as his! The party I was with had to go to the third line, but when we got over there we could not find it, owing to all the shell-holes. The Germans that were there readily surrendered, though one or two showed a little fight.

There were dead Germans lying everywhere past the first line. Some stayed in their concrete dugouts, but a box of ten pounds of gun-cotton placed against their dugout doors soon finished them up.

At a given signal we all moved back, the Artillery covering our retirement. Considering the large number of men who went over, our losses were very light; and most of them occurred before we started when the enemy sent up his S.O.S. signals in reply to our guns and then fired shells upon our Front-line.

On the way over we had to wade waist-deep through a ditch of slush; and the barrage of our guns was like a hailstorm coming across the field. It must be awful to be in Fritz's trench when our Trench-Mortars, Stokes-gun and artillery are on to him.

Private P. Buchanan writes a fascinating account of his war-experiences to his aunt, Mrs. Buchanan, of Witchipool.

A FIGHTING-SOLDIER AT 50.

1917.

"Marvellous experiences come to one and another of us as we journey along the road of life; and I little thought I should ever be writing to you from a soldiers' camp in the Old Country.

You have possibly heard that I joined the Expeditionary Forces? Although someone said that at <u>my</u> age I would never stand roughing it, yet I have gone right through the campaign and have never been in hospital, or had to fall out on a route-march, since I started; and in consequence I am very pleased with myself.

I went into camp on the 3rd. day of September, 1915, and it was the day after my birthday upon which I was 50. I have therefore had <u>months</u> at this game of fighting and I feel as good as ever.

I spent one month training in Egypt where it was very hot (a good deal hotter than it ever was in Donald) but it always cooled down at night, so I slept well.

Then we went over the Mediterranean Sea to France, and we had a lovely trip on the water; and then by train through the beautiful land of France. It was early summer in Europe when we arrived there and I never dreamt there could be such glorious scenery. We saw well-cultivated fields of splendid crops of wheat, oats and barley, interspersed with vineyards and orchards.

Cherry trees grew wild along the railway lines and up the sides of the hills. Here and there were colourful fields of red poppies which are grown for trade purposes. It seemed to me like going into the Garden of Eden. We could not help comparing this green countryside to the deserts of Egypt.

Well, we were about three weeks camped at Etaples (on the French coast) and then we were drafted up the line to "HAVE A GO" at the Huns. Our battalion was holding the line for about six weeks, giving and taking some hard knocks; and I was preserved from all dangers although the bullets and shells dropped around me continually and a lot of my mates fell from time to time.

Then we went back behind the lines for a rest-spell and had a fortnight in peace; but we still trained continually for more fighting to come.

We stayed at Albert for a fortnight, and then marched to the Somme; five days of it, long weary days of carrying heavy packs. Some of the fellows dropped out, but I battled through. On the 15th. September we advanced on a wide front, taking Flers, Martinpuich and Courcelette.

We made our rush against the German lines and hunted them out of their trenches, time after time, losing a lot of our men, but giving it to them far worse so that the German dead and dying were lying about in all directions.

I was in the Front-line for five days with my Company and we went on some bombing-raids where we shook up old Fritz, and cleared him out of some saps with considerable losses; yet we only had <u>one</u> man wounded.

There was another Somme offensive on the 25th. September when we went "Over the Parapet" again towards Polygon Wood. We cleared them out and dug in on top of a rise and stayed there two days, and then we made another advance. But this time we got a great reception from their machine-guns, rifles and shells, and many of my mates dropped as we advanced.

The bullets were spitting all around us like drops of rain; and a tornado of shrapnel and high-explosive shells ploughed up the ground at our feet. It was a positive Inferno.

But onwards our boys advanced, down the slope, across a sunken road and up the next slope, where we settled every German we met; and then, at last, we leapt into their trenches. The Germans jumped out and ran for their lives; but most of them fell as our Artillery was firing over our heads and aeroplane. We could see shells bursting all round an aeroplane, which was only a small speck in the distance. But they must be very hard to hit. I have not seen one hit yet.

The other night we were in reserves, in a big barn, and a battery of ours behind us was banging away, sending the shells over. The row woke me up, but I had dozed off again when suddenly a few German shells came over and almost got our barn; in fact, a few pieces of one did hit it, so we had to get out lively.

All the reports we get show that our side is advancing, so things are going well. We get fed well here — better than we did in the desert in Egypt. I got your last letter just before leaving Egypt.

We had a good trip over, though there were plenty of rumours of submarines. We stopped at Malta for a couple of days, but were not close to the pier so no-one could get ashore. It was on a Sunday and we were allowed to go over the side for a swim during the afternoon. It being fairly hot, there was a big crowd of us in the water of Malta harbour.

Marseilles is a big city. We were about an hour-and-a-half coming into its harbour, passing small lighthouses and buoys about a mile from the shore; and yet we were passing the city the whole of the time. But we were not allowed to see any of it for when we got off the ship they marched us from the wharf straight on to the train which left about 10-30 in the evening.

We passed Paris about 12 miles off, and all I could see of that famous city was the Eiffel Tower sticking right up over everything else. It must be very high as we could see it quite plainly

Lance-Corporal Jack Treahy (of St. Arnaud) writes to a friend, Miss Dolly Osborne.

"SOMEWHERE IN FRANCE".

6TH. MARCH. 1917.   RAIDING A TRENCH

I am still attached to the old battalion. You may be surprised to hear that my cousin. Tom Morrow (of the firm of "Nicholson and Morrow) is an officer in my 'B' Company; and one of the first jobs he was given, in the line, was to take charge of half the company in a "Hop Over" which we had a few weeks ago.

But he did it well, and has gained the confidence of all the boys. This "Hop Over" was not done with the idea of holding the captured trench, but merely to occupy it for 10 minutes. The aim was to gain all the information possible about the enemy, to secure prisoners and documents

Although we learn to take all the good things with all the bad over here, still I don't mind telling you my sleep was slightly-troubled for a few nights previous to the job; and more especially so when the date was finally settled upon.

The assault was to come off on the night of mother's birthday (but I'm glad she didn't know about it). My mates, Alf. Western and Rod. McKay, came back from furlough that very morning, and I felt so pleased when our Captain said they would not take part in it.

Well, the time drew near, and we at last got the order to be ready to move up to the front line. Alf. gave me the soldier's farewell; — "Keep your head down and don't let 'em hit yer!"

We started out and eventually reached our Firing-line. At dark we crawled into "No Man's Land" and took up our positions. I was in charge of a bayonet-team. We lay there for some minutes waiting for our barrage to start.

The artillery was going to support us with shrapnel and trench — mortars, which were to play on our objective (the enemy's trench) for a minute and a half. Then like a flash it would lift to the flanks and the rear, which meant that our turn had come to advance.

Well, we had not been lying there many minutes when our guns started, and every man watched for the barrage to lift. Our captain was lying near me while the heavy bombardment illuminated the sky All at once the barrage lifted, and he gave the order, "Charge!" and away we flew across No-Man's Land.

We had a good run over, although a few enemy machine-guns were causing trouble, but It would have done you good to have heard the shout our lads gave as they rushed the trench. All of a sudden. Fritz woke up to our joke and smothered "No-Man's Land" with shrapnel, but we were already in his trench.

Every raider had his own job to do; and everything worked like machinery. When we had finished, the order was passed to retire; and I tell you I never got through barbed-wire so fast in all my life. We returned through a hail of the enemy's shrapnel. A few of the lads were hit coming back, but I got through safely.

Next day the General thanked us personally for the valuable work our raiding party did, and for the information we obtained. So you see, the old 'B' Company has now got a name which we boys are all proud of.

I have not seen Cliff Crone since we came to France, but Alf. saw him on the Somme Front some months ago. We have been here all winter. Give my best wishes to all St Arnaud friends.

FRITZ WOKE UP TO OUR JOKE

"HE DIED AS A TRUE SOLDIER OUGHT TO DIE, FIGHTING FOR HIS KING, HIS HOME, HIS COUNTRY AND HIS HONOR."

20th. March, 1917

Dear Mrs. Newton (of St Arnaud)

I am writing from "Somewhere in France" to tell you about your son, Pte. Eddie J. Newton, (58th. Battalion) who was killed in action a few days ago. First of all, let me express to you my deep sympathy in your great loss. We in your boy's Company grieve his loss, but I know what you, his mother, must be feeling.

First, let me tell you that I was in command of the Company in which your son served. I had appointed him a Company-Runner, and as such he was required to carry despatches. He had offered himself for the position, and I must state that the work of a Runner is not an easy one, and requires brave men; for messages have frequently to be carried under heavy fire when the telephone wires have been cut by shell fire.

About five days before your son was killed, we were in the Firing-line and the Germans were retreating. I had occupied a German trench the first night we took over; and two nights after this, I sent some of my Company forward to occupy another trench, some 700 yards in advance.

The position was captured, but it became necessary for me to send an urgent message to the officer I had placed in charge of this forward position, so I called for a volunteer to carry it. It was then broad daylight, but your son did not hesitate to volunteer, and he started out on his dangerous mission.

He had to travel across 700 yards of open country which was under constant heavy rifle and machine-gun fire. A man who went with your son crawled into a shell-hole and stayed there, but your boy went on. He had to travel the last 200 yards on his stomach, but he reached the trench safely and delivered his message. Afterwards, I recommended him to the C.O. with these words: -

> <u>"Private Newton, a runner of "C" Company, volunteered to carry</u> an important despatch in broad daylight and in full view of the enemy, a distance of 700 yards. He was under heavy machine-gun and rifle-fire all the way, and was obliged to crawl 200 yards, and make his way through barbed-wire. It was a brave and gallant act."

After we came out of the line, your son was thanked in front of his comrades for his work, and the Battalion-Commander read aloud the citation I had written. The next time we went into the line, I left your son in the support trenches as assistant to the Quarter-Master Sergeant. I thought it would give him a spell after his ordeal.

I should explain that in support-trenches one is comparatively safe, compared with the risks in the Front-line. On coming out of the line, I learned to my keen regret that your son had been killed that afternoon. He was at least a mile-and-a-half behind the Front-line, but a stray shell had killed him, as well as another soldier who shared his dugout.

An ambulance was only a few yards from him and he was

carried at once to the doctor, but died a few minutes after being hit. He lies buried in a little cemetery near the spot; and a wooden cross bearing his name and regiment is erected over him. He was a brave and gallant lad and perhaps these few lines of mine will help you a little in your grief.

All the battalion expressed regret for his death as they had all heard of his brave journey with despatches over No-Man's Land. We all were grieved in his "C" Company and thought it seemed such bad luck to be killed when far back from the Front-line. He had been tried and proved what a brave lad he was. Private Nimmo (of St. Arnaud) was a runner at the same time as your son, and he also did excellent work under heavy fire.

Again I offer you my sympathy, and express to you, his mother, my admiration for your brave and gallant soldier boy. Lieut N. G. Pelton." *(The kind Captain Pelton was himself killed in action two months later, on the 12th. of May, during the Second Battle of Bullecourt.)*

HIS LAST LETTER HOME

Private H. J. Perry, of Corack East, wrote the following letter home while fighting on the Western Front.

27TH. MARCH, 1917.

(Private Perry was killed just a few weeks later)

Dear Mother,

Just a few lines to let you know I am well and hoping this finds you all the same at home. It is some time since I last wrote to you owing to Fritz doing a retreat — and paper was a scarce item, too. But now we are on our way out of the trenches to billets behind the lines for a month or two. We have been in and out of the line for two months, so now we need a rest.

Ben Kerr got badly knocked about on the 20th. March when we came across some Huns. Their machine-guns, snipers and artillery gave us a hot time of it for a few hours. Ben got a shell all to himself, and how he did not get blown to bits I don't know — he is lucky to be alive. He got his left foot blown off; a deep, nasty wound behind the right shoulder; and a few cuts to his right leg. He was in great spirits though and as game as you could make him. I got him a drink and a cigarette and threw a blanket over him until the stretcher-bearers and then I helped to put him on the stretcher — which was the last I saw of him.

They told me at the dressing-station that the doctor operated on Ben and he took the loss of his leg like a hero. But Steve is alright — only got his overcoat riddled with bullets. Luck was smiling on me that morning. We were the first company to march into Bapaume and take possession of that town. So you see, Mother, we have been in the thick of the fray. As paper is scarce I will tell you more when I get my writing-pad out of my pack, as we expect to get them shortly when we reach our billets.

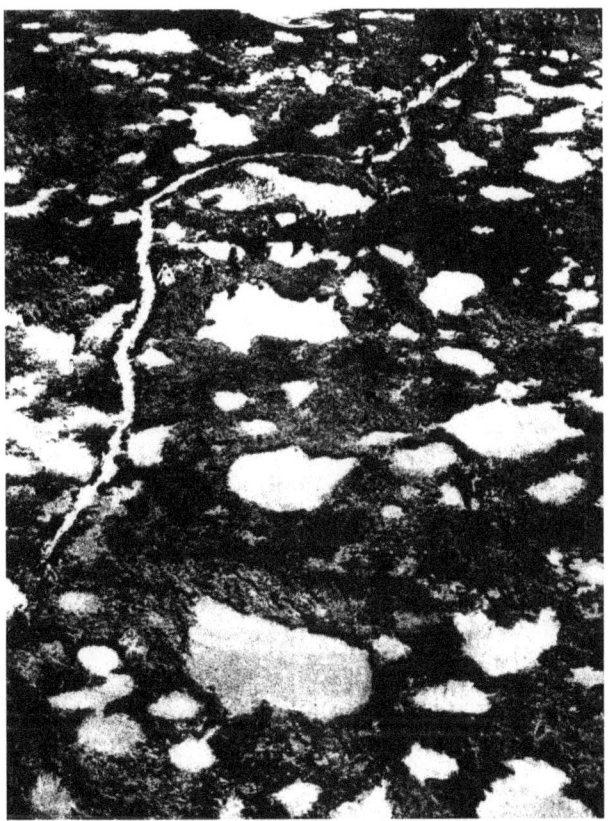

The terrible winter of 1916-7 turned shell-holes into small lakes; and so wooden-boards had to be laid along which the men could walk to their front lines. Yet many men slipped and fell into the deep pits and drowned in the mud, later to be posted as "missing".

Private Andrew Campbell (of Charlton) writes home from a military hospital in Kent, England.

1917.

Dear Mother,

I think I will have to lie in bed for a little while yet. My arm is improving and my hip wound is nearly heeded. The doctor at the first Dressing-Station told me I was a very lucky man, as another eighth of an inch and I would have been either killed or paralysed it was that close to my spine.

There were over a thousand batteries in action on April 9th. when the Canadians advanced and captured Vimy Ridge. One half of the batteries fires for an hour, and then the other half pours the shells over. It is a Hell on earth in France just now, especially for Fritz.

If I have to go back to France I swear that I will never take another prisoner — I'll kill every one, or die. I don't want to go back; yet I'd like to be there again in a big advance for an hour or two.

The Scots are great fighters and I have seen them in action. In the early stages of the war, the Germans put the bayonet in any Scotty lying wounded on the battlefield; and once they crucified a Gordon Highlander sergeant and hung him up in front of their trench.

We saw them going over the top at Armentieres, and it was a grand sight to see the kilts swinging and hear the bagpipes. One would think they were all drunk. But they were not; it was their excitement. Fritz always knows when the Scotties or our fellows are coming. The Germans call them, "The Ladies from Hell".

The night our battalion raided the Germans was a great night indeed. It is a peculiar feeling as you wait in a trench for a certain time to hop out. One hears an officer say, 'Ten minutes to go, boys.'

The next one hears is, "OVER" and a roar of artillery tearing down Fritz's wire entanglements. Our boys got across No-Man's Land at the double and into his trenches under an artillery-barrage. They reached his third line and did good work.

They blew dugouts up and captured machine-guns. Les Bird and I were despatch runners that night. Our casualties were very light. The trenches were so wet our chaps were just covered with mud. Going across No-Man's Land, one is apt to step into a shell-hole and sink up to one's neck. I think my battalion is at Wipers (Ypres) now, and that is a pretty warm corner.

Private Ernie Trollope (of Donald) writes home to his mother from a hospital in England.

KILLED BY THEIR OWN GUNS!

MAY. 1917.

"I am over in Blighty once again, and I am Jolly glad to be here — to be away from the bullets and shells which fly about like rain. I was in the trenches just ten days before I got hit.

On that last night, ten out of thirteen in our platoon were picked out to go and patrol the German Front-line and barbed-wire. We had done that safely, and were returning, and were only 150 yards away from our own trench <u>when our own .machine-guns opened fire on us killing seven out of the ten!</u>

So I was one of the lucky ones, only getting three bullets in the right upper leg, none of which touched the bone. So it wasn't so bad because it has given me five or six months' spell from the trenches.

When I got wounded, I was carried on a stretcher for four

miles, then in a horse ambulance for three miles, and then in a motor ambulance to the dressing-station about ten miles from the firing-line, where they put me straight under an operation and removed the pieces of bullets. I will send them home to you in a little box.

Two days later I was put in an ambulance train and taken to Boulogne. There are a terrible lot of Australians getting killed and wounded here now. One day there were twelve trainloads of wounded came here, besides trainloads going to other hospitals.

After stopping in France for a fortnight. I was sent to the English hospital where I am now. We were treated lovely all the time, but you can see I have had some shifting about. Reg Page is here in Blighty and I have written him to come and see me.

I haven't heard how Willie Humphrey got on, but I know his battalion was all cut up and nearly all were killed and wounded as the Germans surrounded them. But the Australians did some very good work this month at Bullecourt and they have made a name again all over the world."

18th. November. 1916. "This is a photo of our boat that carried us safety to Old England, and evaded all King Billy's tin-fishes — although there were supposed to be seven of them in the English Channel, waiting for us as we came through. I'm having a good time in England at present. Best wishes to all, from LES."

A ruined French village

"TROOPSHIP BALLARAT SUNK BY SUBMARINE."

1917

The story of the "BALLARAT" is one of the most stirring tales of fortitude which could be told — even of the Australians.

The vessel carried 1,400 troops who were practically all reinforcements from Victoria (from the 2nd. and 4th. Australian

Brigades). Throughout the voyage, the Colonel, who was in command of the troops, put them frequently through boat-station drill until they had reduced the time required for assembling at their proper stations to a mere four minutes.

On this particular day — the 25th. of April — the men had arranged an extensive programme for the celebration of Anzac Day, starting with a Memorial Service for their fallen comrades at 2-30 p.m.

At five minutes past two the men were beginning to muster upon deck, in full uniform, when a torpedo was seen moving towards the ship on her port side. The look-out by the gun in the stern telephoned to the bridge and the great vessel swung round quickly.

Another two seconds, and she would have escaped the missile but a dull thud, and then a rending sound of metal, told the men that the torpedo had struck home. Rapidly the ship began to sink down at the stem.

It was soon discovered that the torpedo had torn off one propeller, leaving a gaping hole; while the smashing of the deck had left the gunners helpless to retaliate. No-one saw the submarine; but a few of the soldiers said they saw a periscope about 500 yards away, though nothing was seen of it from the bridge.

Meanwhile the bugle had called the men to their boat stations. With exemplary coolness, every man was in his place inside four minutes and everything was ready for abandoning ship. The soldiers sang a little, but the parade was chiefly notable for their absolute calmness and cheeriness. The sea showed a slight swell, but otherwise all was bright.

The men knew the vessel was adequately supplied with boats

and floats, and all of them wore lifebelts; they had in fact been wearing them continuously for some time under orders.

But the ship seemed to be sinking fast and the officers were anxious. However, the Colonel stood on the bridge, quite undismayed. Several times he called down to his men, "We're all right, boys. Keep steady"; and the men replied, "It's all right, sir. We're all right."

After hearing the engineer's report, the Captain gave the order to abandon ship. Nine boats were lowered in perfect order; and while the men were embarking in the boats they continued to show the most cheerful spirits. One of the officers told his company, "You may smoke on this parade, boys."

Many of them lit cigarettes. Others carried their battalion pets — a squirrel, several dogs, puppies and parrots. When the soldiers were embarking in the boats, they sang, "<u>Australia will be there</u>."

A few minutes later, the engineer reported that the ship was able to go ahead with the remaining damaged propeller; so all the lifeboats were recalled and the men were soon back on deck again. When the Colonel called for volunteers to do Stokehold-Duty, hundreds responded — including the whole of a railway unit.

Forty volunteers were selected; but they were unable, after all, to go below, for the water was rising rapidly and the ship was sinking steadily. The engine-room was soon flooded and accordingly the troops returned to their stations. Three destroyers and two trawlers had come at top speed to the scene, and it was arranged that they should take the men aboard. All the troops and some of the crew were transhipped by 4 o'clock.

Eighty out of every hundred of the soldiers were without their kit. Many of them were coatless and hatless, some were without shoes, and the hospital cases were in pyjamas. During the whole of this time, the only nurses aboard, Sister Tatlow (Victoria) and Sister Lord (Tasmania), had shown conspicuous courage, going from Company to Company and helping the men to fasten their lifebelts. The three Chaplains also gave aid in this way.

Hundreds of the men were allowed to take photographs of the sinking ship and of the final parade; but the officers would not allow them to break ranks in order to go below for their belongings.

The troops were soon taken aboard the rescue ships and <u>all were saved</u>. They landed late at night and were received with the utmost hospitality in British camps and barracks. When the Colonel addressed the men on shore, he had tears in his eyes as he said that Australia would be proud of their soldierly bearing, for it was without blemish.

Among the men present were three who were on the "SOUTHLAND" in 1915 when she was torpedoed, and fifteen veterans of the Landing at Gallipoli."

(From the "London Times" 3rd. April, 1917.)

****

Private Bert. Dewberry (of St. Arnaud) gives his version of the sinking.

<u>SALISBURY PLAIN. MAY. 1917.</u>

"We were on the water nine weeks and three days, and then got torpedoed at the finish. We all kept cool and steady, so we got off safe and no accidents.

I thought at first that the ship could be saved, although the transport started sinking fast until she got her bearings. We could see the destroyers, still miles away, rushing to our assistance when they received the S.O.S. wireless message.

Nobody had noticed the enemy submarine; but the torpedo was seen coming at us from about 500 yards away.

Out Captain quickly steered the boat around sharp, or we would have been struck amidship. We were taken aboard one of the destroyers, and she steamed for Devonport (Plymouth) at top speed, carrying her precious cargo of Australian soldiers.

I was on sentry- duty when the torpedo struck, and I remained on duly three-quarters-of-an-hour after the transport was struck. I should think we waited aboard about an hour-and-a-half to get off.

The boat was hit at the back, the propeller shafting was broken, and the stokehold was flooded; and she sank a few hours afterwards.

We were given a good time at Devonport on landing, and went to the Military Barracks where we were treated well. Next morning we marched two miles to the Royal Naval Barracks with the Royal Marine Band leading us through the town. Our reception was great.

We were dressed just as we were when we left the "BALLARAT" and so we looked a real ragtime army. There were quite a number of men without boots or hats. But I was lucky being on guard-duty when it happened, as I had my best rig-out on.

The ride we had on the destroyer was the best I have ever had on a boat. Sadly, the transport "BALLARAT" sank a few hours after we left her.

On arrival at Exeter from Devonport, we were entertained at

the County Hall and each soldier was presented with a card of welcome from the Mayoress of Exeter and her committee. The card bore the words, "Wishing you Good Luck."

We then entrained for this camp at Salisbury Plain. It is a fine camp here. We have log huts with stoves in, plenty of blankets, all kinds of amusements and moving-pictures. It is a great place and everybody seems to be working for the benefit of this country — our dear old England!"

TRANSPORT S.S. BALLARAT (built 1911)

(PHOTO: SERGEANT ALEXANOER WALDER)

ARRIVAL AT A BRITISH CAMP

"From Salisbury we caught a train for the last few miles of our journey from Australia. We were then turned out into the snow at our destination at 9 o'clock at night. Cold, but dry and cheerful, we learned to our delight that there were waggons to carry our kitbags.

So, carrying only our two blankets, we set out in a long, loose column for the camp, four miles away. It was a merry walk, not without its touch of mystery, almost magic. The still countryside echoed with our songs and whistling; and greetings were exchanged with women and girls whose faces peered out at us from dimly-lit windows of little cottages along our way.

As we marched through one dark village, the column of men had the idea to bark like dogs. We had imitations of every dog, from poodles to mastiffs — displaying that genius for observation and imitation which is so marked in most young Australians.

Then our guide with his swinging lantern turned off the metal road across a rough muddy plain, which even in the dark appeared a harsh and unattractive place. Dim lights reached to the horizon before us, and we knew we were on the threshold of one of those great camps which make up the vast training ground of British troops on SALISBURY PLAIN.

A brisk Sergeant-Major then takes charge of us and we are numbered off — 22 to each hut. Our blankets are increased to six and we get orders to be out at 6-30 in the morning. We sleep on straw bags raised on platforms a few inches from the floor. Those of us who doubt the warmth of our heavy load of blankets, turn in, still dressed in our underclothes and socks; and also add on our greatcoats."

(**written by Gunner H. S. Gullett**)

BULLECOURT — APRIL/MAY, 1917.

On April 11th. the 4th. Australian Division captured a part of the Hindenburg Line. After an heroic fight, lack of reinforcements and ammunition forced them to evacuate.

The "Heads" decided that more preparation and practice was necessary before another attack should be made on the enemy's line.

Thus, the "Second Battle of Bullecourt" began on May 3rd. An eyewitness describes the battle-field————

"Imagine two perfectly-made enemy trenches on the slope of a long rise, protected with four or five belts of barbed wire — 30 yards in depth, and breast high — and sighted so that German machine-gunners could fire accurately along the top of this wire. To reach the first trench meant an advance of nearly 1000 yards over ground which afforded no shelter to our advancing troops."

Brave Diggers flung themselves against this Hindenburg Line with its well-fortified trenches that the Germans boasted were IMPREGNABLE. All along the line, were double machine-gun emplacements protected by concrete; and in the chalky ground, at a depth of 40 feet, the Germans had dug a continuous tunnel that provided them with full protection and comfort. With amazing stubbornness our Diggers fought, and never retreated, in spite of their terrible losses.

SERGEANT ARTHUR CLIFFORD'S WAR CONTINUES INTO 1917 – UNTIL HE IS WOUNDED AT BULLECOURT

PATROL DUTY   14th. March.

About mid-day Mr. Smythe came along and sent me out on patrol with four men. We had to go through a sunken road, over a hill, to a trench on the other side to see what was in it. We got to the road and found it was only sunken on the sides and very little at that. It petered out to nothing on top. I could not take the men along it. It meant certain death. So I crawled over on my belly through the slush, got on top of trench and could see it was occupied on the left as the Huns were walking about. Their snipers were very busy, but we had the luck to get back. Reported to O.C. about it, so arrangements were made to work in from the other end.

****

SALVAGING ABANDONED GEAR AND AMMUNITION__23rd. March.

We are here at Eaucourt-L'Abbaye, near Le Sars, to salvage a lot of the ammunition and equipment that is left lying about. We started on it today. We are collecting a jolly lot of stuff: — rifles, shovels, picks, shell, shell-cases, bombs, machine-guns and equipment of all descriptions. We were told, some days later, that the value of the lot our battalion salvaged amounted to 16,000 pounds. There is a keen competition between battalions to see who can salvage the most material. We are also carrying bricks from the ruined houses in Le Sars to mend the roads.

****

MEDALS   1st. April.

Today at Church Parade, General Birdwood inspected us — we had the usual lot of trouble in cleaning and getting ready for it. He presented a lot of Military Medals — Military Cross etc. and also pulled our legs as usual. While the service was on, several large planes came low down over the Parade and circled around for some minutes. Even the "Heads" laughed at one chap who was leaning right out of his plane and waving at us for all he was worth. We fully expected him to fall out at any moment.

EASTER SUNDAY PILGRIMAGE   8th. April.

Bob Davidson and I went up to Pozieres and Mouquet Farm where we fought 8 months ago. We had a look up Sausage Gully and found the actual holes several of us dug to sleep in. There are plenty of both our Dead and Germans still unburied. I tried to find the place where we buried Jim Bickley, but could not find the spot on account of the trench being knocked about so much. Evidently, the little wooden cross we put over him had been knocked down. At Mouquet Farm the trench we were in was completely obliterated, but could be followed by the rifles sticking out of the ground, and the equipment, and the Dead lying about there. The Farm itself must have been a regular fortress, for the Germans had made underground trenches and dugouts through it. Round both these places are now big camps, dumps and railway lines.

****

PRACTICES   10th. April.

While here at Becourt Camp we have been practising new formations, drilling and a few night stunts. Have had plenty of snow and rain. Today the snow was about a foot thick and the chaps had some great snow-balling practice.

****

PROMOTION   12th. April.

I was promoted to Sergeant today and have No. 1 Platoon.

****

CALL TO WAR   14th. April

Today we had some drill and artillery formation. In the afternoon we shifted our tents over to another spot and fixed them up nice and comfortable and in proper lines, and were just having tea when the order came along to get into fighting order straight away. I had to issue each man with rations for 48-hours. We arrived at a sunken road near Noreuil somewhere about midnight. Everything was wet and muddy, but we found an old blanket or two, and waterproof sheets, and fixed up a bit of covering to sleep under.

LAGNICOURT   15th. April

During the night, a flood of Huns came over and broke through our First Division men in Lagnicourt valley. They advanced right up to our 18-pounder guns in a great offensive — wave after wave of them. Fritz was advancing fast until the 5th. Brigade got on to them and chopped them about, taking a good many prisoners. They reckon about 2,000 Huns were killed or wounded. A lot of our chaps were also knocked and taken. It rained nearly all day, and we were on fatigue-duty tonight, carrying bombs to the Front-line; but it's only about a mile.

****

ADVANCING   16th. April.

We went up to the Front-line tonight and took over. It's a home compared to some we have had. During the day, the Huns shelled the road where we were camped and slaughtered a lot of our lads. Sgt. Tom Francis was badly-wounded; Sid Elliot's leg badly-shattered (since amputated); Charles Matthew's leg was blown off; and Rutherford badly-knocked (since died); and a lot more whose names I will write later. I met cousin Cliff Whitfield, whose dugout was only 30 yards down from mine. I'm taking Tom Francis' place, so I now have No. 3 Platoon — the best in the Company.

****

AUSTRALIAN FRONT — LINE   17th. April.

Our piece of the Front-line is a railway embankment and we have some decent dugouts in it; although not shell-proof. Several of them got smashed in today. Two of our chaps were buried, but we soon dug them out before they could suffocate. Jack Burton got a piece of shrapnel through his wrist this morning, but I bandaged it up with a shell-dressing. Our gallant scouts, Harry Pollard and Bill Fitzpatrick, and some engineers, have been taking gelignite-tubes over and putting them under Fritz's wire and blowing it up ready for our attack later. One of the engineers was badly-wounded when a tube blew up in his hand, and they could not get him back.

RESTING   19th. April.

We got relieved and came out alright, though it was a jolly muddy track on the way to Noreuil. There was a lot of traffic, so we came across country some of the way. We reached our camp at Favreuil during the small hours of the morning. We had to sleep in a big Marquee which had about 3 inches of mud on the floor.

****

PRACTISING   21st. April.

We do a little drill, but spend most of the time practising for the big "Hop-Over". We are getting well-fed and paid. Also, we can buy food at a few canteens in this area.

****

STILL PRACTISING   24th. April.

We put in about 6 hours a day practising for the great Hurdle-Race". Sometimes we have to go out at night. We get up at 1 A.M. and march out to where they have the stunt marked out and we go through the whole performance. They use torches to imitate the barrage. There are to be 7 waves of men, and 17 barrages laid down; with a 3-minute barrage on Fritz's barbed-wire to break it up; a 16-minute barrage on the first enemy trench to demoralise the Huns; and so on! Our Company is to take the first line of trenches.

****

SECOND BULLECOURT   2nd. May.

Fell in at 5 p.m. for inspection before moving off to the Front. We knew the Germans were comfortable in their deep, well-made trenches and protected dugouts, behind a thick maze of barbed-wire; whilst we had nothing but a piece of shattered railway-embankment. Mr. Smythe was in charge of our "A" Company. We marched out of camp with our band playing "Australia Will Be There". About midnight we crept into No-Man's Land and lay in the cold shell-holes; but we had to wait there for over three hours.

****

WOUNDED — THE END FOR SERGEANT ARTHUR CLIFFORD

3RD. MAY.

We hopped over at 3-45 this morning, on the right of BULLECOURT. Our "A" Company was in the first wave to
(*The German "potato-masher" had a convenient handle which gave it a longer throwing range than the Mills grenade our men used.*)
take the first objective — Fritz's Front-line. We got it alright, and the other waves went on and took his second line of trenches. They advanced further, but had to come back as the 5th. Brigade on our left got into difficulties and could not keep up with us. Our rush into the German trench was so sudden that we had little resistance in the hand-to-hand fighting. Soon after jumping into the German trench I got wounded in the left leg and arm by a "potato masher" bomb. I lay there for a couple of hours while the lads were consolidating their position in the trench.

Then I made my way out through the many casualties. But as I crossed No-Man's Land, I got a bullet through my arm, just below the elbow; for the enemy turned his machine-guns on our stretcher-bearers as they carried out the wounded. Before I left for the Dressing-Station, Bill Scales told me that our gallant scouts, Harry Pollard and Bill Fitzpatrick, were killed when we first reached the trench.

****

During the following months, Sergeant Clifford lay in an English hospital, suffering much pain from his wounds. In fact, at the beginning of June, he writes in his diary: -

"My arm is giving me rather a rotten time. It doesn't improve much. There's a bit of bomb pressing on a nerve. The doctor says my arm will have to come off. Don't care if it does!"

However, thanks to the skilful nursing of the hospital staff, Sergeant Clifford's arm improved and he returned to Australia in one piece. He was one of 10 children born to Henry and Alice Clifford, and now he returned home to work again on the family farm in the wheat-belt of North-Western Victoria. He married in 1926 and had two daughters. Arthur Clifford died at the age of 94, and must surely be numbered among the final few of Australia's World War 1 veterans. His daughter, Joan Smith, lovingly preserved his diaries.

WOUNDED AT BULLECOURT

Private Aldag (24th. Battalion) was wounded in the great advance on the 3rd. May, 1917 – now known as "The Second Battle of Bullecourt". He describes what happened to him in this letter to Mr. J. Landrigan.

KITCHENER WARD, MILITARY HOSPITAL,
LONDON. MAY 17TH. 1917.

"I suppose you noted the address, and probably may have noticed my name in the casualty lists. The bullet with my number on it, came along on the 3rd. of this month.

A big offensive on the Hindenburg Line had been taking place for some time. On the 3rd. of May we were lined up in many waves, out in the open, in the early morning; but before our barrage from the Artillery opened up, we were seen by the enemy through the light of their flares. All of a sudden, they turned their Artillery and Machine-Gun fire full upon us.

As soon as our own Artillery started their barrage, we advanced. I had charge of the Rifle-Grenadier Section (8 men) of our platoon. Coming to the enemy's barbed-wire entanglements, we pierced them and then charged the Hindenburg Line, which we took. Thus, the 6th. Brigade was successful in its objective.

Going further, we took two more rows of trenches and were well on to a sunken road when we learnt that the two other Brigades were not so successful, and had not advanced. The 5th.

Brigade's attack failed because of some confusion, due perhaps to the loss of their officers. We could see their men being cut-up badly by German machine-guns. For the same reason the 7th. Brigade also withdrew, leaving us in a rotten position.

So the order was given for us to retire to the last trench taken. (I learned later that the men of the 6th. Brigade refused to retire and held on throughout the night, alone, in the Hindenburg Line, facing the enemy in front and on both sides of them.)

I was one of those furthest advanced, and had scarcely turned when a sniper got me. The bullet entered my left thigh, and penetrating the right leg came out through the right thigh. Of course, I dropped like a log, and I had to lie quite still, as I could see a sniper not far off.

About an hour later, a big shell landed three feet away from me, the explosion raising the earth up under me, and the remainder going up in the air now showered down upon me. Of course, it hurt a bit, but did not cut me.

That night I rolled into a shell-hole and slept for the night, despite the fact that the Germans were all around me. I stayed there next day, hoping to crawl through the enemy's line; but the moon was too bright.

I had to hang on, so I crawled back about 70 yards to a dead comrade to get his water-bottle, my water having given out. The thirst when wounded is intense.

Returning, my home was nowhere to be found, having been blown sky high with my blanket, rifle and equipment, and, worst of all, my rations — including my bread which I had been saving in case I did not get any food for some time. My luck was what you might call rotten.

The night was very cold, and only having a waterproof sheet I was simply perished. The chief thing I was longing for was a long drink of water; but all I could allow myself was a sip at a time.

On the fifth day in No-Man's Land I said to myself that I must take my chance of crawling through the enemy's line, for I was beginning to be afraid of septic setting in. My luck changed, for the night turned out cloudy, which I had prayed for.

About 9 p.m. I started off, bandaging my knees and hands with sand-bags to protect them from the rough, shell-torn ground. Not knowing how far my 6th. Brigade had retired, I did not know whether I was approaching Fritz's trench or not.

After crawling about 50 yards I came to the first trench which I managed to get through unnoticed. Then I was still in No-Man's Land, caught between two fires, our own and Fritz's. After going 70 yards I felt done in and stretched out for a spell; but at once pulled myself together, saying, "This is no place for a rest!"

Proceeding, I had only gone about 50 yards when I found myself on top of a parapet looking down on two bayonets, but no one was in sight. Suddenly Fritz sent up a flare and I could see shadowy figures in the trench.

Being afraid they would shoot, thinking me a German, I called out the countersign as I dropped over the parapet. But a fellow came at me with his bayonet. I said, "For Heaven's sake, man, speak, who are you?" He then spoke to me, and you can imagine how my heart beat with joy to find that I was safe amongst the Australian boys.

I collapsed — utterly exhausted from the exertion, loss of blood, and want of food. The Company-Commander, hearing that someone had crawled in after being out in No-Man's Land for five days, ordered that I should be brought down to his dugout — an old German one, about 30 feet deep.

The captain said, "You have been out for five days, I believe?" I replied, "Yes, sir." At the same time, I recognised him as being one of my old Geelong pals whom I had not seen for two years. I took his hand with both mine and nearly shook it off. He gave me both food and drink, and I soon felt wonderfully-refreshed.

After a rest I gave him some valuable information. I was then sent to the dressing-station, about two miles back; and fritz (small 'f' for the cows) those brutes shelled my stretcher-bearers all the way.

Having a clean bandage put on, I was then sent to the clearing-station and was operated upon the following day. I was then sent to the stationary-hospital, where I spent a pleasant birthday on the 13th. May.

Remember that number (13). I think I told you how many times that particular number comes my way and follows me.

I left England for France on the 13th., returned on the 13th., went into the trenches on the 13th., and the number of my bed here is 13. What a strange coincidence!

The trip across the pond was lovely; and on arrival we were put in a hospital train which was fitted up with decent beds. On reaching London we were sent to this place and I am in the ward which is named after Lord Kitchener.

There are only 21 beds, so one gets any amount of attention and the nurses are great. Nothing is too much trouble for them. The sister is a lover of flowers and so the place is adorned with many pot plants of the flowering variety. The meals are always great, of which we get five per day.

Many outside trips are arranged for the patients and I hope my turn will soon come. The tubes have been taken out of me, and the wounds are wonderfully clean.

Private Fred Baddock (of Charlton)
tells his sister about a big battle.

WOUNDED AT BULLECOURT — ON 3RD. MAY, 1917.

"I was shot through the shoulder at Bullecourt about a month ago. I will try and describe this stunt to you; and I might mention before starting that Fritz knew as much about its coming off as we did. In fact, he had amassed his men and guns especially for the occasion to fight against us.

We (the 5th. and 6th. Brigades) had been feeding up and resting for weeks — we had been doing nothing else much but practising, as no attack by the 2nd. Division had ever before been practised. On two occasions we got up at 12 (midnight) to see how it would go at the real time.

All the boys were in good fettle; and the day before the occasion we were doing the high-jump, hop-step-and-jump, and many different sports.

Half-past four on the day before the stunt, we filed out with our bombs and rifles and were lined up, and a march of 7 miles brought us to the Front-line. It was then 12-30 p.m. and the stunt was not to be until 4-5 a.m. but that time was easily filled up with the troops being supplied with bombs and ammunition, picks, shovels and sandbags; and after we got our loads most of us slept.

I know that I, for one, was fast asleep until awakened by the cry of "GAS" as the Boches had sent some gas-shells over. However, it did not last long and at 8-15 p.m. we started off for the

"Hop-Over Trench". As we moved along, a few shells accounted for about 8 men; but we are that used to it that someone says "Poor Beggars" and then for the time they are forgotten.

As we were approaching the assembly-point, old Boche sighted us and pelted iron foundries very numerously. (I must tell you that on our section alone, which was 400 yards wide, there were 18,000 men went over.) A few got wounded now that old Fritz started shelling us in proper earnest.

With a lot of stops and starts (as every time a flare was fired it lit up the area and we all had to get down on the ground, and I can tell you there were thousands of flares fired that morning) eventually we got to the trench all ready for a go!

We had to wait about a minute for our own barrage to start, and during that time old Boche poured shells and machine-gun bullets into us. (I can tell you that a machine-gun fires from one hundred rounds a minute.) All of a sudden a searchlight played on us from behind the enemy lines, but we forgot all about it as just then our own barrage opened up and the sky was blood-red with the bursting of shells and shrapnel.

In a little while we were hardly able to see the flares on account of the dust and smoke made by bursting shells from both sides, and now the enemy was pouring it in nearly as fast as we were.

As soon as our barrage stopped we pushed forward, and I can safely say that there was not a man who had any fear; as you sort of go mad with the one object in view — to get at them!

As we went along, the firing grew more intense and above the noise of bursting shells you could plainly hear the barking from hundreds of machine-guns. A machine-gun played on us, and to see the men around me getting cut down was a terrible, terrible sight.

I don't mind dead men, but to hear the cries of the wounded was enough to put the wind up any one. At about 4-15 a.m. we neared the Frontline of the Boches and were here met by very strong outposts. It seemed marvellous that any men could be left alive in such a Hell of Fire; but here the Germans were still playing their machine-guns upon our brave boys.

Then, some very accurate bombing was done by our boys who soon took command of the enemy's first trench. I forgot to tell you that we had to cross over two chains of barbed-wire entanglements which protect Fritz's trenches, but our guns had made such a mess of it that we hardly knew it had been there.

After the enemy's first trench had been taken and, leaving one company behind to man it, we pushed on and had to cross another lot of barbed-wire which was as big as the first; and it was here that I saw some blood-curdling sights of men caught up in the entanglements.

I might tell you that two of our boys caught on fire through flares falling on them, and it was very laughable seeing their antics as they tried to put themselves out.

By this time we were nearly deaf from the bursting of shells, and our throats were burning-hot from the gases. We reached the enemy's second line of trenches, but Fritz had done a bunk so there was no fighting.

I cannot tell you any more of the battle, as it ws here that I got knocked flying into a shell-hole, being hit in the left shoulder. I came to my senses, pulled off my equipment, and got like blazes out of there.

There was still another line of trenches to take before my

battalion had finished its bit; and then there were two other battalions behind us — so you can see it was <u>some</u> stunt. It was on a front of 15 miles and we call it "The Grand Battle of Bullecourt" — <u>where Hindenburg's cement trenches were taken und held by the Australians.</u>

Well, you can imagine what it was like. I never hope to see such another. I lost a terrible lot of pals, and I reckon it was an Unseen Power that brought me safely out of it, as I had to pass through as much shell-fire going out as I did when coming in.

The stunt lasted till 10 a.m. but after that, when Fritz counter-attacked, a bombing-stunt lasted for a whole day. Our lads were driven back, but bombed again and again and finally held the line.

I must tell you about wild McDonald. If we had a battalion of men like him there would be no stopping them. He was the first man in the German trench, so he grabbed a machine-gun and drove the Huns out of a sunken road, and then he climbed up onto the bank to give them a parting present. He had just pulled the pin out when he was shot through the wrist. The smoking bomb fell down the bank and he slid down after it. He picked it up and threw it away, thus saving the lives of 10 men who stood nearby. I reckon he was very cool, as these bombs only last 5 seconds before exploding."

STALEMATE IN THE WAR

In 1917 the war was a stalemate. The British front-line stretched all the way from the English Channel almost up to the Swiss Alps.

Miners were digging a tunnel beneath enemy lines — it was just a start, but it would be a break-through for the Allies.

How brave those miners must have been and how clever and careful — for they dared not make any noises that might be heard by the Germans who were listening in nearby tunnels. If their secret was discovered, all their digging would be in vain.

However, when the long tunnels were completed those miners placed explosives in the walls at intervals ready for the great day. The mines were successfully exploded in the early morning of June 7th. and they blew vast craters all along the German front-line, utterly demoralizing the enemy. In Britain the explosions could be heard in Dover and Dublin.

The following letters written home by Australians of the 3rd. Division tell us what happened and what effect those 19 mines had upon the enemy. They completely destroyed Hill 60 which disappeared from view.

19 mines exploded at 3 a.m. on 7th. grmc, 1917. Underneath the german front line.

Amid the human carnage of the Great War, one is often forgetful of the loss of horses. Most people have no idea that eight million horses were killed during that time in various areas of the war.

MESSINES – JUNE, 1917.

The "Battle of Messines" commenced with the explosion of 19 great mines. It is said that this great noise was heard — like heavy claps of thunder — in Southern England.

It was the 3rd. Australian Division that began the Messines attack. This division had been carefully trained on Salisbury Plain for six months (and paraded before the king) before entering the Western Front. Now it was ready to show the older divisions what it could do.

The 1st. 2nd. and 4th. Divisions had been through the horrors of Pozieres and the miseries of the severe winter at Flers, so they were rather sceptical of this inexperienced 3rd. Division which had lately arrived in France.

But the "Battle of Messines" proved beyond a doubt that these men of the 3rd. Division were from the same stock — and possessed the same tenacity — as the Anzacs of Gallipoli and the Diggers of Pozieres.

The severity of the fighting at Messines is reflected in the number of casualties. The 3rd. Australian Division lost 4,122, and the 4th. Australian Division lost 2,676. (*figures quoted from C.E.W. Bean*)

THE 3RD. AUSTRALIAN DIVISION IN ATTACK

WITH THE 3RD. AUSTRALIAN DIVISION

Lieutenant J. B. O'Donnell (38th. Battalion) wrote this very detailed letter to his former employer. His C.O. said of Lt. O'Donnell. "He stands in a class of his own as a machine-gun officer".

THE KITCHENER HOSPITAL, BRIGHTON,
ENGLAND. 23RD. JUNE, 1917,

MESSINES

"You will no doubt have heard ere this reaches you that I have been wounded. I got my left leg shattered with shrapnel while taking part in the big attack at Messines, on the 7th. June, 1917; so I am at present located in the above hospital.

Well, to start from the beginning. We landed in England on August 10th. (1916) and were promptly entrained for Lark Hill Camp, on Salisbury Plain; and, after receiving four days' leave which I spent in London, we started on a very severe course of training, mostly specialist work.

This training lasted till early in November, when we received word that we were to go to France, so the whole Third Division was sent on four days' leave, which I can tell you was very well-spent. A brother officer and I went up to Scotland for two days, which we enjoyed very much, and then spent the other two days in London.

When we arrived back at camp we worked day and night getting the men's papers ready for the Front; and in November we left for France, the trip across taking us several hours. We went into a rest camp for 24 hours and then entrained for an unknown destination — "Somewhere in France" — where we landed 36 hours later.

The train journey was very slow and monotonous as France is a very dull-looking spot in winter-time. We eventually detrained at 3 a.m. and marched 3 miles to our billets; and we then knew we were within sight of the Firing-line for we could hear the continuous boom of the heavy guns and could see the constant glare of the star-shells, which appeared on the distant horizon like a huge fireworks display.

That evening we were informed by our C.O. that we were to take over a part of the Front-line which was being held by the New Zealanders — which we did! We had a fair number of casualties that first time we were in the line; mostly wounded and not a great number killed. There were hardly any trenches there at all as a matter of fact; it was only shell-holes which we were holding.

Being low-lying country and on the banks of the river, it was very boggy and we had to wear boots which came up over the thighs, to keep the water out. We were on the Somme, near Armentieres, and the muddy trenches were just ditches in the slime, invisible except from a few yards away. The whole area was completely waterlogged.

During the winter there was not much doing, although the Artillery were continually straffing and, of course, the poor Infantry were getting it and could not retaliate (except when we sent raiders over).

A number of raids were carried out at different times by our Third Division. A raid consists of any number of officers, N.C.O's and men made up into different parties, each party with a specific duty to perform in the attack.

Raids are nearly always carried out under the cover of darkness, or a smoke barrage, and are preceded by a heavy Artillery bombardment to destroy the enemy's defences.

The largest raid we carried out (<u>and the largest ever carried out on that part of the Front</u>) was undertaken by my 38th. Battalion and the 37th. (a sister battalion). This raid was afterwards known in our Third Division as "<u>THE BIG RAID</u>".

We had a complement of 804 men made up of all ranks. I had 16 machine-guns and teams in it.

<u>Zero hour was 12-30 a.m. on the night of the 27th. February, 1917.</u> A preliminary bombardment took place, three hours before, at 9-40 p.m., to which the German guns replied. When this firing eventually died down, the Germans probably thought the danger was past.

But at 12-30 a.m. our barrage fell again on the German line, and by the light of flares 800 of us advanced at a run across No-Man's Land on a front of half-a-mile.

The raid was very successful and we captured a number of machine-guns, trench-mortars, searchlights and rifles. We penetrated about 200 yards, into the Hun's second and third line of trenches, blowing up all his dug-outs and gun-emplacements. We only captured 17 Germans, as the boys were not out for prisoners. We estimated they killed 250 Boches.

The raid was only a couple of hours' work, but it was very hot work while it lasted, and the poor old Huns got a bad time of it for we took them by surprise.

At 1-10 a.m. the withdrawal began; so you see, we had occupied this line of German trenches for 35 minutes. Our casualties were very light, considering the extent of the operation, and we only lost about 130 men.

Nearly every man in the raid returned carrying a number of souvenirs, which consisted of packs, pistols, German-money, caps, helmets, buttons etc. They said this raid was the most important ever undertaken by the Australians.

The remainder of that 1916 — 17 winter was spent in trench work, which is very monotonous as you always have to be on the alert in case you are attacked by German Raiding Parties.

About the beginning of May it became evident that there was to be a big assault made on a Front, stretching from the River Lys to Ypres Salient, and our Third Division was to take part in it.

At that time the Huns held most of the commanding positions on this Front, which included Messines Hill township, the River Douve, and a number of well-known strong-points. **The day chosen for the Messines offensive was the 7th. June, and the attack was timed for 3-10 a.m.**

We were all up in "No-Man's Land" at our assembly positions by 3 a.m. and waiting for the 19 great mines to explode. And true to the minute they did go off, and as they exploded our Artillery opened up. It was a wonderful sight.

Those mines blew vast craters all along the German Front-Line Garrison. About 300 yards from where we lay, I saw a crater as much as 70 feet deep and 300 feet in width.

Our barrage was on the Huns' Front-line for about three minutes and then it lifted to the Huns' support trenches; and the Infantrymen kept following it up as close as we could with safety.

It was just dawning day at the time, and we could see a

number of Huns trying to get away. The shock of the 19 mines and our heavy barrage completely demoralised them; but those that our boys did not shoot or bayonet got caught in our barrage, so practically none of them escaped.

Nearly every dugout that we captured had a number of Huns inside it, and they came out cringing like beaten animals. They came running out and tried to embrace us, singing out, "KAMERAD".

But they did not get much mercy, I can tell you, and there were dead and wounded everywhere, for Fritz was holding his trenches pretty heavily as he expected our attack and was well-prepared for it.

But our Artillery and Infantry were too good for him and the 19 mines fairly shook him to pieces. It was a wonderful thing to be in and I would not have missed it for anything.

I lasted in the fight until 4 p.m. that day when I was hit just as our 10th. Brigade had taken its final objective.

The Messines Attack was considered to be the most successful ever carried out on the British Front. The Artillery was something terrific on both sides. The casualties were heavy, of course, which is natural in a big attack, but they were nothing compared to the positions we have won.

After I was hit, I was carried on a stretcher to the advanced dressing-station; from there to the casualty clearing-station ; and then by hospital-train to the 3rd. General Hospital, Trefort, France (where I landed 17 hours after I was hit).

It is truly wonderful work, the way the wounded are evacuated in a great battle like this. The organisation of the B.A.M.C. (British Army Medical Corps) and A.A.M.C. (Australian Army Medical Corps) is almost perfect now.

I was operated on in the Trefort Hospital and had some shrapnel taken out of my leg and I was eventually sent along to this Brighton Hospital — where I expect to stay for a couple of months before being convalescent. My leg-bone is shattered in a couple of places and will take a long time to heal up.

This is a fine hospital overlooking the beach, and is run by the Canadians (both doctors and sisters) and they look after you well. Although wounded I can appreciate a rest like this, after having 8 months' solid fighting without a single day's leave.

A number of the boys from up Birchip way were in my 10th. Brigade (Victorian). C. H. Proctor, from Woomelang, died of wounds at the Battle of Messines. Jim Lawler, one of my machine-gunners, was killed a few nights before the attack and I helped to carry him to the dressing-station — his brother, Frank Lawler, was wounded only a few months ago.

Arthur Dillon, from Birchip, is now Orderly-Room Sergeant and was well the last I heard from him. My brother, Andy, is with the Second Division and has been in France for over 9 months now. He was in the fighting at Bullecourt and Bapaume and was doing well the last I heard from him.

The Australian Third Division has made a great name for themselves in the Messines Battle and have received great praise from General Birdwood. Our 10th. Brigade is to be placed on the war list as a unit which has distinguished itself. The other A.I.F. Divisions now recognise that the Third is the best Australian Division that has ever landed in France.

It is now four weeks since I received any mail from home and am beginning to think that the German U-Boats have been at work. I always look forward to receiving the "Birchip Advertiser" to get all the local news, which is very interesting when one is so far away from home.

I have just heard that Matt. Hogan has arrived back home and I hope he is recovering from his wounds. I do not think this war will finish till next Spring for the Huns are hanging out well. If only the Russians had started their offensive in the Spring of this year.

I must now say good-bye, for the sister is waiting to dress my leg and I am tired of writing whilst lying in bed. Please give my kind regards to Mr. Carlisle and Mr. Thompson and all the Birchip folks."

WAITING FOR A STRETCHER

Lance/Corporal J. Bunworth (24th. Battalion) writes home to his mother. He is with the famous "Red and White Diamonds".

THE SECOND BATTLE OF BULLECOURT

JUNE. 1917.

Dear Mother,

Just a few lines to let you know I am alive and kicking. I was wounded on the 3rd. May in a big assault on the Hindenburg Line. I got hit in my left arm, right eye, and right shoulder; but they are only very slight and nothing worth worrying about, mother.

I don't know how my mates got on. but I suppose I shall hear in a day or so. It was very exciting. We had to hop over and push Fritz back a bit, but many of us got wounded and had to leave the battalion.

The doctor operated on my eye and fixed it up a couple of days ago. I can't see out of it yet, but I suppose it will be some time before it heals up. I think it will be alright.

I was very lucky to get out alive as practically everyone around me was either killed, or wounded, and as soon as I got my wounds I lost no time in getting out of that place!

I didn't get very far till I met a pal. He was wounded himself and he said, "I will bandage you and you can do the same for me." Well, the poor fellow had only just started to look in his First-Aid Kit when a shell landed between us and blew him to pieces. All I could find of him was one hand, yet I never got a scratch.

So I thought then it was time to go. I moved a little further on and sat down. I wasn't there long when another shell came and buried me so that I had to scratch my way out I crawled on my hands and knees until I got under cover of an embankment.

I got to the dressing-station and had a drink of water, and then started off to the next one which was over a mile away. Having reached this station. I felt I could go no further on my own as I was weak from loss of blood. Next morning when I awoke, I was in a nice clean bed. bandaged all over and feeling splendid.

BATTLE OF MESSINES 7TH. JUNE, 1917.

Private C. Taylor *(of Charlton) tells Mrs. R. Kendall of a great battle in which the dead and wounded Australians amounted to 6,800.*

BULLETS AND BAYONETS

BELGIUM. 10TH. JUNE, 1917.

"Just a few lines to tell you how I fared during the last three awful days in the Battle of Messines. We have just got back to our billets, about four miles from the battlefield; and now it all seems like a horrible nightmare rather than stern reality.

We left here at midnight on June 6th. to go up to the Front-line from which we were to attack at 3-0 a.m. the following morning. On our way up to Ploegsteert Wood, the Germans sent over a barrage of gas-shells. There were thousands of them and the effect was terrible. We had to walk nearly three miles through the gas, carrying over 60 pounds of fighting-kit, till we reached the high ground of Hill 63 where the atmosphere was clear and the gas could not affect us.

All over the area where Fritz sent the gas, there were thousands of men moving up for the great attack, and it was awful to hear the poor fellows crying in agony from the suffocating gas. **(C.E.W. Bean writes that the possible number of advancing soldiers put out of action by gas was as high as 1,000.)**

Of course, we all had the masks to wear, but some men get frightened and pull off their masks, and then they slowly smother. The masks are very unpleasant to wear, but are absolute protection against the effects of horrible mustard gas.

We reached our assembly trenches and were given a drink of water. We had to attack about 3-0 a.m. (June 7th.) so that meant we only had half-an-hour's rest before we hopped over. The signal for attack was to be the explosion of several great mines under Fritz's trenches (one of which blew a well-known hill completely away). They called it "HILL 60".

The earth for miles around us seemed to rock and it was a great sight instantly after the 19 mines exploded. Fully 1,000 guns of all sizes opened up from then on. Our massed Artillery continued firing till 2-0 p.m. and I can tell you it was Hell let loose.

We swarmed across No-Man's Land over to Fritz's trenches and found the Germans so eager to surrender that they tried to embrace us; and then up we went over the slope of Messines Ridge. When we got to our objectives we had to start at once and dig ourselves in.

This is where our trouble started, for Fritz's aeroplanes came over and saw where we were and told their Artillery. His guns opened on us, and for two days and nights he gave us an awful time.

The last night we were there (June 11th) Fritz massed battalions of his men for a great counter-attack; but, thanks to the observation of the British planes, our Artillery got going and seemed to wither the enemy out of existence.

Our battalion lost just half its strength, but two other battalions in my Brigade lost still more heavily. I came out of it with only bruises. One piece of shell destroyed my gas-mask (which we carry on our chests in a satchel). I was one of a small party which captured a valuable German gun and a number of prisoners.

We had three tanks operating with us — and they are wonderful things as they terrify the enemy and make useful tracks through the barbed wire. Superior to anything, however, is the marvellous Artillery. It was said to be the fiercest artillery bombardment in the world's history. No more words describe it. <u>Nearly every man looks ten years older."</u>

Private Harold Crone writes home to his father, Mr. George Crone, of Lascelles.

BATTLE OF MESSINES

"Somewhere in France". 15th. June, 1917

"We came out of the trenches on Wednesday morning after the most successful battle, the taking of Messines; and there is no doubt it was a great advance for the British.

We went into the front line on Thursday evening, hopped over at 9-30 the following morning, took the trenches, dug in, and made good trenches out of the Hun's mess. That was about three miles from where our trenches were on the previous morning, so you see we had advanced a good way, and our advance is still going on.

There is nothing to compare with our Artillery. With the barrages they put up, I think it would be impossible for even a <u>rat</u> to live under them. Fritz was going to counter-attack the first night we were in his trenches, but our Artillery knocked him back.

We were actually all lined up on the parapet, ready to hop over and meet him with the bayonet, but Fritz never appeared. Our battalion had a lot of successes in the line, and we won every battle. Our officers were very good and looked after us very well. I saw George Proctor the other night, and we had our photos taken together.

It was 12 months last Friday since we landed at Marseilles and entrained for the fighting line, where I have been ever since. I have had some funny and exciting experiences, too, since then.

I have never told you much about a battle, so I will give you a little idea about the battle of <u>Messines</u>. At about 3 a.m. on the 7th. June, there was a big Naval gun just behind us. Everything was silent, but when she fired, the earth shook and trembled. We were all sitting tip at the time with our gas helmets on (for Fritz was sending gas-shells over all night long, in an attempt to slow up and harass our advance) and we went and looked out of the tent door. What a fine sight it was for our eyes!

The explosion of 19 mines along the <u>Messines Ridge</u> made the whole skyline look like one big ball of fire. Messines and Hill 63 faded from view in a fog of smoke and dust. Those mines were exploding, like huge bubbles swelling up from beneath the earth's surface and then erupting into fiery clouds.

With a mighty roar our massed Artillery began to fire, the machine-gun barrage and the bombardment commenced. This was the start of the attack on Messines and all along that front-line for 10 miles.

We had breakfast at 6-30, and then started off to take part in the attack. The New Zealanders went over first and took the ridge. We followed and moved up into a reserve trench, where we watched the tanks advancing, closely followed by our men. There were plenty of shells flying in all directions, so we sat on the parapet and watched it all.

At 9-30 that evening we marched forward and found that the country was nothing but shell-holes, each as big as a dam. We got to our places about 1-30 a.m. At 3 we went out into the shell-holes to take some trenches about 200 yards in front of us; but something went wrong at daybreak and we had to retire to a newly-dug trench.

We were not there long when an aeroplane came over and dived down along the trenches, looking and calling out to us, so that the pilot could tell the Artillery how far we had advanced. The plane put me in mind of a bird flying over her nest, protecting her young ones from someone who was going to rob her of her young.

We signalled back to the plane and away it flew; but it soon came back and stopped with us all the time. At 9-30 an officer said to us, "Come on, boys, now for the Germans," and away we went. We just walked across, nice and quiet, with Fritz sniping at us.

We all got there safe, when Fritz popped into another trench ahead of us. Six of us were picked to bomb him out, and I was "Rifle Grenadier". We sneaked around behind Fritz and got into his trench. But our officer was wounded in the head, so I bandaged him up, and away we went to the dressing-station.

There were a lot of Fritzes at the Battle of Messines, and we could not get all of them on that day — the 7th. of June. He left heaps of his dead behind him, while we lost hardly anyone.

I had a lot of close shaves. One shell landed about 3 feet from me, but it did not burst. Then we had plenty of shooting when we reached a shrubbery. We were shooting into every bush while Fritz was running around a brush-fence. We were all wildly shooting, but the Germans were too numerous and I don't know if we got all of them or not.

Our Artillery knocked Fritz in all directions and there were dead Germans lying everywhere for a distance of five miles. It was a second Pozieres.

28th. June, 1917.
I will be in the fighting-line again tomorrow. I am sending you a little parcel; it is a Fritz belt I found at Messines.

It is 12 months on Sunday next since we first went into action here in France. There were about 1,200 of us then; all fine fellows. Today, we counted up the old boys, including those that had been wounded, and there were only 26 of us left, so you can see the difference. There are three of us, including myself, that have never missed a stunt and have been through the lot.

9th. July, 1917.
I am still in the line; we have been in since last Friday week. I don't know how much longer we have to do in the trenches, but there has been no "hop over" this time. We have had rain and the trenches are muddy and sticky.

When one looks at the country we captured a month ago, it seems marvellous what the Germans had against us. They had reinforced-concrete machine-gun positions everywhere; and their rectangular boxes of concrete were that strong they could withstand a direct hit.

Small shells would just bounce off those concrete-shelters, called PILLBOXES. The Germans had built many of them throughout their lines at Messines and Ypres; yet we got through them all and drove their garrisons out. I might add that things are very dear over here. I had a feed of steak and two eggs the other day, and it cost me 3 shillings."

Frank Wilkinson, of Watchem, describes his part in the war. His brother. Arthur Wilkinson, was killed in France, in October, 1917.

BULLECOURT AND MESSINES

ENGLAND, 12TH. AUGUST, 1917.

Dear Mother and Father: I am at present on furlough in Brighton. It is a pretty seaside place, and the days have been beautiful since I have been over here. I go back to France on the 21st. August.

We are fighting now in the North of France and Belgium. We came from the Somme last May, and I've had a pretty good time as my Company has not been in the line since May, but they will soon be going in again after this rest.

We have had a rough time since last April. We were down at a place called BULLECOURT then, and it was very lively from April 11th. to May 10th. They were fighting for BULLECOURT all the time. We had it one day and the Germans would get it back the next. We were taking it and losing it the whole of the time.

I will never forget the 15th. April when we got all our guns knocked out and more than half our men. There were 15 killed and 8 wounded in less than 10 minutes. We had our guns in the pits ready, but the Germans took us by surprise and came at us along the side of the hill to our right, and we could not turn our guns around to fire on them.

So we pulled the guns out on to the road and fired 30 shots from each gun at them. But the German artillery saw us and played all their guns on to us. They did rock them in, putting 5 of our 6 guns out of action, and killing 15 and wounding 8 out of our 45 gunners. So we had to carry the wounded down to the Dressing-Station.

Our gun was the first one out of action, so we left it — and a good job we did, because our dug-out was blown to pieces. Then we had to take the other guns away to get them repaired and build fresh gun-pits further back from the Front-line. After that, it was not so bad.

But our gunners were getting wounded or killed nearly every day till May 10th. Then they told us the Allies were going to make an advance at MESSINES — that is about 80 miles from the Somme. So we got in the train and went up there as far as we could — and then got off the train and went by road.

We got there towards the end of May and put our guns in position to shell the enemy's roads and cut the barbed-wire in front of the Huns' trenches — and we did all this until it was time for the "PUSH" to start.

Well, it started on June 7th. and it was a tremendous bombardment. We blew up seven lines of craters. The ground trembled for miles around, but we lost only 1 gunner and 3 wounded, during the 21 days we were there. We had a lot of hard work and were fighting for four days and four nights with only a little broken sleep.

We left MESSINES on June 18th. to have 10 days' rest, and we went to a place called Plogstreet (*Ploegsteert*) about 3 miles from MESSINES. It was nice and quiet there, but it was too good to last as the "Heads" only let us stay there for 10 days.

THIRD BATTLE OF YPRES. We were told we were going to push the Germans back at Wipers (*Ypres*). We went up there and got another warm time. We were preparing for the "Push" by cutting the barbed-wire in front of the enemy's trenches, and shelling the roads to wreck the enemy's supplies.

When the infantry attack began, some of our gunners were already dead or wounded, so we had to persevere short-handed till we got reinforcements. Rain started and kept going for 3 days and we nearly had to swim.

* *A British Artillery officer said this about the Australian artillery at Ypres*: — "We were next to the Anzacs, splendid fellows. I remember looking back at the Anzacs who were south of Zillebeke lake, and seeing the Boche fairly pounding it in there; and all the time the Anzac guns kept on firing away, and we wondered how they could do it — how on earth they weren't blown to pieces. Right in the thick of it you would see them firing every time."

WAR IN THE AIR DURING WORLD WAR 1
– 50 BRITISH PLANES AGAINST 50 GERMAN PLANES

(This eyewitness account, by an officer of the Royal Fining Corps, was printed in the "East Charlton Tribune" during July, 1917.)

"There were 50 of our machines stretched across the airfield; and now their pilots gathered in little groups to receive last instructions and to study maps and photographs. At last a bugle sounded and we scrambled into our machines. All along the line, engines began to throb and splutter as the planes came to life.

Our Squadron-Commander, with his observer behind him, soared up into the air, and the other 49 machines followed him into the heavens; and we swooped and manoeuvred like a flock of swallows until the formation was right.

A loud crack from the Commander's pistol was our signal; and we were off, like bees following the Queen Bee, straight for the enemy's lines.

We faintly heard the cheering of the mechanics and riggers from the aerodrome beneath us, but we mounted so swiftly that soon it was lost. We climbed higher to six — eight — ten thousand feet. Soon we were over the British trenches and I could see tiny specks that were men beneath us.

Now we were flying over No-Man's Land, a desolate waste. A stone's throw ahead were the German trenches. Suddenly, tiny specks began to rise from far in the rear of the German lines. They were aeroplanes coming to meet us. Later, I learned that by some strange coincidence there were 50 of them. We would like to have fought them, but that was not our mission.

We had been sent out to bomb the German Front-Line and Support-Trenches; thus smashing the enemy's morale before our Infantry boys went yelling across the pock-marked earth to bayonet them.

My observer, seated behind me, was watching the Commander's aeroplane. He saw the signal and let go our first rack of bombs. Forty-nine other observers did the same, almost simultaneously. Hell was let loose in the Heavens as bombs fell crashing on the men beneath who could find no shelter.

We flew lower, and another rack of bombs was turned loose from each of our fifty machines. I could clearly see our bombs strike and scatter earth, and men, and parts of men, all over the ground.

Lower and lower we flew. I could make out their anti-aircraft guns in the pits below. Directly ahead of me a column of flame shot out from one of our planes, and I caught a glimpse of the pilot's face — it was as grey as the dawn-sky under which we were now fighting. His petrol-tank had been hit, exploding in a sheet of flames. His machine swooped and then spiralled swiftly towards the earth.

I have read descriptions of Cavalry charges, but I do not know if any man lives who has yet described a charge of aeroplanes. We had been dropping Death into that thin, grey line of enemy trenches below; and their anti-aircraft guns had been barking at us (rather ineffectively), but now we faced a real enemy, an enemy as strong as we!

The German squadron was flying in mass-formation until it was upon us, and then it scattered. Just to the right of me, one of their planes dropped out of sight. My partner had just let go another rack of bombs when suddenly an explosion directly underneath me caused the plane to give a dangerous lurch upwards. I tightened my grip on the levers as the plane jerked about.

Our formation had now ceased to exist, for all we cared about was to dodge the German planes and to keep on pouring explosives and bullets into those trenches although their air-patrol was trying to knock us out of the sky.

One drum of our machine-gun ammunition was already

spent, so my observer whirled about on his little stool, grabbed for another drum, and slammed it into the machine-gun. He was just about to send a parting message to the Boches, when suddenly he lurched forward. He was hit.

Not a word from him — not even a sigh. I took a quick look, but now, above all else, I must concentrate on saving my machine. I could see a thin stream of blood trickling from his hair down his face. I headed my plane westward and just then came the Commander's signal to retire.

We raced along like the wind, the German planes spitting lead at us from behind; and those of our machines who had observers left alive, cracked back at them with what little ammunition remained unspent.

As we whirred back over the British trenches, the Scots were just clambering out of them and dashing across that bullet-swept No-Man's land to fight with steel the Boches — who call them the "Ladies from Hell" because of their kilts.

It was grim work, flying back to quarters after that first fight. The wind whistled through the torn sides of my plane, and my partner leaned against the empty bomb rack — silent.

As I walked towards the aerodrome, I noticed the plane (which had been beside me for most of the return journey) glide safely down to earth; but neither the pilot nor his observer got out. I walked over to look.

The observer was shot through the head — and had been dead for some time. The pilot was hit in a dozen places, yet he made a perfect landing; and afterwards he fell forward in his seat — dead!"

In this letter from Belgium, Lieutenant Hal. Young (of St. Arnaud) describes his part in the British advance along the Menin Road on September 20th. 1917.

THE BATTLE OF MENIN ROAD

23RD. SEPTEMBER, 1917.

"We have just been through one of the biggest and most successful battles along this front. The attack began just at dawn. Exactly to the second, all our guns along this 10-mile front opened fire, also the machine-guns. You can imagine the noise, with thousands of guns firing at the same time. Every man hopped over the top at once. It was a great sight.

I got caught in some barbed wire and thought I was done for, as machine-gun bullets were flying all around me. I assure you I didn't take long to get away, leaving bits of my trousers behind on the wire.

In Glencorse Wood we struck a bit of opposition, running into a nest of German dugouts with five machine-guns. They showed a bit of fight and shot dead an officer with me. After that — well, I'm afraid they won't trouble anyone else again.

Our troops went mad at the death of their officer. They swarmed around the enemy dugouts and filled the place with bombs. Our men bombed and bayoneted about 30 of the Huns, until, growing tired of killing, they allowed a few to go to the rear as prisoners.

We took a lot of prisoners and machine-guns and the Him lost a terrible lot of men, killed and wounded. But Fritz has a nasty habit of firing at you with his machine-gun until you get right up to him, then he throws up his hands and cries, "KAMERAD! KAMERAD!"

This battle will be a big blow to Fritz as he has now lost all his observation of Ypres and the roads running round it. I have not seen our men so eager to fight since the Landing at Gallipoli. Our  losses were extraordinarily light. We could hardly credit it when we called the roll afterwards.

But I lost several good pals, including * Major Tubb, 7th. Battalion whom I was with when he won his V.C. at Lone Pine. He was shot in the spine by an enemy sniper.

[* However, official accounts of the death of Major Tubb state that <u>he was wounded by his own artillery</u> and died that evening. Apparently, his company had just captured nine enemy pillboxes when they came within range of a British barrage. Understandably, it is better to announce that a German sniper shot Major Tubb, of Lone Pine fame, than to admit he was killed by his own side.]

We were relieved last night and taken well back behind the firing-line for a spell. I was slightly gassed, which made me feel a bit off for a while. I suppose we will be going in again shortly, but I won't mind turning my sword into a ploughshare again. It is just three years and one month last Friday since I left dear old St. Arnaud".

———— OVER THE TOP ————

Here is the filth and stench of war.
The corpses on the parapet,
The maggots on the floor.

Here is the filth and stench of war.
The corpses on the parapet,
The maggots on the floor.

---- WAR IN THE AIR ----

Here are the two WILLEY brothers of DONALD. Sapper Victor Willey is seated on the left of the picture. He enlisted at the beginning of the mar, serving at the Dardanelles throughout the eight months of the Gallipoli Campaign. His brother, Harold, joined near the end of 1915, and so the two brothers mere together in Egypt at the beginning of 1916. They appear to have stayed together whilst training in Egypt. Then they mere both sent to the Western Front in 1916 — and served

PRIVATE EDWARD CONINGSBY WRITES HOME —
"I have been in the front-line twice, 5 days each time. We get well looked after by our officers. Why, we even get hot stew and tea

every night in the trenches, and in the mornings we get our issue of bread, butter, bacon, jam, cheese, pork and beans, so you can see we are well-fed which is the main thing. I suppose you have heard of this new gas that Fritz is using. It is causing a lot of casualties, but most of them are only away from their unit for 14 days. You are quite safe with the respirator on, but it blisters the exposed parts of your body. It smells like mustard and is sent over in shells."

Private Coningsby took part in the Great Offensive of September, 1917, which proved to be a great success for the Australians who had Fritz completely demoralised.

"Throughout the woods, Fritz was hiding in concrete 'pill-boxes' and out of these solid buildings Fritz had his machine-guns playing on us as we advanced across the open. Only for the help from our artillery we would never have got near them. Our barrage was marvellous and the minute it lifted we rushed forward with fixed bayonets to take our objectives. As soon as we got up to them, Fritz would rush out with his hands in the air crying, "Mercy Kamrade" which I can tell you was hard to give him as only a few minutes before that he had killed or wounded our best cobbers; but one has to play the game and fight clean although it was hard to do. The poor creatures were trembling as we got near them with our fixed bayonets. Some of the prisoners told us that they had been warned the Anzacs would cut their throats if ever we caught them. I suppose they are told this kind of thing to make them fight and not surrender. Fritz puts up a good fight until you get right up to him then up goes his hands for mercy. It makes one's blood boil to think he is getting off scot free after killing some Mother's son. There is no doubt the British are too humane."

In the 'Big Push' of October, 4th. 1917, Private Ted Coningsby was struck down by a piece of shell to his face and was sent for treatment behind the lines. On his return to the front lines he had the misfortune to be buried alive in a shell-hole, but was dug out unharmed though obviously suffering from shock.

"I have not regretted in the slightest that I came and I have had a good experience of what war is. No one can realise the full horrors until they spend some time at the front, take part in several advances, get into trenches after a heavy bombardment to find heads and limbs severed with shells, look at reeking corpses lying for days and weeks in front of the trenches, and be pestered by flies in their millions. Where is the world's boasted civilization now? Germany's old 'Kaiser Billy' will go straight to Hell when he dies, according to all accounts."

Edward's last letter to his family was written sometime in late August, 1918, only ten weeks before the end of that terrible war. He was killed in action and is buried in France amongst thousands of other young soldiers who paid the supreme sacrifice.

"My word, it is hard to lose such good pals as I have lost lately. One thing I know, they laid down their lives for their friends. It is hard to think such good fellows have been killed while there are a lot of shirkers in Australia. I don't know what kind of conscience they must have to stay safely at home in comfort when other poor fellows are dying on the battlefield to keep them in safety. Surely if this war lasts much longer they will answer the call of their country and come over here and give us a hand?

Soldiers inspect a wrecked gun

Corporal Leslie Harrison writes home.
[of Meyer Street, Donald]

SOME NEAR MISSES

Dear Mother,

"Since I last wrote we have been having a busy all about our doings in the papers long before you receive this letter.

I wasn't actually in the fighting-line, but was one of a carrying-party that was supplying the boys in the front line with ammunition. It was rather a hard job, and pretty risky, as a lot of Fritz's heavy shells were dropping all around the sector where we were carrying. All the same, I was glad to be doing something to help the boys in the Front-line.

One night we had got into bed and were just about asleep, when someone poked his head in the tent and called out my name. He told me to get up and get dressed and be ready in full marching order as soon as possible. Then there was a mad scramble!

Outside, it was pitch-dark and raining. Nevertheless after scrambling about in the dark for a while, somebody managed to light a candle and it wasn't long before we were ready. There were 48 of us altogether and it was about 11 o'clock at night by this time, and the rain was still pouring down.

We had to march a good distance to a place where we would find motor lorries that were to take us to our destination. The track we walked along was slippery and everything was in darkness. I wasn't the only one that fell into the mud during that march, and by the time we got to the two lorries we were wet through.

There were 24 of us in each lorry, and with all our equipment, I can tell you, we were packed in like sardines. All aboard, and then our joy-ride started. For the first part of our journey the road was level, then we came on to a road where shell holes were plentiful. The "Rocky Road To Dublin" was not in it compared to that road on our way to the Front-line.

After about two hours of this bone-shaking journey, the motor lorries came to a halt and we had to get out. We were told to get our packs off and get ready in fighting order. When our packs were left behind, we got into the lorries once more and made another start for the front line. This time when we stopped, there was an officer waiting for us, who informed us that we were to be a carrying-party for our Brigade.

Off we went to the ammunition-dump. It was about 3 o'clock in the morning, so we had to set to and build our own dugout (or log huts, as we liked to call them). There were plenty of wooden slabs there and it wasn't long before we had it built.

"I Wouldn't Leave My Little Wooden Hut For You" says the song. But that's a lie as I would have left it for anybody; and what's more I had to leave it for Fritz's shells before we came away.

The guns were pretty busy all night, and I was just dozing off to sleep when our barrage opened up to cover the boys' advance. And what a barrage! I've heard a few bombardments in my time here, but never one like this. Guns of all sizes and shapes spoke from every direction and the sky was on fire. The roar of the guns was deafening and it was useless to try and speak to one another although only a few feet apart.

Then some of Fritz's heavies started to drop around our dwellings. It wasn't long after the guns opened fire that German prisoners started to come down past us, then we knew our boys were on the Great Advance. Soon afterwards, we started on our carrying job, taking two bombs each.

As we went up the line, we passed some wounded that were on their way back to the Dressing-Station. Quite a number were only slightly-wounded, but others were very bad, poor fellows. Yet all seemed to make light of their wounds and called out to us in cheery tones about having a good time in Blighty. One chap, wounded through the hand, called out when passing us that he wouldn't sell his wound for a tenner *(ten pounds)*.

When the battle first started there was a light rain falling, but that did not last long; and as soon as it cleared, our aeroplanes began to appear and it wasn't long before the sky was alive with machines.

Prisoners continued to pass us, and a sorry-looking lot they were! All the fight seemed to have been knocked out of them.

Later on that day we saw the British tanks moving about. There is no doubt they are queer-looking affairs, and one would never think that they were machines by the way they move about. They more resemble some big beast. It is marvellous what they can crawl across, and even shell-holes cannot stop them. I don't wonder at them frightening Fritz as there is nothing very enticing about them, especially when their guns are spitting fire from both sides.

Our party was carrying up ammunition all that day, and we also helped with some of the wounded on the stretchers — which wasn't very light work. It was wonderful the way in which the stretcher-bearers stuck to their work; and if anybody deserves praise, it's these men. They were carrying all day and well into the night, having to put up with a lot of heavy shell-fire.

I had a bit of dinner about 12 o'clock, and then another snack about 7 o'clock that evening. About 9 o'clock we set off, each carrying two cans of water for the Front-line, but we got lost. Goodness only knows how far we walked, but it was four hours before we found the right place.

Carrying up water to the Front-line was the easiest part of our night's work, as when coming back we had to carry out stretchers with wounded on them. This is a bad enough job in the daylight when you can see where to go, but in the dark with no one to guide you, it was almost impossible. I tell you it's not nice, blundering into shell-holes and getting tangled up in barbed-wire.

The lads on the stretchers never complained, although they were getting a rough ride. By the time we got down to the ambulances, I was just about knocked out. I have been tired at times in my life, but never before was I as tired as I was on that morning when I crawled into my little wooden hut.

From the top of my head to the tip of my toes, I felt as if someone had hammered me with a stick; and my shoulders felt raw where the stretcher had been resting on them. But I wasn't the only one — there were plenty more just as tired, if not worse, than I was.

I tried to sleep, but it was rather cold for sleeping as we had left our blankets behind with our packs and only had waterproof sheets to cover us. The 'chats' also were on the move all night; I think they must have been digging in.

{~?~PG: @277@}{~?~IM: insert DaringDeedsOfDiggersOnTheSomme-part2-p277.jpg here.}

A British Tank in trouble

An Australian soldier helps a wounded officer hung up on the enemy's entanglements.

A British tank puts enemy soldiers to flight and silences their machine-gun.

ON BOARD A TROOPSHIP

(Driver Harry Budge continues his well-written narrative of an unforgettable trip on an army transport across the seas to Europe.)

THE HALIFAX HORROR

"Now our transport reaches the shores of Nova Scotia and its capital city of Halifax — or rather what is left of it. For this is the ill-fated Halifax, which on that memorable day a few months ago was reduced from a happy, thriving city into a desolate ruin. On that tragic day, the population of this handsome city was lessened by 1800 souls. Let me tell you all about it.

The morning of December 6th. 1917, dawned brightly, and gave promise of a beautiful day. Then, without any warning, the heavens opened with a thunderous crash and molten metal rained down upon the heads and buildings of the people, changing this glorious morning into one of the blackest days in our human history.

The powder-ship, MONT BLANC, loaded with 7,000 tons of that most deadly explosive T.N.T. was rammed accidentally by the Belgian relief steamer, IMO, whilst passing through a narrow part of the Bay. The powder-ship caught fire, so the captain and his crew took to the life-boats and made off into the hills.

There was no red flag, or any sign, to denote that the MONT BLANC was carrying such a dangerous cargo. The ship burned for twenty minutes before the first explosion occurred.

A grocer called Upham, saw the collision and subsequent fire, so he telephoned the Fire Brigade which arrived at the pier just as the powder-ship blew up. Every man was killed and the cars shattered.

When a large party of sailors from a British warship ran their hoses alongside the MONT BLANC, several more explosions occurred and those brave men were blown to pieces.

To make matters worse, thousands of people were drawn by curiosity down to the pier to see the fire, not realising that their lives were in danger from flying metal. At the time, the people of this city were going about their normal, daily activities.

In the homes, women-folk were proceeding with their household tasks. In some schools, the children were in the yard being marshalled into lines. Many little mites were on the streets, walking to other schools which did not open till 9-30 a.m. In fact, the nearby streets were filled with pedestrians on their way to work.

In an instant, almost every living thing within an area of 2 square-miles was killed or badly-injured by the force of the explosion; or by the flying shells and torn pieces of iron and steel with which the air was filled.

Human beings with shattered limbs dragged themselves out from under the ruins of their collapsed homes. These sufferers were looking for help, but there was no one to render it. Others ran aimlessly about, whimpering and crying, with blood streaming from their wounds, with faces so blackened by soot and grime as to be almost unrecognisable.

A hundred fires broke out simultaneously, and live electric wires dangled from poles broken in half like toothpicks from the shock. Trees were denuded of their branches, and left stark and black; some had only stumps remaining. Every house and factory for miles had felt the shock and suffered from it.

Windows were broken up to 62 miles away. A negro was seen cutting the fingers of a dead woman, to steal her rings, and was shot dead by a soldier.

Witnesses declare they saw the bottom of Halifax Bay; and one man declares he stood on the solid rock on the bottom, but when the sea rushed back he was washed up on to the hills.

Men of good standing in the city told us stories of many marvellous happenings. For instance, a gun weighing about 8 tons was blown into a lake 3 miles away. A stone weighing 5 tons was blown from the bottom of the Bay (a depth of 127 feet) on to the deck of a boat lying at one of the piers.

I, myself, picked up pieces of iron, twisted like melted candy, 3 miles away on the hills. Whilst visiting a place, I saw an old woman scratching among the ruins of what had once been her home, and, whilst talking to her, she picked out of the debris her wedding ring. You can just imagine the joy of that old woman!

One little Halifax school had a death roll of 58. In the ruins of another home I saw a piano that had been split in half by the force of the explosion, yet was still standing; and on the rack was the music of that old familiar hymn, "Rock of Ages". One can almost picture a child playing it when this dreadful shock came. But what happened to that little pianist, I wonder?

While things were at their worst, there was a sudden change in the weather, and the town had one of the heaviest falls of snow for years. This exacerbated the people's suffering.

One man had returned home to find his wife and eleven children killed and his house reduced to burning ashes. There are still two or three hundred people missing. During our stay in Halifax, the body of a little boy was found under the ruins of a house.

Another tragic consequence of that morning was the death of forty, wounded soldiers returning home from the war, whose boat happened to be in the harbour, taking on coal.

Also, a four-mast schooner, with 250,000 bushels of wheat on board, was blown ashore and 58 men killed. There are still 15 bodies trapped under the engine-room of this boat. She is being unloaded as speedily as possible.

On the deck of the IMO, which lost the pilot, captain and 20 crew, I saw the stern pole (a piece of iron about 3 tons) which had been thrown there from the MONT BLANC. An undertaker told me that the majority of bodies recovered from the immediate area of the disaster, had to be picked up with shovels and buckets.

I visited the cemetery and saw the mass grave of the victims who had not been recognised. It was a shock to find the coffins were half-uncovered, owing to the fact that when they were buried, the diggers had to delve through 4 feet of snow. Did you know that 55 bodies from the TITANIC disaster are also buried in this cemetery?

The death roll of that awful day (6th. December, 1917) was 1,800 killed, 3,000 injured, 6,000 homeless, and damage to the extent of 50,000,000 dollars.

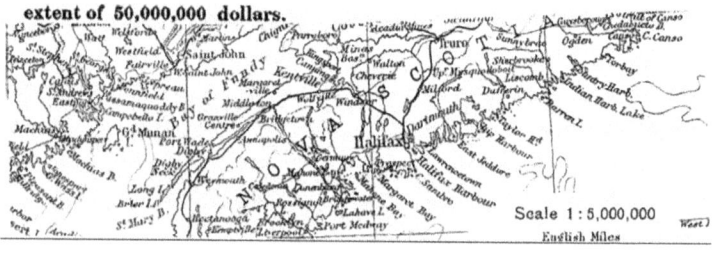

To increase the misery of these unfortunate inhabitants, within the next two days a succession of blizzards blew up and buried the city beneath heavy falls of snow. Icy blasts blew through nooks and crannies and broken windows, and many delicate folk, forced to unaccustomed exposure, fell victim to ailments which later caused their deaths.

Once the outside world heard of their disaster, there was no lack of assistance and money flowed in from nearly every nation on earth.

Within only two hours of the explosion, a train with 100 doctors and nurses on board left Boston for Halifax; and this American contingent of doctors and nurses took over the local hospitals and did marvellous relief-work. Most of them had had previous experience in the Frisco (San Francisco) Earthquake of 1906.

The basement of a large school was turned into a gigantic morgue, and here for weeks lay the unidentified remains — merely charred bones and pieces of jewellery. But many were never identified and were therefore given public funerals from the mortuary. They buried 712 on one day.

I was told that one peculiar effect of the explosion was that almost all the corpses had their clothing blown right off.

I visited a hill on the east side of the Bay, and there is hardly a square-foot that is not covered with pieces of twisted iron relics from the ill-fated Mont Blanc.

I could go on and on with these gruesome details, but I just wanted to give you a brief account of the most terrible disaster which has ever befallen a Canadian city. It is now up to the survivors of Halifax to rise, Phoenix-like, from its ashes and build a more beautiful city than ever.

After three days in Halifax, our boat, in company with many others loaded with Yankee and Canadian soldiers, left the Bay, and in the midst of a dense fog, headed for the Homeland. The fog sirens were kept going at one-minute intervals. We almost collided with a steamer of 1,000 tonnage which came right across our bows.

We must have had a Jonah on board, for a few nights later during a violent gale, whilst the pots and pans were rolling around the galley and no man was allowed on deck, our steering went wrong and we drifted towards another transport.

PRIVATE EDWARD PALMER PEARSE

- the life of a Stretcher-Bearer -

When war broke out in 1914, Ted and Ged Pearse (of Donald) were among the first volunteers to answer Australia's Call. Ged was accepted, but Ted was knocked back as he was 1/4 inch below the required height of 5ft 6ins. After six weeks' training at Broadmeadows Camp, Ged sailed away to war, leaving behind his disappointed brother.

But Ted refused to take "NO" for an answer. He volunteered again in June 1915 after the height-requirement was lowered (no doubt due to the heavy losses suffered by our Anzacs upon Gallipoli Heights).

Ted's group of trainees became part of the Third Division, but at this stage Ted had decided on his own particular course of action for the war. He felt for humanitarian reasons that he did not want to shoot at the enemy; so when there was a call for volunteers to be trained as "Stretcher-Bearers" he saw his chance of running risks without endangering others' lives. In fact, as a stretcher-bearer he would be helping to save lives.

Ted was 20 years old when his transport-ship left Melbourne Docks in July, 1915. They travelled across the Indian Ocean to South Africa, where the troops marched through the Cape Town and were entertained to a dinner and concert, and taken to beauty-spots like Table Mountain, the Botanic Gardens and Camp Bay.

Back on board, Ted suffered severe stomach pain which was diagnosed as appendicitis. The ship had to stop its engines opposite Cape Verde to enable the doctors to operate — on Ted's 21st. Birthday!

After about seven weeks at sea, the troops landed at Plymouth and entrained for Salisbury Plain where the huge, Army Camps were situated — about 640 acres of Wooden Huts stretched across this wild and lonely place.

Here, Ted trained in the "10th. Field Ambulance Corps" (Third Division) and, in due course, was sent to France. He landed at Le Havre May 10th. Then they told us the Allies were going to make an advance at MESSINES — that is about 80 miles from the Somme. So we got in the train and went up there as far as we could — and then got off the train and went by road.

We got there towards the end of May and put our guns in position to shell the enemy's roads and cut the barbed-wire in front of the Huns' trenches — and we did all this until it was time for the "PUSH" to start.

Well, it started on June 7th. and it was a tremendous bombardment. We blew up seven lines of craters. The ground trembled for miles around, but we lost only 1 gunner and 3 wounded, during the 21 days we were there. We had a lot of hard work and were fighting for four days and four nights with only a little broken sleep.

We left MESSINES on June 18th. to have 10 days' rest, and we went to a place called Plogstreet (*Ploegsteert*) about 3 miles from MESSINES. It was nice and quiet there, but it was too good to last as the "Heads" only let us stay there for 10 days.

THIRD BATTLE OF YPRES. We were told we were going to push the Germans back at Wipers (*Ypres*). * We went up there and got another warm time. We were preparing for the "Push" by cutting the barbed-wire in front of the enemy's trenches, and shelling the roads to wreck the enemy's supplies.

When the infantry attack began, some of our gunners were already dead or wounded, so we had to persevere short-handed till we got reinforcements. Rain started and kept going for 3 days and we nearly had to swim.

* *A British Artillery officer said this about the Australian artillery at Ypres*: — "We were next to the Anzacs, splendid fellows. I remember looking back at the Anzacs who were south of Zillebeke lake, and seeing the Boche fairly pounding it in there; and all the time the Anzac guns kept on firing away, and we wondered how they could do it — how on earth they weren't blown to pieces. Right in the thick of it you would see them firing every time."

STRETCHER-BEARERS

IN PRAISE OF STRETCHER-BEARERS

Stretcher-bearers, stretcher-bearers,
Running in the rain
Out amongst the flying shells
Seeking those in pain.
You carry in a wounded man
Then go out to seek again.
From danger's fire you never shrink,
Nor hide when others can;
Your work is far more deadly
Than that of a rifle-man.
Fatalistic, faithful, fearless,
You never crouched, but ran.
In sticky mud through sharp barbed wire
You searched where many fell;

Looking for a sign of life
In a bloody place like Hell.
Then run with him on your stretcher
To escape each killing shell.
Stretcher-bearers, stretcher-bearers,
To you our thanks are due.
You never shirked the danger
When there was work to do.
For we have seen and know your worth
And sing in praise of you.

F.B.

STRETCHER-BEARERS BRING IN THE WOUNDED (British Official Photograph)

RUNNING ACROSS A BATTLEFIELD

Private Charles Bertie Gilchrist (of Watchem) won three citations for his courage as a runner. As a result (according to the Canberra War Museum Records) he was awarded the Belgian
CROIX DE GUERRE.

"This soldier has at all times displayed exceptional coolness and conspicuous bravery under fire. As a Company runner he has proved himself invaluable to his Commanding-Officer in the difficult work of keeping touch with his command under very severe bombardment. He has taken part in all the recent battle operations and in all has rendered splendid service; and has never failed in getting through with information, and has always shown an absolute disregard for personal danger."

{**10TH. AUGUST, 1918. J. MCARTHUR. LIEUTENANT-COLONEL.**}

"This soldier acted as a runner during the operations near MORLANCOURT, south-west of ALBERT, on the night of 28th./29th. July, 1918. No matter where his Company-Commander sent him, he found his way and safely delivered his despatches. He displayed a total disregard for personal danger under a heavy enemy barrage, and kept his Company-Commander in touch with his command throughout the operation."

{11TH. AUGUST, 1918. MAJOR-GENERAL E. TIVEY}

WEARING THE DREADED GAS-MASK

A RUNNER ON THE BATTLEFIELDS

A runner in World War I was not a professional athlete in the modern sense of the word, but a soldier who ran with important messages across the battlefields, regardless of danger from enemy bombardments and machine-gun fire. When the telephone lines were cut, making communication impossible, a very heavy responsibility rested upon a runner's shoulders as he was expected to deliver his Commander's orders.

Threading his way amidst huge craters, six feet to eight feet deep, a runner had to cross open ground upon which shrapnel and high explosive shells were continually bursting.

As well as runners, there were also 'Dispatch Riders'. These were soldiers who used motor-bikes and were handed messages at any time of the day or night. They had to ride across country as speedily as possible, in blinding rain or in pitch darkness.

Usually, officers had to rely mainly upon runners to carry

their messages through the enemy barrage. When facing such dangerous missions, in many cases a runner did not bend down, or even turn his head, because he knew his mates were expecting him to show them an example of fearlessness.

A runner had to carry messages, for the most part, across open fields and along exposed roads. Sadly, during the shelling of Pozieres (in July, 1917) runner after runner was killed as each crossed the sunken road that was continually under heavy bombardment.

The demands upon runners were heavy because they had to travel straight through the constant, dreadful barrage from the Germans. One runner was so exhausted after a run that after delivering his message he lay down to rest and then shot himself. He found it more than he could bear, but he went without complaining.

The spirit of many runners might be judged by the courage of Private P. I. de Jongh (of St. Arnaud) who was taking a message from the front-line back to Headquarters, when a shell burst behind him. De Jongh was blown into a shell-hole and later pulled out by some passing soldiers who then left him there, thinking he was dead. Recovering consciousness, de Jongh cut off with a penknife his leg which had been almost severed and was just hanging by some thin skin. It took him five hours to crawl along the track and reach a first-aid post. When he arrived, the badly-wounded de Jongh asked for a cigarette and said, "Now tell me, Doc, have I a sporting chance?"

Let us also praise 'stretcher-bearers' whose job was to get the wounded off the battlefield, bandage their wounds and carry them back to the regimental Aid post for treatment by their Battalion's medical officer. Other soldiers admired these stretcher-bearers who were unarmed and worked under fire, carrying wounded to safety. They wore 'SB' armbands, but sometimes the enemy would still shoot at them.

Pte. Frederick Olive (of Donald) was a runner for his 4th. Machine Gun Battalion and won the Military Medal for conspicuous bravery while acting as a forward runner during the operations near Demancourt on 5th. April, 1918. He carried several messages through very heavy barrage fired by the enemy near the Albert-Amiens Road. He also went forward during a fierce attack by the Germans in an effort to find certain lost guns. The next time he brought back valuable information concerning the whereabouts of the enemy. Sadly, Pte. Olive's luck ended and he died of wounds on 3rd. May, 1918.

We cannot possibly imagine how runners and stretcher-bearers were able to deal with the horror of so much death on the battlefields of the Western Front — and let us not forget that the suffering of the German soldiers would have been similar to that of Australian soldiers. (In fact, the total number of Germans killed in the war is stated as 649,000.)

There were runners in the German army, too, who also faced speeding bullets and shrieking shells whilst carrying messages. One of their runners was a soldier called Adolf Hitler and although he was wounded and blinded by mustard gas in 1918, he recovered and twenty years later led the German nation into a war against Britain. The one man responsible for all the murders and damage wrought by the Nazis during World War 2 was Adolf Hitler. They say the Devil looks after his own — so did Hitler survive to turn this world into another Hell years later?

A RUNNER'S LAMENT

I used to love running, but it's not quite the same
When shells fly around me and snipers take aim.
I'm carrying a message and that must be done,
For lives now depend on how fast I can run.
Crawling through mud that is sticky and brown,
Avoiding the shell holes in which I might drown.
I dare not look back through the dust and the haze
So arrive at headquarters, my mind in a daze.
Runners must pass through a barrage each day,
So I'm lucky, but next time might die on the way.

*Signaller Matt Hogan —
dispatch rider*

On the Road to Pozières. Helping an Ambulance up.

Charles Gilchrist

THE KIND OF LETTER THAT PARENTS DREAD TO RECEIVE IN WARTIME

France
14. 2. 18.

Dear Mr Lofts,

It is with the very deepest feelings of sorrow and sympathy for you and your family that I have been caused by the Will of God - to write you. On the night of the 12th, whilst on Duty, your Son, Charles, received a severe head-wound which caused his death today without having regained consciousness. In such a case, Mr Lofts, words seem very trivial, from one unknown to you, but his loss is very severely felt by myself and every member of this Company, let alone by his immediate friends, the members of my Section.

Your son, by his very gentlemanly spirit of coolness and courage, has, many a time, carried us successfully through very trying hardships; whilst his grand example of patience and endurance muchly endeared him to the hearts of all.

Such as Charles can little be spared, but, in these troublous times we must all bow to the inevitable.

Please, Mr Lofts, do not put yourself out to reply to this as I, too well, know your feelings, unless there is something I may be able to do for you; but, believe me, I, as his Section officer and all the members of my Section very deeply feel your loss with you.

With deepest sympathy, I am
Yours sincerely
A. L. McIntyre. Lt.

EXPERIENCE OF A SOLDIER ON THE SOMME BATTLEFIELDS.

"From out of the darkness I could hear the groans and wails of wounded men — faint, long, sobbing moans of agony and despairing shrieks. It was obvious that dozens of men with serious wounds must have crawled for safety into nearby shell holes and now the water was rising about them as it rained — and as they were powerless to move they were slowly drowning in those deep pits."

British soldier helps a wounded German to first-aid post

The Conscription Referendum in 1917
Majority votes for 'NO' was 184,832

THE CONSCRIPTION REFERENDUMS IN 1917 – MAJORITY VOTES FOR 'NO' WAS 184,832.

Do not disturb, but leave in peace
That hallowed place where sleep the brave;
Here lies our Youth, forever fair,
More lovely now in sombre grave.
Do not disturb, for they do dream
Of battles fought and victories won;
Their bones entwine and mingle there,
Each man a mother's son.
Do not disturb that sacred place
Where youthful heroes lie;
Above them poppies blossom red
And stars adorn the sky.
Do not disturb our soldiers brave
Who sprang to war and won the fight
And died that joy and freedom
Might be every person's right.
Do not disturb our bonnie lads
Who fought 'gainst hateful wrongs
And now beside their comrades dear
Sing Heaven's angelic songs.
Fair France — guard well the men who wear
The badge of the Rising Sun;
Do not disturb the blessed bones
Of those whose war is won.

BURIED AT FROMELLES
(On hearing of the intention to dig up this mass grave outside the village.)

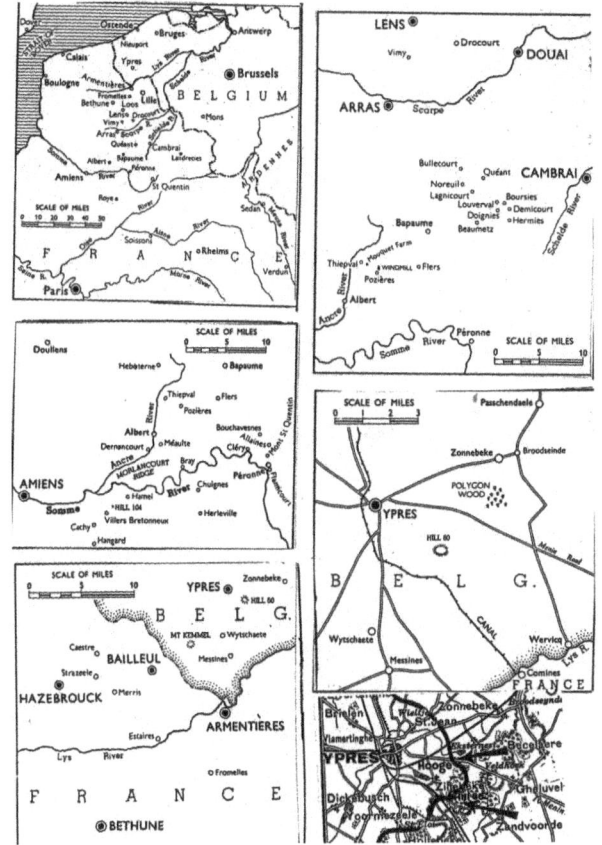

The scene at Hooge Dump on September 25, 1917, after its explosion.

THE BIG GERMAN OFFENSIVE

On 21st. March, 1918, the Germans launched their big attack on the Allied line in a last, desperate attempt to reach Paris. They broke through on a wide front and were advancing every day. For the Germans, this was their last chance before the Yanks arrived.

CORPORAL VICTOR WILLEY ("Somewhere in France") 15th. April, 1918. "Dear Mother and Father, Things are not the same over this part of the world as they formerly were, as no doubt you will read in the papers that we have been getting 'carved up a treat' by old Fritz. But so far, he has not driven us back into the sea. Only God knows what will happen to us this week.

Fritz has got the wind up over our "Heads" properly, and no wonder, as the land it took us nearly three years to wrench from him, he took back (with more added) in a few days. Bapaume has fallen — and that is very painful to our men as we remember only too well what it cost Australians to win that town a year ago.

I don't think the war can last long at the pace it is going. It is a perfect Hell let loose. It is practically open warfare now, so it is a case of keep your head down low if you can.

Thousands are being killed and wounded as the German hordes press on towards the Somme. You must excuse this short letter as we have been racing on foot from one end of France to the other, trying to stop Fritz from breaking through the lines.

I think that his dash is over for a time, but, by Cripes, the

Australians have suffered. We have been put into almost every part where Fritz has broken through, and I am glad to say our boys have stopped him every time. The bloodiest engagements known in history.

Our "boys" are all in good heart, and confident of holding on; but, alas, God only knows how many of us will come out of this terrible carnage. But cheer up, dear parents, as I truly believe God will see me safely through this great German offensive."

A ruined church at VILLERS-AU-FLOS

Photo of a German found in a trench at Villers-Bretonneux

Australian Machine-gun shooting at a German Aeroplane during the Fight near Bullecourt.

EXTRACTS FROM WAR LETTERS (1917-18)

11ᵀᴴ. FEBRUARY, 1917.

We are now in 'Thistle Trench' and in the vicinity are dead Germans, old bayonets, gas helmets and guns. One of our boys, rather anxious for souvenirs, ventured out in the daytime for the purpose of searching the dead Germans. He told us he kept very low by crawling along the ground. "There are numerous dead," he said, "including Tommies and Scots. Their faces are black and some of their teeth are showing like wild beasts." He told us that in an attempt to pull a gold ring from a German finger, he pulled the arm right out from the shoulder.

1ˢᵀ. MARCH, 1917.

Some of the walking track was so muddy and we just had to do our best to keep our feet standing on the duck-boards. It was after we had done about three trips over the same track that it was discovered in one particular spot a dead German had been used to replace a shattered duck-board and that we had walked over him time after time. I felt a tinge of horror run through my veins. Whether he was a German or not, it was an inhuman thing to do.

6ᵀᴴ. MARCH, 1917.

We are now in a place called Le Sars, a village that is now just a heap of ruins and not far from Bapaume. We visited the ruins and the rats — they were having great fun — and yet I thought the war was doing some good by blowing up rats. We discovered a great number of dead Tommies and Scotties lying around the Butte — it seems their units had failed to drive the Hun from the Butte.

14ᵀᴴ. MARCH, 1917.

When I left the dug-out in search of fresh air, I wondered if God had sent down fire from heaven because in every direction I could only see mountains of angry flames. Later I discovered that the Germans had set many villages on fire before evacuating. This news brought about a hurried attack on Bapaume by our men and the local cemetery soon became the scene of a very fierce struggle. Men were hiding behind tombstones hurling bombs at one another, until gradually we could only find an isolated German here and there. The smoke and heat and flames from houses and stores in the village of Bapaume stopped any further advance on our part — but, undoubtedly, our men had performed a wonderful feat to capture the village of Bapaume.

7TH. AUGUST, 1918.

On the afternoon of the seventh day of August I slept with several of my companions in a dug-out just in front of Villiers Bretonneux. I was quite stiff in the limbs when I awoke and before me stood our officer. He held in his hand a large sheet of paper and he gazed into my eyes without speaking. There was a sadness about his expression and a lump seemed to come into his throat. "Wake the men up," he said. I shook them and they lifted their weary eyelids. "Is Peace declared?" cried one of the troops as he rubbed the sleep from his eyes. "I have a message from the general," the officer continued. "We are to attack tomorrow in company with the whole of the Australian and Canadian divisions. Two English regiments will be on our extreme left. This battle will be the greatest that Australians have been called upon to face and every officer and man will do his best. For Australia's future and the liberty of the peoples of the nations fighting by our side, we are asked to put the full strength of our wills into the battle." Well, the determination to be victors slowly crept into our minds and the very thought of gaining a decisive victory made Australian shores appear closer than ever. We prepared our equipment and ammunition right away and by eleven o'clock that night the area around us was one mass of eager troops from the shores of Australia.

8TH. AUGUST, 1918. DER SCHWARZE TAG.

We moved to the right of Villiers Bretonneux, just in front of a battery of 18-punder guns. It must have been two o'clock in the morning when we settled down in our trench. At two-thirty stew was served up and I thoroughly enjoyed it. It was hot and there was plenty of it. We also had a good, hot cup of tea. This nourishment had a wonderful effect upon the troops for it seemed to regenerate their strength and warm their bodies. The hurry and bustle were now becoming very regular with quite a lot of noise. Thousands of troops were on the move and huge tanks were coming forward — some of them were crawling right over our trench as if there were no trench there at all. The high parapets were broken down. Activity increased with every minute and so our excitement grew greater and greater. The words, "For those we love", came into my mind and the emotion brought tears to my eyes. But they were not tears of sadness, nor were they tears of pain, but tears of joy for what our boys from Australia were about to undertake.

THAT SAME DAY.
All the troops were carrying explosives, as many as their strength would permit. Tanks were conspicuous and their noise was deafening. The enemy was only eighteen hundred yards away so he quickly surmised an attack. It was only a few minutes past three when he sent over a terrific barrage which disorganized our movements. Men were losing their units and the longer we waited the more intense was the enemy's barrage. Worst of all, he then directed his fire right on our unit. Every member turned ghastly pale and was lying flat down on his stomach along the bottom of our trench. Shells were bursting right on the broken parapet, slowly breaking up the only bit of protection we possessed. The earth was being hurled high into the air and then falling down upon our backs like massive hailstones. With our faces turned to the sod, we felt that any second would end our lives — but God watched over us.

FOUR O'CLOCK THAT SAME DAY
Suddenly our mighty instruments of war opened up their challenge and the roll of the cannon sounded like many powerful drums. It gave us fresh hopes and brave hearts. The great battle had started and our boys went forward full of confidence with the tanks assisting them to combat the enemy in this great battle of blood and iron. After a few yards of advance we came

in contact with the enemy and many of our men fell before our eyes, but many of the enemy were shot down. Bombs were hurled at us and we retaliated. Our determination was growing, whilst the enemy's will was weakening. The sights of the wounded and killed were awful. Men with long gashes in their heads, parts of their bodies torn off them, legs blown off and arms with deep cuts. Their clothes were torn and hanging from their blood-stained bodies. At this stage many Germans surrendered and the prisoners we captured numbered a thousand or more. Some of the enemy wounded were in a shocking condition and one in particular had his breast torn right off and he was suffering great pain. We gave him water and a cigarette. Our casualties were very slight considering the class of battle, but the enemy suffered heavily in killed, wounded and prisoners of war.

9TH. AUGUST.

The enemy was now on the run and I had an opportunity to look around the captured area because the German reserve lines were shattered to pieces. Dead Germans were everywhere lying about in very queer positions — some were half-buried with dirt because the ground had been ploughed up by the thousands of shells that fell like rain. At eleven o'clock we took over the attack again and pushed forward some five or six kilometres. Some of our planes were brought down and some of the enemy planes came down in flames. During the day field guns were captured, troop trains were captured and hundreds of prisoners. We even captured German nurses. Many souvenirs were taken such as anti-tank guns, whiz-bangs, miniwherfer guns, watches, pipes, rings, watches and wallets.

10TH. AUGUST.

On the third day we did not advance and I was glad to get some sleep. Whilst I was inspecting the captured villages of Weincourt and Goullancourt the battalion which had taken over the attack captured a huge gun — it was an 11.9 naval gun and I was photographed with it. I spent the rest of the day watching exciting air battles.

11TH. AUGUST.

On the fourth day we took over the attack again and pushed the enemy beyond a ridge near Harboneires. A number of prisoners were captured, but then we were stopped by a nasty issue of gas from the Germans. When we were waiting I viewed the battle area and saw many German soldiers mangled and mutilated by our gigantic tanks.

16TH. AUGUST.

We are still attacking and many officers of high rank have been captured and several valuable war trophies have been collected by the men. I found a complete wireless set in a deep dug-out, but after carrying it about three miles it was taken from me and I was accused of stealing Government property.

18TH. AUGUST.

On the evening of the tenth day we were bombed by enemy planes, but no casualties were inflicted. Night bombing seems to be very common just now — it seems the enemy is only game to come out after the sun has set.

19th. August.

Early in the morning we caught sight of a very queer-looking heap just to our left and it aroused our curiosity, so several of the boys, including myself, ventured across the fields. We had only got within a hundred yards when we could smell the dead bodies. Some of the boys turned back as the odour was becoming too strong and the sight was as much as I could bear to look upon. There must have been a train carrying horses, troops and nurses belonging to the enemy and we guessed that this train was bombed by our aircraft and caught fire. The horses, troops and nurses were roasted — their bodies were black and in a shocking condition. A few yards away was one of our aeroplanes which had crashed to the ground. Several dead Australians were lying about and quite a number of dead Germans filled a nearby trench.

20th. August.

We have not had a good night's sleep for quite a long time and it is very open and cold at night. The little gully in which we live is full of crawling insects, and most numerous of all is a horrid-looking blood-sucker. They crawl down your neck and up your arms, making it so uncomfortable that we cannot sleep. We seem to be advancing faster than the rear troops, but we are getting a poor lot of food rations just now. Last night a patrol party was sent out around "No Man's Land" and discovered the enemy in hiding. A new type of attack has been introduced and it is called "Peaceful Penetration". There is no artillery support and we just march up in the broad daylight and capture the enemy trenches. Once we found four Germans asleep in their dug-out and they had no boots on their feet and told us they had not had anything to eat for four days. They were glad to be our prisoners.

22ND. AUGUST.

Our next attack was not satisfactory on account of the numerous gas shells that were hurled at us, causing us to wear our gas-helmets. But the enemy gained nothing by this, because we attacked again in a most determined manner, taking prisoners and capturing another two thousand yards of his trenches. He did not have time to sit down when we launched another attack and sent him further back to the Rhine. Another brigade passed us and took up the chase and we followed, acting as a support to them.

26TH. AUGUST.

Quite unexpectedly our guns opened up a most terrific bombardment on the enemy. We thought there was to be a repetition of the eighth of August, but instead it was a plan to enable us to cross some very marshy, exposed ground. The marshy ground was more like a young sea and the water was in places up to our chests. The tall reeds and grass made travelling most trying and I thought I would never wade through it. I was knocked up and I thought we had gone miles instead of a few hundred yards. I was soaked to the skin and there was perspiration on my face and under my steel hat. The enemy was nowhere to be seen so the officer said we had better have something to eat and have a smoke. But very few had anything and those who had bread in their packs found it wet like sop. We rested that day in a trench near Mont St. Quentin.

30th. August.

During the rest spell we were told that Mont St. Quentin was to be our next task. We all looked upon this battle as being something harder than any in the past. The high position held by the enemy was to their advantage and our handicap was the tiring effort of climbing the hills.

31st. August.

We attacked early in the morning with the support of the artillery. The rain fell upon us making the conditions very difficult. By four o'clock one of the bloodiest battles of the war was in progress. The fighting was most stubborn and neither our men nor the enemy would give an inch — and in and out of the shallow trenches men were dropping, killed or wounded, almost as fast as you could count them. The battle raged all morning and I could see our men with blood-stained face looking up at the enemy strongholds with their teeth clenched. Others were curled up in the various saps groaning with pain. It was close on midday before the fierce struggle eased, but we had failed miserably to gain the heights, yet we did not lose one inch of ground. It was the loss of our brave men and the flow of precious Australian blood that stirred us to anger.

We had sixteen men left at midday. They talk of the charge of the Light Brigade, but our attack that morning was real war. At half past one we were gathered together and an officer spoke to us about the importance of capturing Mont St. Quentin. He told us that our brothers from Australia were waiting news of the capture. They were held up at Peronne and could not advance until we had captured the Mount. As he spoke I noticed a gutter of blood below our feet — the blood of Australian soldiers. Along the sap I could see the dead lying on top of one another. Germans and Australians were all in heaps and beyond them I saw the Mount that was to be captured.

Later we were attached to another battalion and our officer told us to stick, but before he could say anymore he dropped at our feet, dead — a pellet from a shell had caught him in the throat. At two o'clock our guns gave a wild roar and we moved towards the Mount. Bit by bit we forced the enemy from his strongholds and there was great relief when we reached the village. The battle was very severe in the village and more of Australia's sons fell before our eyes, but with determination we stuck our ground and cleaned up the village. Groans from all directions were now piercing my ears and I was beginning to feel that I could go no further. I was staggering like a drunken man — I was done!

After his brave part in the capture of St. Quentin this soldier was struck down with a piece of shell in his back and was sent to England for an operation in the military hospital there. He was informed that it was nothing too serious and in October he was able to enjoy his well-deserved weeks of leave looking around the Mother Country. The war ended on November 11th. 1918, and he was able to join in the wonderful celebrations. On the 5th. January, 1919, he wrote home to his folks to say his name was on the list for returning soon.

Pte. Charles B. Gilchrist — runner

Signaller Matt Hogan — dispatch rider

A RUNNER'S LAMENT

I used to love running, but it's
not quite the same
When shells fly around me and
snipers take aim.
I'm carrying a message and
that must be done,
For lives now depend on how
fast I can run.
Crawling through mud that is
sticky and brown,
Avoiding the shell holes in
which I might drown;
I dare not look back through
the dust and the haze
So arrive at Headquarters, my
mind in a daze.
Runners must pass through a
barrage each day,
So I'm lucky, but next time
I could die on the way.

LT. J. V. LARKIN AND FRIENTS (8th. BATTALION)

(Photo - Lt. John Foott)

"You will have read in the papers about the great work done in the Battle of the Somme. No one can realise the horror of war till they go through it themselves. It was terrible trampling over all the dead bodies, I thought my time had come."

(**PRIVATE ALBERT PICKERING**)

"Our boys encountered the advancing line of Huns! Bullets and shells were everywhere and the wounded men were pouring back. I was there all night; not that I wanted to be, but soldiers obey orders without question. We later found Ypres to be a doomed city, once the capital city of Fanders, and where the German Kaiser promised himself he would be crowned King of Belgium. To my mind he should be crowned 'KING OF HELL.'"

(**PRIVATE GILBERT OLIVE**)

"Fun usually starts with the roar of cannon, shells screeching, bullets flying, comrades dying. It is in these gory battle lines that all the best knowledge and science of the different Powers are being fought. Which one will be the winner? Surely it will be the one who can find the strongest guns and ammunition and has the most money. Yet we long to face the fight — to slaughter and exterminate the savage beasts who would destroy our civilization."

(**PRIVATE MARK NEYLAND**)

"As for our boys, they are just splendid. They are looked up to as the best fighting troops of the world — an honor which they have won by their gallant and ever-ready devotion to duty in face of all dangers. And if they fall, remember that, 'No greater love hath any man than this, that he lay down his life for his friends.'"

(**SERGEANT ALEXANDER WALDER**)

THE BRITISH EXPEDITIONARY FORCE IN BOULOGNE.

AN HONOR FOR AUSTRALLA FRANCE.

20TH. APRIL, 1916.

"I received your welcome letter dated February 9th. and am always glad to receive letters from over that side of the world, as it makes a man feel happy to hear that you are all well. It is very disappointing when a mail comes in and there are no letters for me.

We are up against it at present and going for our lives. I think we have proved in the present crisis, without a doubt, to be the finest soldiers that the British have got! Fritz has never broken through us yet and we are always given the hardest points of the line to stop him; so it should be a great honor to Australia.

No doubt the papers have told you all about it Fritz is making a desperate effort to break through before the Yanks can get a decent army here. If Fritz fails now, he is finished. It is just as well if he is, as it will end the war.

The pity is that, in this final effort, there will be so many broken homes, as a terrible number (both German and British) will be slaughtered. It is a cruel, cruel world at present.

Thank God that Australia is so far away, as very few of you

realise what an awful thing war is. It is a pity we have not been sent any reinforcements from Australia, as we will soon be all wiped out at this present rate of casualties. Though few in number, we still have to bear the brunt of German attacks and stop him."

BUT ...... Help is at hand!
Early in the summer of 1918 a U.S. Army of 1,000,000 men, well trained and well equipped, landed in France to help the Allies.

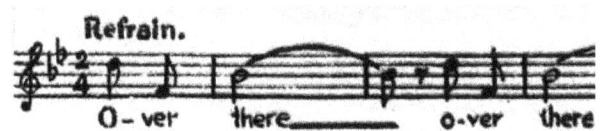

George M. Cohan's "Over There" became the theme song of America's fighting men.

Driver P. M. Short writes to his brother, Mr. Elton Short, of Donald, about his part in the sudden German advance.

A LULL BEFORE THE STORM

"Somewhere in France" April, 1918.

"At the beginning of this great offensive stunt of the Boches, we were moved very quickly from Flanders, down here to the scene of operations on the Somme. We had to keep our waggons loaded and hold ourselves ready to move at a moment's notice.

Horses and waggons were entrained. The Journey took about sixteen hours, but as I slept most of the time, I didn't notice. Six horses and three men in each truck, plus bed and bedding, horse rugs etc. Needless to say, we slept in full marching order.

Our first billet down this way was in a village which was visited by Fritz's armoured cars. Two of them were captured there a couple of days before we arrived.

We stayed there only a day, and then moved into another village. Fritz dropped a good many gas and highly-explosive shells on this village before we left, but he didn't do any great amount of damage.

From there we moved up to within about 3,000 yards from the line. Our 18-pounders were playing over our heads, so we only stayed there about six days before we moved further out, where we are now. Up to the present, this village has not been shelled or bombed, and you can guess none of us are anxious that it should be.

Fritz aeroplanes are overhead at the moment, dropping their

bombs somewhere about. Our anti-aircraft guns are having a shot at him, but it is such a common occurrence that one does not trouble to go outside to watch.

Everything, with the exception of our aircraft and artillery, has become quiet here now; but it is only the lull before the storm!

Well, at 2-30 this morning the storm broke when Fritz made a determined effort to break through. As usual. Fritz prepared his movement well. He started off with intense shelling of our area, including the back areas; and our village received its fair share of gas-shells.

But when his men "hopped over" the barrage sent over by our artillery was magnificent. It was a constant bubble of sound, as though a mighty cauldron was boiling furiously. I cannot describe it any other way. The noise was intense.

There was no more sleep for any of us, and we spent the rest of the time until we had to get up, in speculating as to his chances of success. We agreed that they were remote, and in this we were right. He failed in every way, and by our counter-attack he was driven back beyond his own lines.

My little company had its share of casualties — one killed, one wounded, and eight gassed. In fact, wounded and gassed men were streaming into the Dressing-Station all day.

Our man (who was killed) was driving past a First-Aid Post and saw his mate who was wounded. So he jumped off his waggon to go over and have a few words with him. A high-explosive shell suddenly landed nearby, killing him and one of his horses; but it left the other man and horse untouched. Had he remained on his waggon he would have escaped.

I saw two French-women and a young girl have a marvellous

escape. A shell landed in their house. Up it went, leaving only the skeleton standing. The only damage done to the people was a scratch on the child's face."

FRANCE. 25TH. APRIL, 1918.

"A few nights ago, several villages in this area suffered a heavy gas-shelling. The effect of this German gas is awful. A big dose turns a man yellow, and the agony he endures is heart-rending. The man who first invented gas as a weapon of warfare deserves all the torments of Hell and Damnation.

Men are blinded by it for some time, with bums to their faces, and eyes and noses running and they feel awfully sick. In addition to our casualties of over 90 men in the transport section, we had one horse killed, four wounded, and a good many horses were gassed. You would be sorry to see the poor brutes, blind and gasping for breath. Just like men.

Our artillery has been giving the Boche hell all day and all night it is now nearly 3 a.m. on the 25th. April (1918). I am on picket-duty, hence the reason for being up at this time. The Hun is sending over more gas-shells, but they are falling some distance away.

It is now 8 p.m. on the 25th. April; and to celebrate Anzac Day our 15th. Brigade "hopped over" last night in a counter-attack. They met with great success and their own casualties were light. They captured over a thousand prisoners who have been streaming into this village all day.

*Our boys had a feast with their bayonets, showing no mercy and settling old scores. They cut down a big lot of Huns; and many of the enemy are now surrendering in large batches. I have seen most of them coming in today. The majority of them are men of rather good physique, but to me. anyway, they are a bad-looking crowd.

There is no doubt that our infantry are fine, fighting men, and their complaint is that Fritz will not stand up to them in an open fight. The more I hear of our lads, the prouder I am of being an Australian. The position all along the line is, I hear, very satisfactory.

Before you get this letter, I fancy the whole aspect of the war will be changed, and we will take the ascendancy over Fritz.

I cannot close without saying a word about the British Air Service. A couple of nights ago I counted about 50 planes in formation. They looked grand.

On April 21st. there was great excitement near us when the Boche Air-Champion, Baron von Richthofen, who had 80 victims to his credit, was brought down by Australian machine-gunners. He was evidently a wonderful airman. His red plane crashed quite near us.

I saw another enemy plane brought down close to us recently. This machine, which carried two men, fell from a great height and was smashed to matchwood. One of the men was wounded in four places; and both men were, of course, badly knocked about by the fall, yet both were conscious when we picked them up. However, they died the same night.

I got a new mare yesterday, a Percheron. She is a beautiful-looking beast — a dark chestnut with a fine body and a crest such as I have never seen on any horse before. She is very light-legged, and her breed resembles the Suffolk Punch in some ways.

I am driving her with another dark chestnut mare — a real beauty and as staunch as can be. The pair look tip-top in harness.

I reckon I have the best team in the Company. I must close now and go to sleep."

This ferocious counter-attack, which drove the Huns out of Villers-Bretonneux, brought great fame to the Australian Infantrymen. It is said that they attacked the enemy "with a cheer that would have turned a tribe of Red Indians green with envy" (C.E.W. Bean).

Gunner Frank Young of Donald, writes about France to his former school-teacher, Mrs. Rowland, of Natte Yallock.

"SOMME" MUD

HURDCOTT CAMP, NO. 4,
SALISBURY PLAIN. 19TH. JULY, 1918

Dear Mrs. Rowland,

There was an Aussie mail in today so I got my issue and your letter of the 21st. March was among the number. I was very pleased to hear from you, even though the news was old. Your letter has been chasing me from one hospital to another and it has just caught me in time as I expect to leave here tomorrow for Sutton Veny Camp.

I expect to be there about 10 days and then go on to our Machine-Gun depot. I may stay three weeks there (if I'm lucky) before going back over 'the pond' again.

Anyhow, I've had a good run. When I left the Front-line, gassed on April 24th, I hadn't the slightest idea I would end up in Blighty. I was almost totally blind. I say "almost" because I walked out of the line to the First-Aid Post on my own, and a blind man couldn't very well do that! But it's surprising what you can do when you really have to. I thought I would just have some treatment for my eyes and then get sent back to the line.

There were shells dropping all around me as I came out. I was feeling my way along the sunken road, falling down shell-holes, and getting caught up in barbed wire. But you know the old saying, "The Devil takes care of his own." I'd tell you the whole rigmarole, but I don't ask you to believe it. (They say you can't believe half of what a soldier tells you.)

I was in France only two months to the day I was gassed. I was on three different fronts, so saw a fair bit of war in that short time. The first was at <u>Messines</u>. Then at <u>Kemmel Hill</u> where I saw one of Fritz's observation balloons brought down (part of which I sent home as a souvenir). Fritz owns ail that country now, but he only got it after the Aussies were shifted from there.

The next front was at <u>Seatvilliers</u> where we stayed for Easter week, living off a Frenchman's fowls, pigs and cattle. I was only twice in the Frontline there when we got word to shift up to the Somme, as the Boche was breaking through up there, near <u>Albert</u>. So our 25th. Machine-Gun Company went to <u>Corbie</u>, or rather a smaller village just separated from <u>Corbie</u> by a canal off the Somme River.

The name of our village was <u>Fouilloy,</u> and the civilians had all left there at the "Toot sweet" (Hurry up). My French vocabulary is very small, but I use it at every opportunity. Talk about a mess! That village took the prize, and brought home to me the horrors of war far more than all the bullets and shells in the Front-line.

The villagers must have left in a terrible hurry when Fritz was making his big push, as they left behind all their furniture, pianos, wardrobes (full of priceless silks and satins) and everything else.

The Tommies went through all these houses, pulling things about in search of valuables. Of course, I don't say our boys would have behaved any better, but I wouldn't blame the Tommies so much for looting if they didn't leave everything scattered over the floors. I could write a book about it all if I had the time and inclination — but the old "cocky's" life will satisfy me if I have the good luck to return home.

We started up the Communication-trenches one night at 1 a.m. to relieve the Tommies. It had been raining all day and was still pouring. I suppose you've heard of the "Somme" mud? Well, it is certainly "Some" mud; and marching along, carrying full pack and machine gun and ammunition, and expecting to meet Fritz at any time, was "No bon" (No good)

After we had wandered about for a considerable time, lost, we found ourselves luckily not in Fritz's trenches, but our own. It was 4 a.m. and you bet the Tommies were "some" pleased to be relieved.

Well, we put in four days and nights in that open trench, and it didn't stop raining. We were only 900 yards from the enemy's Front-lines. He was very quiet, but at times he would put over a barrage of shells; and then we had to lie down in the bottom of our muddy trench and have more mud thrown over us by shells bursting within three yards. I don't think I ever felt so miserable as I did in those four days.

Then to crown things, Fritz sent over gas, and amongst all that mud it was just lovely to have to put down our muddy rifles and put on our muddy gas-masks. But we all came through that experience safely and I went into the line a few times after that in far better circumstances. We were usually in the line three days and nights, and then we would be relieved and come back into Fouilloy for a couple of days' rest.

On the night I was gassed (April 24th) we were getting ready to go up the Front-line again, and we were sitting down above the cellar (which we used as a shelter) when Fritz started shelling Corbie, the nearby village. He was using gas-shells.

We had our masks ready, and as I walked across the yard the first gas-shell fell between my mates and me. It missed me by three yards. I went flat down on the ground at once, then jumped up and put on my mask. I looked around and the lads were scuttling into the cellar like a mob of rabbits down a burrow — and you can bet I joined them.

Fritz put about 2,000 shells into the village, so you can guess the air was pretty thick with gas. We blocked up the door and ventilators with blankets and then took off our masks. The boys were all laughing at my extraordinary agility after that first shell landed. We little knew that we were all breathing in the deadly "mustard-gas" which has very little sniff. When the bombardment ceased about 11 p.m. we went up the trenches to relieve our mates. We were feeling all right then, till we struck another heavy barrage.

Pte. Young as a machine gunner in World War I.

There were only four of us on our machine-gun, so we had a bit of a rush. Towards morning one little fellow in our dug-out was wounded and said he was gassed in the eyes. I bound up his wound and he went to the Dressing-Station. By this time, my own eyes were feeling pretty sore, too, but I did not leave the line till after day-break."

(Gunner Frank Young is seated second from right)

ON THE BACK OF THE PHOTO-CARD:-

Salisbury. 12th. Aug. 1918

Dear Mum and Dad,

What do you think of this group of tent mates?

They don't look down-hearted, do they? We are going to London on leave next Friday. Hoping all are keeping well as this leaves me. I am, ever you loving son Frank.

TRANSPORT DIFFICULTIES AT THE FRONT.

OVER ONE HUNDRED TANKS TOOK PART ON THAT FIRST DAY

EXTRACT FROM THAT IMPORTANT MESSAGE BY JOHN MONASH FOR THE TROOPS ON THE 8th. AUGUST, 1918

"Because of the completeness of our plans, of the magnitude of the operation, of the number of troops employed, and of the depth to which we intend to overrun the enemy's positions, this battle will be one of the most memorable of the whole war; and there can be no doubt that by capturing our objectives, we shall inflict blows upon the enemy that will make him stagger and will bring the end appreciably nearer. I entertain no sort of doubt that every Australian soldier will worthily rise to so great an occasion . . . . . . and be animated by no other resolve than a grim determination to see through, to a clean finish, whatever his task may be . . . . . . for the sake of AUSTRALIA, the Empire, and our cause. I earnestly wish every soldier of the Corps the best of good fortune and a glorious and decisive victory, the story of which will re-echo throughout the world, and will live for ever in the history of our homeland."

During that attack in September the vital hill of Mont St. Quentin was captured by a brilliant Australian feat of arms — as partly described here by a local soldier:-

"The fourth Company was on the left with 2 Platoons to move forward to exploit success on this flank, and 2 Platoons to form refused flank. We had 2 Companies of the 30th. Battalion also.

(PLAN. Capt. A.M. Robertson. M.C. is in charge of B Company on right. Lieutenant E. Thomas is in charge of D Company in centre. Lieutenant C. E. Davis is in charge of A Company on left. C Company is on the left of A Company for the purpose of exploiting success on that flank under Captain A. J. Ainslie. D Company of 30th. Battalion, under Captain Barbour is needed as reserve and to hold the front line on right half. C Company of 30th. Battalion, under Captain C. D. Savage, with instructions to hold left-half of old Front-line.)

At Zero plus three minutes, the line advanced and rushed the first position where the enemy tried to make a stand using their bayonets; but they were quickly overcome, the whole of the garrison being killed excepting very few who ran forward without weapons and hands up.

A Boche picked up one of our wounded and carried him in and seemed very pleased to get away from his trenches. This prisoner was rather funny because he thought we were English troops, so he had quite a lot of chatter like, "Englishmen are good comrades". But when we told him we were Australians, his jaw dropped and he looked very frightened and appealed for mercy, saying he was a married man with two children. {Evidently, the Germans have been told dreadful tales about us.}

On moving to our second objective, large numbers of the enemy garrison bolted, a few showed fight, a number threw up their hands, and a very large number were killed. There were six and seven Germans lying in heaps in different places. Those who would not come out of their dug-outs were promptly killed.

Some of our Platoons swept over the objective and were racing towards another trench, about 400 yards in advance, when our protective barrage came down too soon, thus forcing them to return.

One Sergeant got right up to a trench and saw it full of the enemy, who seemed rather disorganised owing to the fleeing ones having fallen into this trench on top of them. He came back with the intention of taking forward his platoon, but our standing-barrage came down and he could not take them forward. The enemy casualties inflicted by our artillery at this point were very great.

The advance posts moved out from 200 to 300 yards in advance of main position, but, owing to our artillery's protective barrage, the line had to withdraw about 100 yards. If the barrage-line had been thrown 300 yards further forward, the bag of prisoners would be much larger.

Two captured machine-guns were promptly turned on them

by our men and several thousand rounds fired and a large number of casualties were caused by these weapons. The position was quickly consolidated.

Small counter-attacks were beaten off. In one case, a party of 25 of the enemy tried to rush our position gained on the left. Two Lewis guns on either flank waited until they had got to within 100 yards and then they opened fire and completely wiped them out.

A large number of casualties were inflicted and I do not think there is much use in preaching mercy to mv men. They fight to kill, if the enemy shows resistance: but are extremely kind to prisoners who are captured by them.

A number of very brave deeds were performed. Private Bolger on the right rushed a Machine-gun which was troubling our right flank, and single-handed he killed the crew of 5 and captured the gun.

Another case of devotion to duty was a Runner, Private Baulch, who was wounded early, but still carried on. He was wounded a second time, but still remained on duty. When on his way to deliver an important message to Battalion-Headquarters, he was blinded by a mustard-gas shell which exploded right in his face, and I found him feeling his way along the Communication-trench, and when I spoke to him he said, "I have a message for you, sir." I found then that he was totally-blind."

LETTER OF CONDOLENCE

The death of <u>Private Tom Taynton</u> (14th. Battalion) is sympathetically recorded here by one of his officers, Lieutenant William Jacka, (the brother of Captain Albert Jacka who was Australia's first V.C.)

SOMEWHERE IN FRANCE

20TH. JUNE, 1918.

"I write on behalf of the officers and men of B Company, to tell you how very sorry we are that your son has been killed. He has been with us a very long time, and proved himself to be one of the finest soldiers in the 14th. Battalion.

He had been in a great many big battles, and his officers have nothing but praise to offer for his good conduct. With reference to when and where he was killed. I will tell you all I can.

We had been in the Front-line for 16 days, not far from Villers-Bretonneux, and during our time in the Front-line we carried out a raid on the enemy's trenches. Your son, Tommy, was one of the first to volunteer, and went through the raid without getting a scratch. He worked well, and Lieutenant Thompson, who was in charge of the raiding-party, speaks very highly of your son's conduct.

After the raid, which took place on the 15th. of June, we were relieved by the 13th. Battalion and we came back into the Reserve-line. We all had very good dug-outs, but had to go out each night digging trenches.

Last night, the 19th. of June, the men were just getting ready to go to work when the Huns began to shell our trench. Unluckily, one shell burst in the trench, and five men, one of whom was your son, were seen to fall.

We rushed up with stretchers, but, I am sad to say, we were too late to do anything for three of the boys, including your son. Death was instant, so he suffered no pain.

The place close to where your son is buried is called Corbie, and is situated on the River Somme. A nice little cross has been erected over your son's grave, and, if possible, I will take a photo of it and forward it to you later on. I have handed all your son's personal effects into Battalion Headquarters and trust they will reach you safely in time.

Though you have suffered a great loss, it will be something to know that your son stood out as one of the noble defenders of sunny Australia; and, that though he will not reap his reward in this world, he will reap it with you in the Great Beyond, and though he returns not, you will know that in a far-off foreign land there is a sacred piece of soil which is for ever Australia."

The following letter was found on the body of <u>Private Roger Hogan,</u> *by his mate,* <u>Private Eric Wilkinson.</u> <u>Private Roger Hogan</u> *was a stretcher-bearer at Morlancourt on the morning of 29th. July, 1918, when his 29th. Battalion attacked the German lines. He was doing his duty when a shell fell between him and a mate, killing them both instantly. They are buried in the Military Cemetery at Merricourt.*

IN THE FRONT LINE. FRANCE.

My Dearest Mother,

We have been in the Front line several days and are to go back just a little tonight. Then we advance to left or right, then a "Hop over" so I'm told. I don't know when it is coming off.

I am a stretcher-bearer and so far it is not a bad job. If this comes off I hope to do my best for the lads and to keep my end up; and if I should get wounded or "Go west", well, dear Mum, you need not worry as I'll be alright.

I'm just writing this in case anything happens. Well, goodbye, dearest mother, my fondest love to you and all. From your ever-loving son, ROGER HOGAN.

P.S. Just keep on praying for me. Times like this makes a chap think of home and loved ones.

God Bless You Always.

Mates in the 29th. Btn. Eric Wilkinson (left) Roger Hogan (standing) and friend.

Trench warfare

EATING CATS AND DOGS

The success of the British Allies throughout September, 1918, eventually resulted in the destruction of the Kaiser's German Empire. Let us not forget that Britain's Royal Navy had successfully blockaded enemy ports, thus preventing food supplies from reaching the German population — and great credit should also be given to the British Army who successfully crashed through the German lines during the Autumn of 1918.

Australians played a great part in the Allies' success on Germany's 'Black Day' (der Schwarze Tag) which was the 8th. August; although German historians claim that the Allies' success was due to its tanks — 'fire-vomiting iron dragons' and 'black monsters' those scared enemy soldiers called them.

Consequently, throughout the month of October, the German people were starving as their country crumbled around them. Its soldiers who returned home after suffering defeat, refused to fight any more. There was civil unrest throughout the land as people turned against the Kaiser and his military Government — yet these same people had given him their full support in the beginning and had fully agreed with his ambition to dominate Europe.

But now a lack of food meant they had to eat their cats and dogs and use the skins for leather. Let us remember that only four years previously the German people had enjoyed boundless confidence in their leaders and believed in military supremacy.

However, just four years later these same people who had so

eagerly supported the Kaiser's evil ambitions were now just a despairing nation of human misery. Thousands of their young men had perished in the fight on the Western Front, white at home their old people and children were slowly starving to death.

By the end of October the German people no longer wanted the Kaiser and his military dictatorship. At last, the Germans realized that their Emperor and his wicked son, the Crown Prince, were responsible for the wrongs committed during that terrible war and for their present suffering.

The British Prime Minister had promised that the Kaiser would be hanged for his sins when Britain won the war and Peace was eventually declared. Unfortunately, the crafty Kaiser escaped to Holland and was never punished.

General Ludendorff, the enemy's commander, stated that August 8th. was the blackest day for the German army in the history of the war — known as "Der schwarze Tag" — and afterwards, realized they could not win.

Although the bodies of the fallen littered Europe across the land from the English Channel to the Adriatic Sea, something far worse than the war was happening at that moment. It was the Spanish flu, ripping around the world, killing many victims within hours of their first symptoms. It was the deadliest pandemic since the Black Death six hundred years earlier — this Spanish flu would kill more lives than all the battles of World War 1 added together.

The August 8, 1918, "Battle of Amiens" was successful by Aussies and Canadians, but at the cost of 6,000 casualties "The Weeping Angel" statue is in the Amiens' cathedral and sent on postcards from France by soldiers.

Nurse M. Cannard, of St. Arnaud, describes the way in which Spanish Influenza is killing soldiers. By the end of the war, this disease was spreading throughout the world and killing millions.

GERARD FREEMAN THOMAS WAR HOSPITAL, INDIA.

6TH. NOVEMBER, 1918.

SPANISH INFLUENZA PANDEMIC

"Since I wrote to you last, I have been having a bad time. In August I went on night-duty in a Malaria Ward. Most of the "Tommies" who were in there suffering from Malaria, caught the Spanish Influenza; and talk about a time, it was dreadful. A silent pneumonia seemed to steal upon them, and within 24 hours they would die.

One was powerless to help them: and the hard part is, they were all boys who had fought in France and Mesopotamia. To think after all the battles and fighting they have been through, to die of this wretched epidemic. I can tell you, it was just heart-breaking to see it.

The Indian natives died like flies from it. There were 700 to 800 deaths a day in Bombay alone, and their cremation-ground was a pitiful sight, as well as disgusting, being littered with dead bodies. They could not get enough fuel to cremate all their dead.

At the end of the month I went down with a bad attack of the Spanish Flu myself, and I can quite understand the natives just turning their faces to the wall and giving up. I was prostrate with weakness, and developed a cough that tore me to bits both day and night.

When I was strong enough to walk they sent me to Nasik on 15 days' leave. My cough cleared up, but I began to feel ill again, running a temperature up to 105 degrees. I was too weak to leave my bed, so they sent me up to Nasik Convalescent Hospital for Army Officers.

Much to my horror and disgust the doctor said I had B.T. (that is Tropical Malaria and Malignant Malaria together). I had a bad time and just dread another attack, I may get Malaria attacks for the rest of my life. Some doctors say you can get clear of it, others that you never can."

Many of our sisters are now suffering from B.T. Malaria. One poor girl died. She had a funeral larger than any General, and it was a very sad and impressive sight. There were many Tommies; and the officers made a Guard-of-Honour; and the medical officers carried the coffin from the gun carriage to the church and grave.

She had been very good to the Tommies and terribly busy nursing the soldiers who had the Spanish Flu — so obviously she caught it from her patients. She was only sick for four days. It was a great shock to us.

There are 15 of our sisters down with flu at the moment, and one is very bad with pneumonia. It is a great worry to our Matron as these girls are so far away from their own people in Australia."

The military campaigns fought the first Australian Imperial Force (AIF) in France and Belgium between April 1916 and November 1918 cost the lives of more than 45,000 Australians

Lance-Corporal Albert Jacka, the first Australian soldier to be awarded the VC in the First World War

TELEGRAM THAT ENDED THE WAR

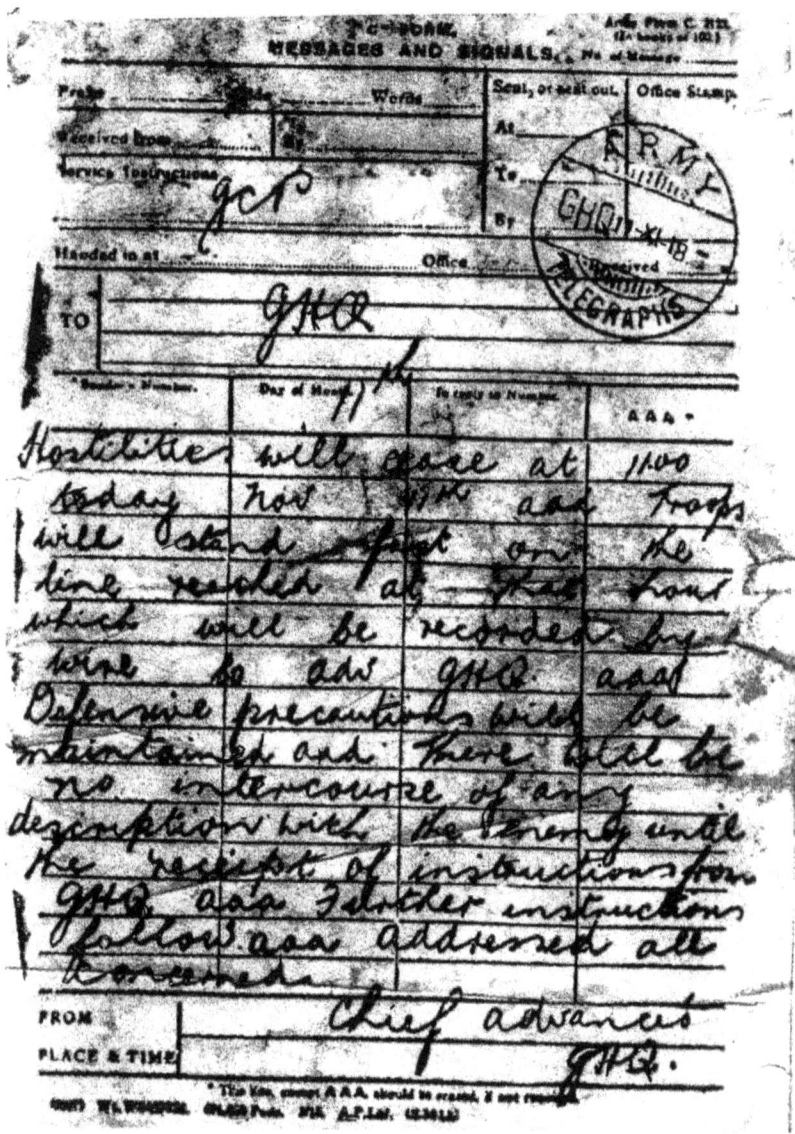

Above is a reproduction of the famous "Cease Fire" telegram that ended hostilities in the Great War at 11 a.m. on November 11th. 1918.

PEACE.

GERMANY SIGNS ARMISTICE.
HOSTILITIES CEASE.

1918

(At the 11th. Hour, of the 11th. Day, of the 11th. Month.)

Summary of Armistice Terms: -

(A) Immediate evacuation of Belgium, Prance, Alsace Lorraine and Luxemburg within 14 days. Occupation by Allied-Forces to keep pace with enemy evacuation.

(B) Surrender by the German armies of their 5,000 guns, 30,000 machine-guns, 3,000 Minenwerfer and 2,000 aeroplanes.

(C) Evacuation by the German armies of territory on the left bank of the River Rhine; and this territory is to be administered by local authorities under the control of the Allied armies. Occupation by Allied Forces of the three main crossings on the River Rhine — at Mayence, Coblenz and Cologne, together with the bridges.

(D) A neutral zone of about 30 kilometres to be left on the east bank of the Rhine.

(E) Immediate repatriation, without reciprocity, of all Allied prisoners-of-war. (In addition, there are clauses in regard to the handing over of locomotives, waggons, means of transportation, and so forth.)

(F) Germany must surrender to the Allied Governments her 160 German submarines; and any other submarines are to be paid oft and placed under the supervision of the Allies.

(G) Germany's Navy is to be interned in neutral ports under Allied supervision: — 10 battle ships, 8 light cruisers and 50 destroyers. All other ships to be paid off, disarmed, and placed under the supervision of the Allied Powers.

(H) There must be freedom of access to the Baltic for the Allies.

(I) The blockade upon Germany is to be maintained (with a number of minor clauses added to this).

THE FINALE OF WORLD WAR 1

Did it really come to an end at 11 o'clock on the morning of the 11th. day, of the 11th. month, in 1918? The mighty guns of war fell silent as two mighty armies packed up and went home: and they all lived happily ever after?

Is it possible that men, returning from a great war in which so many thousands were killed and maimed, could blot out from their minds the horrors of what they had experienced? How could they ever live in Peace again — haunted by nightmares of bloody bayonet-charges and horrific bombardments? Were they consumed by guilt for having come through it alive while their mates were blown to pieces? Their only consolation — there was no Hell to fear in the next world because they had already been there.

Would their family and friends understand the enormity of what had happened to them at the Western Front? No — only the comrades who had lived through it with them could possible know!

We saw the physical scars of war on these men — missing limbs, blindness, deafness — but what about their mental and emotional scars?

Major-General Elliott died in 1931, a gallant officer and gentleman. Newspapers said that he had died from "haemorrhage supervening upon protracted treatment for blood pressure", but we <u>now</u> know that he shot himself. So, why did society hush up the suicide of a distinguished soldier — and how many other returned soldiers took their own lives?

We will never know because it is an ugly aspect of war that most people go to great lengths to hide. I have heard of returned men who drowned themselves, or shot themselves — accidentally?

Gunner Frank Wilkinson won a Military Medal in 1917 for outstanding bravery. Alone, he extinguished several fires lit by enemy shells in an ammunition dump. After the war, Frank married and worked hard on a soldier's settlement farm, and it seemed as if he had forgotten all about the war and the death of his brother in the battle of Polygon Wood.

Not so! In 1927 his mental state was such that he stabbed to death his wife and only child, and then himself. Do they not count as innocent victims of that First World War — the "War to End All Wars"?

OUR GALLANT DEAD

By the end of 1918, the reburial of the remains of Fallen soldiers became an urgent problem; and so the "Imperial War Graves Commission" was formed to deal with it. Eventually, it was decided to remove all bodies to special cemeteries, where their graves could be cared for with the special reverence that was due to our heroes.

This was indeed a formidable operation, because over 150,000 isolated graves had been dug in France and Belgium — mainly on the Ypres and Somme battlefields. During the course of this bloody war, bodies had been thickly-strewn over areas that covered several miles in length and breadth; and, usually, soldiers were buried by their comrades on the very spot where they were killed.

In 1919, when the blood-stained fields of France and Belgium had to be returned to their original owners, it would have been very painful for the relatives of the Fallen (and also unfair to the Belgian and French farmers) if the War-Dead were not removed.

As most people could not afford to exhume the body of a loved one to take him back to his native land, the Commission felt there should be "Equality of Treatment" towards all those who paid the Supreme Sacrifice.

Accordingly, volunteers from among the comrades of the Fallen were asked to carry out reburials under the supervision of Army-Chaplains. A Donald man, Private Arthur Pascall, was stationed in Belgium at the time, awaiting transport home.

Arthur was one of those who agreed to go back into Villers-Bretonneux with the War Graves Commission to bury the dead in cemeteries created for this purpose.

"It was a job no one wanted, but it had to be done," Arthur Pascall said philosophically, many years later. "We dug up and reburied 23,000 service-men, <u>and after a while it became almost as impersonal as going around the sheep.</u>"

Later, the War Graves Commission, acting again on its principle of Equality, decided to mark each grave with an identical headstone. It would be 30 inches high and 18 inches wide, and engraved with the fallen man's rank, name, regiment and date of death.

Relatives were invited to compose a few words, of no more than three lines, to be inscribed on the headstone. One can imagine the agonising hours spent around the kitchen-table in the performance of this last and loving chore for a loved one.

Rudyard Kipling, the English poet, was asked to compose an inscription to be placed in all the special war cemeteries; and from the book of Ecclesiasticus he chose these inspired words: -

PTE. Arthur Pascall

 # "THEIR NAMES SHALL LAST FOR EVERMORE"

A section of the Tyne Cot Memorial, skirting the north-eastern boundary of Tyne Cot Cemetery
Silent, they lie in their last long line while the lark sings overhead.

WHO REALLY WON THE WAR?

Could we have won this war without the help of America? That is a question which is often debated, but there is no doubt that by September, 1918, the Germans were retreating all along the Western Front unable to deal with America's superior numbers of soldiers that had arrived there in July.

The Americans were very well-equipped with tanks and artillery and it was said "their guns filled the small ravines and valleys with such a rain of shells that the enemy was unable to concentrate".

By the beginning of August, there was a great army of 1,145,747 Americans on the Western Front fighting beside the British and French forces — and President Wilson promised to send another three million men before the end of 1918.

So we may well ask, "Did America win the war for us?" or "Did France win the war?" or "Did Britain win the war?"

Surely, although America powerfully contributed to a great victory, the true answer is that it was the Allied Powers fighting TOGETHER that determined this victory — with each country making massive sacrifices of men and money.

At first, those inexperienced Americans fought beside the British, Australian and French troops to learn from them all about battle-tactics, but eventually they formed an independent army of their own and on 12th September a successful attack upon St. Mihiel proved beyond doubt that this huge American army was very successful. The Yankees' characteristic fast progress staggered the Germans and left them no time to prepare fresh defences as soon as their Hindenburg line was smashed.

The American tanks crushed down all obstacles, forcing their way through the enemy's maze of trenches and bursting through seemingly impassable barbed wire, while their keen infantry followed behind with great enthusiasm, leaping "over the top" of the German trenches

The next day those brave, conquering soldiers marched through the streets of St. Mihiel where the Belgian inhabitants greeted them with enthusiastic cheers — but just imagine how surprised they were to see it was American troops who were their saviours and conquering heroes.

However, during the last week of September, heavy fighting took place when the Australians and British attacked the German lines north of St. Quentin — while in Flanders the Belgians captured Passchendaele and Messines.

The American army under General Pershing continued its success and Monfaucon was taken on September 27th., capturing 8,000 prisoners and 100 guns. No wonder by the beginning of

October the Germans were becoming desperate, realizing they faced military defeat on the Western Front.

Yet only six months previously they thought they were winning the war when they almost drove the British into the Channel and nearly reached the gates of Paris. Although the British retreated towards the coast for thirty miles they did eventually turn the enemy around — and now the great German military machine was crumbling because, since July, the French and the British, ably assisted by a vigorous young American army, struck blow after blow, turning the German invader out of those parts of France and Belgium which he had held for four years or more.

But let us not forget it was the battle-hardened Australians who demonstrated to those fresh young Americans the best way to fight — and the last brilliant action of the war in 1918 was undertaken by Australian Infantrymen with the capture of Montbrehain, a village on the Hindenburg Line, that had been occupied by the Germans for a long time. It was on the 5th. October — this successful action cost the Australians 30 officers and 400 men.

Amongst those who died was a local soldier, Private Joseph Gordon Wright, who suffered severe gun-shot wounds in that battle for Montbrehain and died from his wounds in a French hospital just a week later. He was the last local casualty of the war.

Later, in October, a captured German told an Australian officer that they were sick of the war and had they known Australians were attacking them they would not have fought at all.

O sacred land called Flanders
Where tall, wild poppies grow
And weave a blood-red carpet
That covers, row on row,
The bodies of our youthful dead
Who fell there long ago.
Those daring Diggers on the Somme
Whose deeds our Freedom bought;
Their courage never faltered
In the bloody battles fought.
For no-one can fight better
When in fear of being caught.

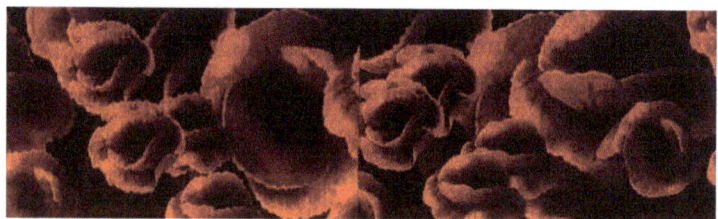

Infantry filing past bomb craters

A wrecked British tank on the battlefield

The German Fleet surrenders at the end of the war.

SURRENDER OF GERMAN FLEET

It is estimated that the ships surrendered by Germany at the end of the war cost considerably over 50 million pounds. Today they lie, rusting, at Scapa Flow in the Orkney Islands. A Donald man, <u>Lieutenant Horace Platt</u>, of H.M.S. RENOWN, witnessed this unique event in British History. He writes about it in his diary: -

"<u>Today is the most memorable day in the history of the world</u>. We have just come in from sea (4 p.m.) after bringing the mighty German Fleet to its place of surrender.

My ship, RENOWN, had the pleasure of the company on board of Lord Lemington (ex-Governor of Bombay); Major Clarke of the Scottish Army; and the prominent French Attache, Captain Vandier. In addition, we had the famous French naval-correspondent and other Press Officials. They all dined with us in our ward-room, and many fine speeches were made.

These prominent men were amazed beyond description at the magnificent sight of the day; and realised that the Kaiser was prevented from becoming the Conqueror of Europe by the overwhelming and efficient power of the British Navy, which enabled our gallant British, Colonial and Allied armies to gain such a marvellous victory on land.

For nearly a week we have suffered a most awful sea-fog; so thick that it made navigation almost impossible. But today — the one chosen to go down in our History books — turned out to be a most glorious, clear and sunny day. The whole Grand Fleet of our Royal Navy steamed out of the River Forth, beginning at midnight and finishing about 5 a.m.

QUEEN ELIZABETH (the Commander-in-Chiefs ship) led 33 battleships; and LION led 8 battle-cruisers, including RENOWN, REPULSE, AUSTRALIA and NEW ZEALAND. Following us were 49 light-cruisers and 106 destroyers. The RENOWN was the largest and most modern out of the whole lot, and that includes the German ships. I might mention that we had the American squadron of 6 Dreadnoughts with us, as well as the old French cruiser, ADMIRAL AUBE.

The British squadrons split up into two divisions, forming two complete single lines, steaming in formation, one behind the other. These great lines of ships met the Germans at 9-30 next morning. The enemy ships came over the horizon in a slight haze and smoking heavily from their after-funnels. When they had a look around, they found themselves hemmed in on both sides with lines of British ships that stretched from one horizon to the other.

This present assembly of fighting-ships was far and away the greatest in the history of the world.

We took every precaution to guard against the enemy's nasty tricks. So at 9 a.m. every British ship of the line ordered its sailors to "Action-Stations", absolutely ready to pump 15 in. shells and 21 in. torpedoes into Fritz if he showed the slightest inclination to fight. Then boarding-parties were sent to each of the German ships to see they were not armed.

The returning sailors reported that there were no signs of ammunition or firearms, and that the breeches had been removed from their guns and left at Wilhelmshaven. They said the German sailors were depressed and sulky; their mess-decks dirty; and there was a lack of general discipline. However, after the inspection, the Germans had enough sense to come along with us quietly.

The whole affair is too wonderful for words. Just imagine, here is the second largest sea-power in the world, surrendering, and handing over to us their magnificent ships, the cream of their navy, their hope and pride for years and years — and all this <u>without a single murmur</u>! They gave us eleven battleships, five huge battle-cruisers, seven light-cruisers and fifty destroyers.

This German-Fleet was led by the nose by one of our light-cruisers, which piloted them through our mine-fields and led them to their final anchorage in the River Forth. They are fine ships; and I must say their men showed great tact and capable seamanship in forming a straight line, three deep. They could have given us a very nasty shaking during the war if they had only been brave enough to come out of hiding and face us.

Year after year during the war, unbeknown to the public of the British Empire, our Grand Fleet steamed thousands and thousands of miles in German waters, knocking at the door of the Hun, asking him to come out and fight; but he would not budge. We used to be at our action-stations, day and night, ready for a bugle-call to be up and fight at any moment and always ready to meet them.

I never dreamt that one day we would lead them into our own base, without a single scratch, just like leading a horse to the water-pond. Really, it is too wonderful for words. Never in the annals of history has such a glorious victory been achieved.

Even now as I write, the German Fleet is lying a short distance away from us, being inspected by the First Battleship Squadron. Next Monday, we shall escort them to a place called Scapa Flow, a large bay (big enough to hold twice their number) situated on the wild and lonely east coast of North Scotland where nothing but snow and ice can be seen.

The ROYAL OAK, a fine British destroyer, took the German Rear-Admiral and his Flag-Officers to the QUEEN ELIZABETH where they were piped aboard in the customary manner. They saluted the Captain and were received very courteously. However, the Royal Marines were lined up on decks with fixed bayonets, just to show them we still meant business. Then the Germans were escorted to the Commander-in-Chiefs cabin where they received a formal reception.

They were then put in a room where a good meal awaited them; consisting of a quart of Claret each, half-a-bottle of Port Wine each, a leg of mutton with vegetables etc., etc. They were left entirely to themselves, and when our officials returned the Germans had mopped up the whole bally lot and then had the audacity to state there was no shortage of food in Germany.

The Conference between both sides lasted all night Sir David Beatty sat at his table, with his Flag-Officers on each side of him and the Germans facing him. At the same time, the Germans were looking right at the picture of Lord Nelson hanging on the bulkhead behind our Admiral. This historic scene was witnessed by a famous artist who will paint a picture of the occasion which will hang among all the other glorious pictures of our Empire.

The German Officers eventually left Rosyth with their sailing orders, expressing their appreciation of the courteous manner in which they had been treated. It is unanimous among the British Naval Officers that the German Officers were fine fellows. Yesterday we had the King and the Prince of Wales to visit us, and it was a very patriotic and thrilling day."

CONCLUSION

A Donald soldier, Sergeant Edward George Spencer, died of wounds on 8th. June, 1918, at the Casualty Clearing Station at Ebblinghem, on the main road between St. Omer and Hazebrouck, and is buried in the Ebblinghem Military Cemetery.

A BURIAL ON THE SOMME BATTLE-FIELDS (Photo: Roy Gilchrist Cllection)

Ypres in Ruins

ON THE WESTERN FRONT

using duckboards

Tanks, invented by the British, support the infantry in 1918

AN AUSTRALIAN ON PEACE DAY

On the 19th. of July, in 1919, there were peace parades throughout Great Britain to officially mark the victory of the British Empire over her enemies; so many of the Dominion soldiers, who were waiting in holding-camps to go home, were given leave-passes to take part in the great celebrations. Four terrible years of slaughter and mayhem were finally over and everyone was filled with so much thankfulness and happiness. This day of rejoicing ever afterwards was referred to as "Joy Day".

All the Allied nations were well-represented in a huge procession that marched through the city of London. It was a spectacular event witnessed by millions of people and amongst the crowds was a young Australian soldier from Donald named Godfrey Morgan, who describes what he did on that auspicious occasion.

"It was almost impossible to get a decent view of the procession. Mounted police and barricades, together with foot police and soldiers, kept the great crowd under control. I jumped up behind a mounted policeman and in spite of his objections stayed there on his horse with him until the procession had passed. I gave him ten shillings with my grateful thanks and told him to have a drink on me. The crowd was so dense that I just had to go where the people carried me and it was hours before I could manage to disentangle myself from the crowds and find my way back to the hotel."

This special day was the last opportunity for Colonial soldiers to enjoy themselves in the Mother Country before they were repatriated and placed on transport ships for home.

Sent by Private Austin Davey in Belgium in 1916 to Miss Clementine Pope of Donald

Nurse M. Cannard, of St. Arnaud, describes the way in which Spanish Influenza is killing soldiers. At the end of the war this disease spread throughout the world, killing millions.

SPANISH INFLUENZA PANDEMIC

GERARD FREEMAN THOMAS WAR HOSPITAL, INDIA.
6TH. NOVEMBER, 1918.

"Since I wrote to you last, I have been having a bad time. In August I went on night-duty in a Malaria Ward. Most of the "Tommies" who were in there suffering from Malaria, caught the Spanish Influenza; and talk about a time, it was dreadful. A silent pneumonia seemed to steal upon them, and within 24 hours they would die.

One was powerless to help them; and the hard part is, they were all boys who had fought in France and Mesopotamia. To think after all the battles and fighting they have been through, to die of this wretched epidemic. I can tell you, it was just heart-breaking to see it.

The Indian natives died like flies from it. There were 700 to 800 deaths a day in Bombay alone, and their cremation-ground was a pitiful sight, as well as disgusting, being littered with dead bodies. They could not get enough fuel to cremate all their dead.

At the end of the month I went down with a bad attack of the Spanish Flu myself, and I can quite understand the natives just turning their faces to the wall and giving up. I was prostrate with weakness, and developed a cough that tore me to bits both day and night.

When I was strong enough to walk they sent me to Nasik on 15 days' leave. My cough cleared up, but I began to feel ill again, running a temperature up to 105 degrees. I was too weak to leave my bed, so they sent me up to Nasik Convalescent Hospital for Army Officers.

Much to my horror and disgust the doctor said I had B.T. (that is Tropical Moleria and Malignant Maleria together). I had a bad time and just dread another attack. I may get Malaria attacks for the rest of my life. Some doctors say you can get clear of it, others that you never can; but the best thing you can do is to live in a good climate and keep your blood at its best.

While the blood is strong enough to fight the germ, attacks won't trouble you. My headache could never be described, and I had an ice bag on my head for days. I am nearly 2 stones lighter than when I left Australia, but that won't matter.

Each day there is a marked improvement in me and I am getting a good colour again. I looked the colour of an old, tan boot. I have to take Quinine for four months; and I mean to persevere with it, although it is awful-tasting stuff. I shall spare nothing to get better.

Many of our sisters are now suffering from B.T. Malaria. One poor girl died. She had a funeral larger than any General, and it was a very sad and impressive sight. There were many Tommies; and the officers made a Guard-of-Honour; and the medical officers carried the coffin from the gun carriage to the church and grave.

She had been very good to the Tommies and terribly busy nursing the soldiers who had the Spanish Flu — so obviously she caught it from her patients. She was only sick for four days. It was a great shock to us.

There are 15 of our sisters down with flu at the moment, and one is very bad with pneumonia. It is a great worry to our Matron as these girls are so far away from their own people in Australia."

THE STORY OF TWO LIENTENANTS

(Lt. John V. Larkin and Lt. John Foott served together in Gallipoli and France with the 8th. Battalion. In 1918, Lt. John Foott was wounded on the Western Front, and as a result he lost a leg. He returned home to work on the family farm, and later married.)

Dear Jack,

18th. June. 1918.

For goodness sake don't get a mild form of shell-shock when you see whom this note is from, but all the officers in the 8th. are writing to you.

You have my deepest sympathy, Jack, in the loss of your leg, but I hope it has not affected your ever-lively spirits. I agree with your surgeon who said, "It is better to be alive with one leg, than to be dead with two." Anyway, I reckon you are dead lucky to be finished with all this ghastly business and to be able to return once more to that best home of all in sunny Australia.

No doubt you will be surprised to hear they have given me my star. Now I am a full-blown "Ossifer", as my men say in "B" Coy."

Jack Larkin.

(Lt. John V. Larkin died for his country and Empire after over three years' service, at the age of 26. He was killed on the 9th. August, 1918, when his 8th. Battalion was advancing towards Lihons during the great Allied Offensive. His death is described in the following extract.)

Dear John (Foott)

Frankston <u>3rd. June, 1919.</u>

It was a fine surprise to hear from you so soon and thank you very much for the "Welcome Home" letter.

Yes, I'll bet you were surprised and sorry to hear that our mate Jack had gone under. It seems so hard that good men such as Jack should go west, and chaps who spend their time in the clink should stay alive. But that is war.

Jack was taking his platoon ahead towards Rosieres when someone asked him to allow them to go over to the right, but Jack saw that doing so would cover some other party, and so he went straight ahead. German machine-guns turned upon the irfantry and a bullet hit Jack in the pit of his stomach and he fell. Asked how he felt, he said, "A nice Blighty". He was carried away; but as you know, stomach wounds are the worst, and the most dreaded."

TRIBUTE TO A SOLDIER WHO ENLISTED – TWICE.

<u>Sergeant Edward Spencer</u> died on June 8th. 1918, from wounds received in the fighting on the Western Front.

Before he enlisted in 1915, <u>Sergeant Edward Spencer</u> was the Presbyterian missionary of Laen and Lawler churches for two years. People of both churches respected him for his sincere, kindly manner and for his devotion to his spiritual work; and spoke highly of his ability as a preacher. In fact, he was very popular with alt sections of the community.

He enlisted early in the war, and served with the 8th. Light Horse in Egypt and then in Gallipoli, where his right arm was seriously injured in a bomb explosion. After treatment in England, he was invalided home and became a Sergeant-Major on the Headquarters Staff in Melbourne to instruct the troops.

When Conscription was rejected for the second time at the end of 1917 — and the volunteers became scarce — there was a desperate need to repair Australia's great losses. So <u>Sergeant Edward Spencer</u>, wanting to rejoin his pals, returned to France where Manpower was scarce.

He requested to be drafted into the infantry; and consequently fell in action during the German offensive on the Aisne. The double newspaper announcement, below, tells its own tragic story of this war's horrors.

Birth

SPENCER.—On 24th June, 1918, at Nurse Hoare's Private Hospital, Donald, the wife of the late Sgt. E. G. Spencer—a daughter.

Death

SPENCER.—Died of wounds on 8th June, 1918, in France, Sgt. Edward George Spencer, beloved husband of Mollie Spencer (nee Pearse). Aged 28 years.

BROTHERS-IN-LAW at a Melbourne Camp.
EDWARD PEARSE and EDWARD SPENCER

BRIDAL STATISTICS

Statistics make interesting reading at the best of times, but the number of war-brides who left Britain for the colonies at the end of WW1 is quite astonishing and the immediate disadvantage to Britain was to lower her birth-rate during the post-war years.

It was a sad loss to Great Britain of potential mothers. One only needs to look at the number of women who married colonial soldiers to fully realise the extent of the problem.

The following statistics from the Registrar-General's Office in Britain cover marriages up to 10th. May, 1919, but more marriages took place during the following year while thousands of soldiers were in British camps awaiting repatriation to their homelands.

AUSTRALIA

Total number of men sent over: between 250, 000 and 300,000.
Marriages to British women: 10,545.
The marriage rate averages about 400 a month.

NEW ZEALAND

Total number of men sent over: 99, 822.
Marriages to British women: between 2, 500 and 2,750.
Number remaining in England is very small.

CANADA

Total number of men sent over: 549, 349.
Marriages to British women: 32, 000.
Number remaining in England is very small.

SOUTH AFRICA

Total number of men (white) sent over: 30,755.

Number of marriages: 1,000.

There were quite a number of Austalian soldiers who, in spite of being engaged to an Aussie girl before they set sail for the war, brought back a foreign bride.

Young war-brides arrive in Australia

SHOT AT DAWN

A British soldier faces a firing squad during World War I

This punishment was widespread in the army during W.W.I. and there are records of the cases of 306 British soldiers executed between 1914 and 1920 for cowardice, or desertion, or sleeping on guard duty.

A MAIDEN'S PRAYER

I'd like to go over to Berlin
And visit that Palace so grand
Where dwells the illustrious Kaiser –
You bet I would take him in hand.
I'd make him account for the murders
Of women and children galore,
And with one solid blow
I'd lay that brute low
Then finish him up on the floor.
If I were a man, not a woman,
I'd leave fair Australia today
And without much delay
I'd seek out the treacherous Kaiser
And give him just what he deserves.
I'd love to meet the Kaiser
Just for an hour or two;
For he killed my gallant sweetheart,
My lover, brave and true.
And the poison I'd give
And the short time he'd live
Would certainly finish his nerves.

ANON

In the First World War thousands of young men were killed on the battlefields of Belgium and France and this 'Lost Generation of Men' produced a tragic problem known as 'Surplus Women'. The sad fact was that there were 3,000,000 more women than men in the British Isles after that great war — and, consequently, most women ended up as spinsters for they had no men to marry.

Suicide figures for returned soldiers is about 550, mainly in 1919 and 1920.

Private William Davison — of Donald

WILLIAM DAVISON, died on the 28th. February, 1919, aged 30. They said "he took his own life while of unsound mind" but we know that, like so many others, Private William Davison was suffering severe mental trauma caused by the cruel, grim realities of war.

William was severely wounded at Armentieres in 1916 and was almost killed. As a result, his right arm was badly scarred and useless — which would have made life very difficult for him to find a job after the war.

He tells of his experience in a letter (written by a helpful padre) in which we see what horrors he suffered. "I got a piece of shrapnel through the right forearm which shattered the bone," he says. "The Germans were slinging over a good few bombs. One just missed me, but killed a chap alongside me. He fell over dead and I fell on top of him. You ought to see some of our chaps who get hit with shells. They are chopped into pieces. You would wonder how some of them manage to survive after such horrific injuries."

When William Davison returned home after prolonged treatment in an English hospital, he lived on the family farm at North Laen, but he must have felt physically helpless. Still suffering from shell-shock, is it any wonder that he decided life was too difficult — and, consequently, drowned himself in a nearby dam. He was yet another sacrifice to that terrible God of war.

The Anzacs found themselves in the "best billets" once they reached Belgium, near the end of 1918. They had been used to barns and sheds, but now they occupied the spare rooms of houses and slept in real beds with white sheets and clean blankets. The Belgian people welcomed their liberators and treated them as honoured guests.

(Photo: Gunner Jack Whittaker Collection)

CITIZENS OF ST. ARNAUD GATHER IN FRONT OF THE TOWN HALL TO WELCOME HOME LT.-COL. B. DUGGAN AT THE END OF THE WAR.

"Australia is the best country in the world, and the Australians were the best soldiers in the world," said Lt.-Col. B. Duggan at a great reception in St. Arnaud on Thursday, 22nd. May, 1919.

THE WORLD'S OLDEST MAN

AND ONE OF THE LAST THREE BRITISH W.W.I. VETERANS

Henry William Allingham died in Brighton, England, on the 16th. July, 2009. He was the world's oldest man at 113 years of age, but he was also a veteran of the First World War. During the Battle of Passchendaele in 1917, he remembers taking refuge in a shell-hole. It must have been a very frightening experience for he says: -

"Going forward at night to salvage parts of an aircraft, I fell into a shell-hole. It was full of arms, legs, ears, dead rats — a lot of decaying, rotten flesh. I was almost drowning and up to my neck in freezing water and mud. I can't describe the smell of flesh and mud mixed up together. I nearly gave up, but then turned to my left and I was able to lift myself out of the water. I lay there in the dark on the rim, too terrified to move in case I fell back in. Cold and with my uniform stinking, I was scared and terrified. I was so relieved when it finally got light and I could see to move."

WAITING FOR A STRETCHER

When I see the boys returning.
My heart does throb with pain.
To think you're not there, dear Gordon.
And will never come home again;
Could I have raised your dying head,
Or heard your last farewell,
The blow would not have been so hard
To those who loved you well.
Australia mourns her hero's fate,
Who died to bring her fame,
True to country, King, and mate,
Leaving a spotless name.

Somewhere in France is a new made grave
Where lies my only son;
God spared his life through the terrible strife
Till the victory it was won,
Then he called him away, Gory could not stay,
For the summons must be obeyed.
And the meeting, I pictured here on earth, is for a little
time delayed ;
But when I meet my darling son,
It will be in that bright land
Where every tear is wiped away ;
It is then we'll understand.
Somewhere in France, no matter where,
He was just as near to heaven
As though he had laid on his bed at home,
When the signal cease was given.

In Fond and Loving Memory

OF OUR DEAR AND ONLY SON
AND BROTHER,

TROOPER GORDON COLOLLO RILEY

(GORY)

NO. 417.

13TH LIGHT HORSE, A.I.F.

WHO DIED FROM BRONCHO PNEUMONIA AT
THE 5TH CASUALTY CLEARING STATION,
FRANCE, ON FEBRUARY 17, 1919.

ENLISTED 1914.

AGED 27 YEARS 3 MONTHS.

INFLUENZA, THE POST-WAR KILLER

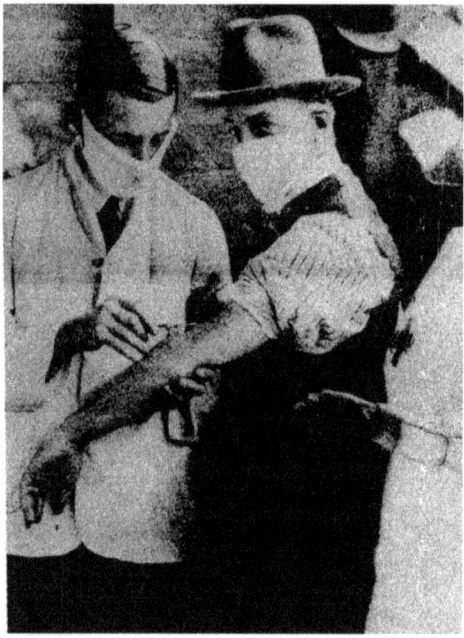

1 An "inhalatorium" in a factory with employees inhaling zinc sulphur fumes as a protection against influenza

The treacherous sinking by the German crews of the interned ships in Scapa Flow (as in other allied ports) was meant to impress the world that Germany still had the will to revenge and had no intention of carrying out the terms of the Armistice.

• The German Fleet in Scapa Flow, November 28, 1918. The Germans left on board treacherously scuttled their ships here in June, 1919.

(Old postcard) german Fleet at Scapa Flow — 1919 (just before scuttling their ships)

The Germans' last deadly deed

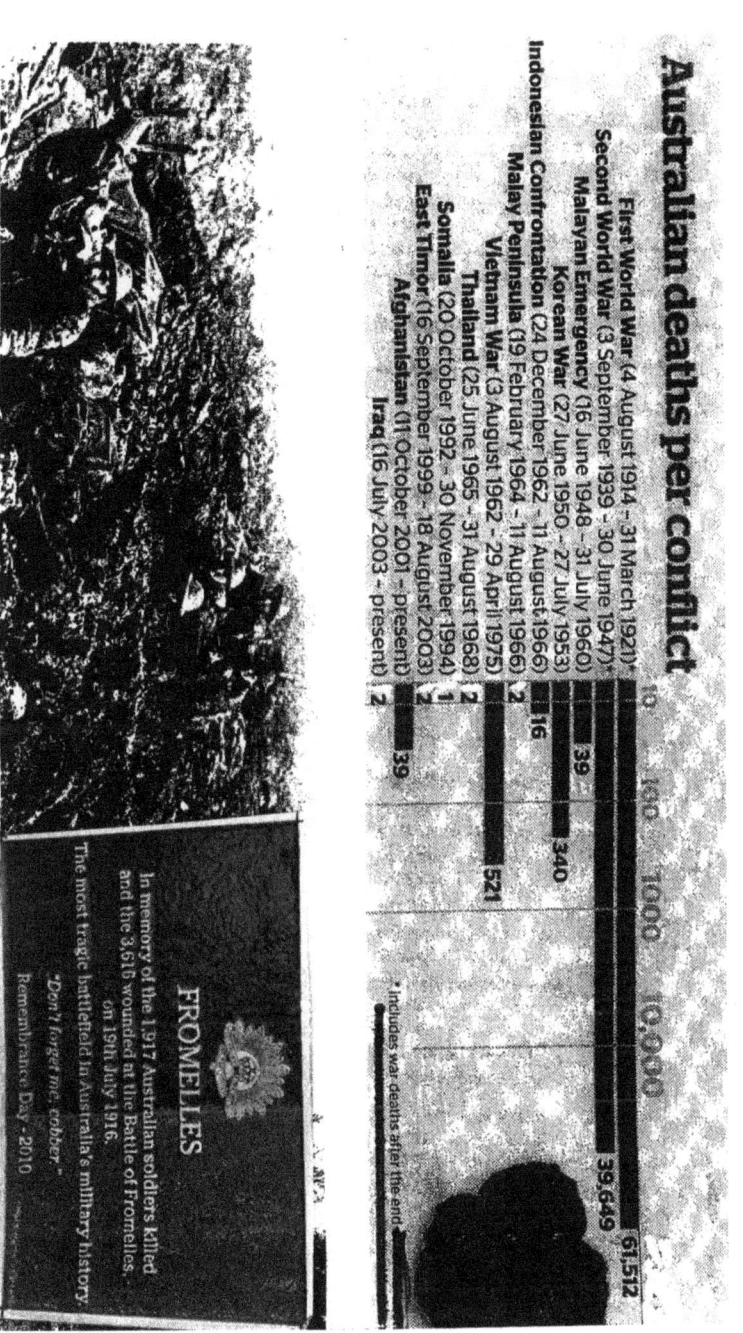

Going into Battle

A 'Dead Man's Penny'

Next-of-Kin Memorial Plaque

www.ingramcontent.com/pod-product-compliance
Lightning Source LLC
Chambersburg PA
CBHW041955080526
44588CB00021B/2749